# The Prophec:
# Saint Bridge

# Table of Contents

3

# Book 1

The words of our Lord Jesus Christ to His chosen and dearly beloved bride, Saint Bridget, about the proclamation of His most holy Incarnation and the rejection, desecration and abandonment of our faith and baptism, and how He bids His beloved bride and all Christian people to love Him.

## Chapter 1

"I am the Creator of the heavens and the earth, one in Divinity with the Father and the Holy Ghost. I am the one who spoke to the patriarchs and the prophets and the one whom they awaited. For the sake of their longing and in agreement with my promise, I assumed flesh without sin and concupiscence, by entering the womb of the Virgin like the sun shining through the clearest gem. For just as the sun does not damage the glass by entering it, likewise the virginity of the Virgin was not lost when I assumed Manhood. I assumed flesh in such a way that I did not have to forsake my Divinity, and I was no less God - with the Father and the Holy Ghost, governing and upholding all things - although I was in the womb of the Virgin in my human nature. Just as brightness is never separated from fire, so too, my Divinity was never separated from my Humanity, not even in death.

Thereafter I allowed my pure and sinless body to be wounded from the foot to the head, and to be crucified for all the sins of mankind. That same body is now offered each day on the altar so that mankind might love me more and remember my great deeds more often. But now I am totally forgotten, neglected, despised, and expelled as a king is from his own kingdom and in whose place the most wicked robber has been elected and honored.

I have indeed wanted my kingdom to be within man, and by right I should be King and Lord over him, for I made him and redeemed him. However, now he has broken and desecrated the faith which he promised me in his baptism, and he has broken and spurned my laws and commandments which I prescribed and revealed to him. He loves his own will and refuses to hear me. In Addition, he exalts the most wicked robber, the devil, above me and has given him his faith. The devil really is a robber, since he steals for himself, by way of evil temptations, bad councils, and false promises, the human soul that I redeemed with my blood. But he does not do this because he is mightier than me; for I am so mighty that I can do all things with a word, and so just, that even if all the saints asked me, I would not do the least thing against justice.

But, since man, who has been given free will, willfully rejects my commandments and obeys the devil, it is only right that he also experiences his tyranny and malice. This devil was created good by me, but fell by his own wicked will, and has become, so to speak, my servant for inflicting vengeance on the workers of evil.

Yet, even though I am now so despised, I am still so merciful that whoever prays for my mercy and humbles himself in amendment shall be forgiven his sins, and I shall save him from the evil robber - the devil. But to those who continue despising me, I shall visit my justice upon them, so that those hearing it will tremble, and those who feel it will say: "Woe, that we were ever conceived or born! Woe, that we ever provoked the Lord of majesty to wrath!"

But you, my daughter, whom I have chosen for myself, and with whom I now speak in spirit: love me with all your heart - not as you love your son or daughter or parents, but more than anything in the world - since I, who created you, did not spare any of my limbs in suffering for your sake! Yet, I love your soul so dearly that, rather than losing you, I would let myself be crucified again, if it were possible. Imitate my humility; for I, the King of glory and of angels, was clothed in ugly, wretched rags and stood naked at the pillar and heard all kinds of insults and ridicule with my own ears. Always prefer my will before your own, because my Mother, your Lady, has, from the beginning to the end, never wanted anything but what I wanted.

If you do this, then your heart shall be with my heart, and it will be inflamed by my love in the same way that anything dry becomes rapidly inflamed by fire. Your soul shall be so inflamed and filled with me, and I will be in you, so that everything worldly becomes bitter to you and all fleshly lusts like poison. You will rest in the arms of my Divinity, where no fleshly desires exist, but only spiritual delight and joy which fill the delighted soul with happiness -

inwardly and outwardly - so that it thinks of nothing and desires nothing but the joy which it possesses. So love me alone, and you will have all the things you want, and you will have them in abundance. Is it not written that the oil of the widow did not decrease until the day the rain was sent to earth by God according to the words of the prophet? I am the true prophet! If you believe my words and follow and fulfill them, the oil - joy and jubilation - shall never decrease for you for all eternity."

Our Lord Jesus Christ's words to his daughter - whom He now had taken as His bride - about the articles of the true faith, and about what kind of adornments, tokens and desires the bride must have in order to please the Bridegroom.

# Chapter 2

"I am the Creator of the heavens and the earth, and the sea and of all the things that are in them. I am one with the Father and the Holy Ghost - not like the gods of stone nor the gods of gold, as were used by people of old, and not several gods, as people once thought - but one God: Father, Son, and Holy Ghost, three persons but one in divine nature, the Creator of all but created by none, unchangeable and almighty, everlasting - without beginning or end. I am the one who was born of the Virgin, without losing my Divinity but joining it to my Manhood, so that I, in one person, should be the true Son of God and the Son of the Virgin. I am the one who hung on the cross and died and was buried, yet my Divinity remained unharmed. For even though I died in the Manhood and flesh that I, the only Son, had assumed, yet I lived on in my Divinity, being one God with the Father and the Holy Ghost. I am the same one who rose from the dead and ascended into Heaven, and who now speaks with you in my Spirit. I have chosen you and taken you to myself as my bride in order to show you the ways of the world and my divine secrets, for this pleases me. You are also mine by right; for when your husband died, you entrusted all your will into my hands and, after his death, you also thought and prayed about how you should become poor and abandon all things for my sake. For this reason, you are mine by right because of this great love of yours, and I will provide for you because of this.

Therefore, I take you to myself as my bride and for my own pleasure, the kind that is becoming for God to have with a chaste soul. It is the obligation of the bride to be ready when the bridegroom wants to celebrate the wedding so that she will be properly dressed and pure. You purify yourself well if your thoughts are always on your sins, on how I cleansed you in baptism from the sin of Adam, and how often I have been patient and supported you when you fell into sin. The bride should also have the insignia of her bridegroom on her chest, which means that you should observe and take heed of the favors and good deeds which I have done for you:

such as how nobly I created you by giving you a soul and body, how nobly I enriched you by giving you health and temporal things, how lovingly and sweetly I redeemed you when I died for you and restored your heavenly inheritance to you - if you want to have it. The bride should also do the will of the Bridegroom. But what is my will, except that you should want to love me above all things and not desire anything but me?

I created all things for the sake of mankind, and placed all things under his authority, but he loves all things except me, and hates nothing but me. I bought back the inheritance for him which he had lost because of his sin. But he is so foolish and without reason that he prefers this passing glory - which is like the foam of the sea that rises up for a moment like a mountain, and then quickly falls down to nothing - instead of eternal glory in which there is everlasting good.

But if you, my bride, desire nothing but me, if you despise all things for my sake - not only your children and relatives, but also honor and riches - I will give you the most precious and lovely reward! I will not give you gold or silver, but myself, to be your Bridegroom and reward - I, who am the King of Glory. But if you are ashamed of being poor and despised, then consider how I, your God, walked before you, when my servants and friends abandoned me in the world; for I was not seeking earthly friends, but heavenly friends. And if you now are troubled and afraid about the burden and difficulty of work and sickness, then consider how difficult and painful it is to burn in hell! What would you not deserve if you had offended an earthly master as you have me? For even though I love you with all my heart, still I do not act against justice in the least point.

Therefore, as you have sinned in all your limbs, so shall you also make satisfaction and penance in every limb. But, because of your good will and your purpose of atoning for your sins, I shall change my justice into mercy by foregoing painful punishment for but a little penance. Therefore, embrace and take upon yourself a little work, so that you may be made clean of sin and reach the great reward sooner. For the bride should grow tired working alongside her bridegroom so that she may all the more confidently take her rest with him."

Our Lord Jesus Christ's words of wisdom to His bride about how she should love and honor Him, the Bridegroom, and about how the evil love the world and hate God.

# Chapter 3

"I am your God and Lord, whom you worship and honor. I am the one who upholds heaven and earth with my power; they are not upheld by any pillars or anything else. I am the one who is handled and offered up each day on the altar under the appearance of bread as true God and true man. I am the same one who has chosen you. Honor my Father! Love me! Obey my Spirit! Honor my Mother as your Lady! Honor all my saints! Keep the true faith which you shall learn by him who experienced within himself the battle of the two spirits - the spirit of falsehood and the spirit of truth - and with my help won. Maintain true humility. What is true humility if not to behave as one really is, and to give praise to God for the good things he has given us?

But now, there are many who hate me and my deeds, and who account my words as sorrow and vanity, but instead, with affection and love, embrace the whoremonger: the devil. Whatever they do for my sake is done with grumbling and bitterness. They would not even confess my name or serve me, if they did not fear the opinion of other men. They love the world with such fervor that they never tire of working for it night and day, always burning with their love for it. Their service is as pleasing to me as that of someone who gives his enemy money to kill his own son! This is what they do to me. They give me some alms and honor me with their lips in order to gain worldly success and to remain in their honor and in their sin. The good spirit is therefore hindered in them and they are prevented from making any progress in doing good.

However, if you want to love me with all your heart and to desire nothing but me, I will draw you to myself through love, just as a magnet draws iron to itself. I will place you on my arm, which is so strong that no one can stretch it out, and so firm that, once outstretched, no one is able to bend it back, and is so sweet that it surpasses every fragrance and is beyond comparison to any sweet thing or delight of this world.

# Explanation

This man, who was the teacher of the bride of Christ, was the holy theologian and canon of Linkoping, named Master Mathias of Sweden. He wrote an excellent commentary on the whole Bible. He was ingenuously tempted by the devil with many heresies against the Catholic faith. However, he overcame all of them with the help of Christ and could not be conquered by the devil, as is shown in the written biography of Saint Bridget. It was this Master Mathias who composed the prologue to these books which begins thus: "Stupor et mirabilia," etc. He was a holy man with great spiritual power in both word and deed. When he died in Sweden, the bride of Christ was living in Rome. While she was praying, she heard a voice saying to her in spirit: "Happy are you, Master Mathias, for the crown that has been prepared for you in heaven! Come now to the wisdom that will never end!"

One may also read more about Master Mathias in this Book (inChapter 52), in Book V (in the answer to question 3 in the last interrogation), and in Book VI (chapters 75 and 89).

Our Lord Jesus Christ's words to His bride about how she should not fear or think that the revelations told to her by Him come from an evil spirit, and about how to discern an evil spirit from a good one.

# Chapter 4

"I am your Creator and Redeemer. Why did you fear and doubt my words? Why did you wonder whether they came from a good or an evil spirit? Tell me, what have you found in my words that your conscience did not tell you to do? Or have I ever commanded you anything against reason?

The bride answered: "No, all you told me was completely true and reasonable and I was badly mistaken." The Bridegroom, Jesus, answered her: "I showed you three things from which you could recognize the good spirit: I invited you to honor your God, who made you and gave you all the good things you have; your reason also tells you to honor him above all things. I further invited you to keep the true faith, that is, to believe that nothing has been created without God nor may be made without God. I also invited you to love reasonable work and continence in all things, for the world was created for man's sake, in order that he may use it according to his reasonable needs, and not in excess.

In the same way, you may also recognize the unclean spirit, the devil, from three opposing things: He tempts and advises you to seek and desire your own praise, and to be proud of the things given you. He also tempts you into unbelief and intemperance in all your limbs and in all things, and makes your heart inflamed by them. Sometimes he also deceives men under the guise of a good spirit. This is why I commanded you to always examine your conscience and reveal it to spiritual men of wisdom!

Therefore, do not doubt that the good spirit of God is with you when you desire nothing but God and are completely inflamed by him! Only I can do this, and it is impossible for the devil to come near you then. He also cannot come near to any evil man unless I allow it, either because of his sins, or some secret judgment that is known only to me. For he is my creature like all other things - he was created good by me, but made himself evil by his own malice – therefore, I am Lord over him.

Therefore, those who accuse me do so falsely when they say that those who serve me with great and godly devotion are insane and possessed by the devil. They consider me to be like a man who gives his chaste and trusting wife over to adultery. Such a one should I be, if I allowed a righteous and God-loving man to be handed over to the devil! But because I am faithful, the devil will never rule over the soul of any man who devoutly serves me. Although my friends sometimes seem to be insane or senseless, it is not because the devil is tormenting them, or because they serve me with fervent and godly devotion. It is rather because of some defect or weakness in the brain, or some other hidden reason, which serves to humble them. It may also happen, sometimes, that the devil receives power from me over the bodies of good men for the sake of their future reward, or that he darkens their consciences. But he can never rule the souls of those who have faith in me and who love me.

The loving words of Christ to His bride in the wonderful parable of a lovely castle, which signifies the holy Church militant, and about how the Church of God will be rebuilt by the prayers of the glorious Virgin and of the saints.

# Chapter 5

"I am the Creator of all things - I, the King of Glory and the Lord of Angels! I built for myself a lovely castle and placed my chosen men in it, but my enemies undermined the foundation and overpowered my friends so much so that the marrow is violently forced out of my friends' feet as they sit chained to the wooden stocks. Their mouth is beaten by stones, and they are tortured by hunger and thirst. Moreover, enemies are persecuting their Lord! My friends are now praying with tears and groans for help, and justice is calling for vengeance, but mercy says to forgive.

Then God said to his heavenly host that stood around him: "What do you think about these who have conquered my castle?" They all answered as with one voice: "O Lord, all justice is in you, and in you we see all things. You are without beginning and without end, the Son of God, and all judgment is given to you. You are their judge." He answered: "Although you know and see all things in me, still for the sake of my bride who stands here, tell me the just sentence." They said: "This is justice: that those who undermined the wall should be punished as thieves, that those who persist in evil should be punished as intruders and violent criminals, and that those who are captive should be freed and the hungry be filled."

Then Mary, the Mother of God (who until now had remained silent) spoke: "Oh, my Lord and most dear Son, You were in my womb as true God and man. By your grace you sanctified me, who was but an earthen vessel. I beg you, have mercy on them once more!" Then the Lord answered His Mother: "Blessed be the words of your mouth that ascend like a sweet fragrance to God. You are the Queen and glory of angels and all saints because, by you, God and all the saints are made happy! Because your will was as my own from the beginning of your youth, I will do as you wish once more."

Then He said to the host of saints: "Because you have fought manfully, and for the sake of your love, I will let myself be appeased for now. Behold, I will rebuild my wall because of your prayers. I will liberate and heal those who were oppressed by force, and honor them a hundredfold for the indignity they have endured. But if the violators and wrong-doers pray for my mercy, I will give them peace and mercy. However, those who despise my mercy will feel my justice."

Then he said to his bride: "My bride, I have chosen you and brought you into my Spirit. You hear my words and those of my saints. Although the saints see all things in me, nevertheless, they have spoken for your sake so that you might understand, since you, who are still in the flesh, cannot see all things in me in the same way as they who are spirits. I will now also show you what all these things signify.

The castle I spoke about previously is the Holy Church and the souls of Christians, which I built with my own blood and that of the saints. I cemented and joined it with my love and placed my friends and chosen men in it. The foundation is true faith, that is, to believe that I am a righteous and merciful judge.

Now, however, this foundation is undermined because all believe and preach that I am merciful, but almost no one preaches or believes me to be a righteous judge. They view me as an unjust judge! Unjust and unrighteous, indeed, would the judge be who, out of mercy, allowed the unrighteous to go unpunished, so that they could oppress the righteous even more! But I am a righteous and merciful judge; for I do not let even the least sin go unpunished, nor the least good go unrewarded. By the undermining of this wall's foundation, there entered into the Holy Church people who sin without fear, who deny that I am a righteous judge, and who torment my friends as severely as those who are placed in the stocks. My friends have no joy or consolation given to them but, instead, every kind of mockery and torment are inflicted upon them as if they were possessed by the devil. When they tell the truth about me, they are rejected and accused of lying. They have a fervent desire to hear or speak the truth about me, but there is no one who listens to them or speaks the truth to them. And I, the Lord and Creator of all things, am being blasphemed and rejected, for they say: 'We do not know if he is God and, if he is God, we do not care!' They overthrow my banner and trample it under their feet calling out: 'Why did he suffer? What benefit is it to us? If he wants to satisfy our lust and will, it is enough for us. He may keep his kingdom and heaven!' I want to go into them, but they say: 'We would rather die before giving up our own will!'

Behold, my bride, what kind of people they are! I made them, and could destroy and damn them with a word if I wanted to. How bold and arrogant they are toward me! But because of the prayers of my Mother and of all the saints, I am still so merciful and patient that I will send them the words of my mouth and offer them my mercy. If they want to accept it, I will be appeased. Otherwise, they will come to know my justice and be publicly humiliated like thieves in front of all angels and men, and be judged by every one of them. For just as the men who are hanged on gallows are devoured by ravens, they will also be devoured by demons, yet not die. Just as those who are punished in the stocks have no rest, they too, will have pain and bitterness all around them. The most burning river will flow into their mouths, but their bellies will not be filled, and their punishment will be renewed each day.

But my friends will be redeemed and consoled by the words that come from my mouth. They will see my justice joined with my mercy. I will clothe them in the weapons of my love and make them so strong that the adversaries of the faith will fall back like filth and feel ashamed for all eternity when they see my justice. Yes, they will surely be ashamed for having abused my patience."

The words of Christ to His bride about how His Spirit cannot remain with the unrighteous, and about the separation of the unrighteous from the good, and how good men, armed with spiritual weapons, are sent to war against the world.

# Chapter 6

"My enemies are like the most violent beasts that can never be filled or have rest. Their heart is so empty of my love that they never allow the thought of my suffering into it; and not once has a word like this been uttered by their inmost heart: "O Lord, you have redeemed us, may you be praised for your bitter suffering!" How could my Spirit remain with the people who have no divine love for me, and who willingly betray others in order to satisfy their own will? Their heart is full of vile worms, that is, full of worldly desires. The devil has left his filth in their mouths, and that is why my words do not please them.

Therefore, I will sever them from my friends with my saw, and just as there is no more bitter way to die than to be sawn asunder, so there will not be a punishment in which they will not partake. They will be sawn in two by the devil and separated from me! They are so abhorrent to me that all who cling to them and agree with them will also be severed from me.

Therefore, I send out my friends in order that they might separate the devils from my members, for they are truly my enemies. I send my friends like knights to war. Anyone who mortifies and subdues his flesh and abstains from forbidden things is my true knight. For their lance, they will have the words that I spoke with my own mouth and, in their hands, the sword of the true faith. Their breasts will be covered with the armor of love, so that no matter what happens to them, they will love me no less. They shall have the shield of patience at their side, so that they may suffer and endure all things patiently. I have enclosed them like gold in a vessel; they should now go forth and walk in my ways.

According to the ways of justice, I could not enter into the glory of majesty without suffering tribulation in my human nature, so then, how else will they enter into it? If their Lord endured pain and suffering, it is not surprising that they also suffer. If their Lord endured beatings and torture, it is not too much for them to endure words and contradictions. They should not fear, for I will never abandon them. Just as it is impossible for the devil to touch and divide the heart of God, so it is impossible for the devil to separate them from me. And since they are like the purest gold in my sight, I will never abandon them, even though they are tested with a little fire, for the fire is given to them for their greater reward and happiness.

The words of the glorious Virgin to Saint Bridget about how to dress and with what kind of clothes and ornaments her daughter should be adorned and clothed.

# Chapter 7

"I am Mary who gave birth to the Son of God, true God and true man. I am the Queen of Angels. My son loves you with all of his heart. Therefore, you should love him. You should be adorned with the most proper clothes, and I will show you how and what kind they should be. Just as before you had an undershirt, a shirt, shoes, a cloak, and a brooch on your chest, so now you shall have spiritual clothes.

The undershirt you shall have is contrition for your sins; for just as an undershirt is closest to the body, so contrition and confession are the first way of conversion to God. Through these the mind, which once enjoyed sin, is purified, and the unchaste flesh restrained from evil lusts. The two shoes are two intentions: namely, the will to make amendment for your past sins, and the will to do good and refrain from evil. Your shirt is hope in God; and just as a shirt has two sleeves, so may justice and mercy be paired with your hope, so that you will hope for the mercy of God, yet not forget his justice. Think about his justice and harsh judgment in such a way that you do not forget his mercy, for he does not work justice without mercy, or mercy without justice. The cloak is faith, for just as the cloak covers everything and everything is enclosed in it, man can likewise comprehend and attain all things by faith. This cloak should be decorated with the tokens of your Bridegroom's love - namely, how he created you, how he redeemed you, how he raised you and led you into his spirit and opened your spiritual eyes. The brooch, which should always be on your chest, is the frequent consideration of his suffering: how he was mocked and scourged, how he stood alive on the cross, bloody and wounded in all his limbs, how in death his whole body shook from the most bitter pain and anguish, and how he commended his spirit into the hands of his Father. May this brooch always be on your chest! There should also be a crown on your head, which means that you should be chaste in your desires, so much so, that you would rather endure a beating and pain than to be further stained.

Therefore, be modest and polite and do not think about or desire anything but your God and Creator - for when you have him, you have everything! Adorned in this way, you shall await your Bridegroom."

The words of the Queen of Heaven to her beloved daughter, Saint Bridget, teaching her how she should love and praise the Son of God together with his blessed Mother.

# Chapter 8

"I am the Queen of Heaven. You are concerned about how you should praise and honor me. Know and be certain that all praise of my Son also is praise of me, and those who dishonor him also dishonor me. This is so because I loved him and he loved me so ardently that both of us were like one heart. He so magnificently honored me, who was an earthen vessel, that he raised me above all the angels. Therefore, you should praise me like this: "Blessed be you, God, Creator of all things, who deigned to descend into the womb of the Virgin Mary! Blessed be you, God, who wished to be within the Virgin Mary without burdening her, and deigned to take immaculate flesh from her without sin! Blessed be you, God, who came to the Virgin, bringing joy to her soul and her whole body, and who went out of her without sin, to the joy of her whole body! Blessed be you, God, who after your heavenly ascension gladdened the Virgin Mary, your Mother, with continuous comforts and visited her with your consolation! Blessed be you, God, who assumed the body and soul of the Virgin Mary, your Mother, into heaven and honorably placed her above all the angels next to your Divinity! Have mercy on me for the sake of all her prayers!"

The words of the Queen of Heaven to her beloved daughter about the wonderful love the Son had for His Virgin Mother, and about how the Mother of Christ was conceived within the most chaste marriage and sanctified in the womb. She tells how she was assumed, body and soul, into Heaven, and about the power of her name, and about the good and evil angels assigned to men for their protection or trial.

# Chapter 9

"I am the Queen of Heaven. Love my Son, for he is most worthy; when you have him, you have all that is worthwhile. He is also most desirable; when you have him, you have all that is desirable. Love him, too, for he is most virtuous; when you have him, you have every virtue. I want to tell you how wonderful his love for my body and soul was and how much he honored my name. My Son loved me before I loved him, since he is my Creator.

He united my father and mother in a marriage so chaste that there could not be found a more chaste marriage at that time. They never wanted to come together except in accordance with the Law, and only then with the intention to bring forth offspring.

When an angel revealed to them that they would give birth to the Virgin from whom the salvation of the world would come, they would rather have died than to come together in carnal love; lust was dead in them. I assure you that when they did come together, it was because of divine love and because of the angel's message, not out of carnal desire, but against their will and out of a holy love for God. In this way, my flesh was put together by their seed and through divine love. Then, when my body had been made and formed, God infused the created soul into it from his divinity, and the soul was immediately sanctified along with the body, and the angels guarded and served it day and night. When my soul was sanctified and joined to its body, my mother felt such great joy that it would have been impossible to describe it!

Afterwards, when my lifetime had been accomplished, my Son first raised up my soul - for it was the mistress of the body - to a more excellent place than others in heaven, right next to his Divinity. Later, he also raised up my body in such a manner that no other creature's body is so close to God as mine. See how much my Son loved my soul and body! Yet, there are some people with a malevolent spirit who deny that I was assumed into Heaven, body and soul, and also others who simply do not know any better. But this is a most certain truth: I, with body and soul, was assumed to the Divinity!

Hear now how much my Son honored my name! My name is Mary, as it is said in the Gospel. When the angels hear this name, they rejoice in their mind and thank God for the great mercy that he worked through me and with me and because they see my Son's Humanity glorified in his Divinity. Those within the fire of purgatory rejoice exceedingly, just like a sick and bedridden man does if he receives a word of comfort that pleases his soul: he is suddenly overjoyed! When the good angels hear my name, they immediately move closer to the righteous for whom they are guardians, and rejoice over their progress in good deeds and virtues.

All humans have been given both good angels for their protection, and bad angels to test them. The good angels are not separated from God; they serve the soul without leaving God. They are constantly in his sight. Yet they work to inflame and incite the soul to do good. All the demons, however, shudder with fear at the name of Mary! When they hear the name, "Mary", they immediately release a soul out of the claws with which they had held her. Just as a bird or hawk, with its claws and beak embedded into its prey, releases it immediately if it hears a sound, but soon returns when it sees that no action follows, so do the demons - frightened when they hear my name – release the soul. But they return and fly back as fast as an arrow if no improvement follows.

No one is so cold in his love of God (unless he is damned) that he will not experience the devil releasing him from his habitual sins if only he invokes my name with the true intention of never returning to his evil deeds. The devil will never return to him unless he resumes the will to commit mortal sins. Sometimes, though, the devil is allowed to trouble him for the sake of his greater reward. However, the devil shall never own him.

The words of Virgin Mary to her daughter, presenting a useful lesson about how she should live, and describing many wonderful things about the suffering of Christ.

# Chapter 10

"I am the Queen of Heaven, the Mother of God. I told you to wear a brooch on your chest. I will now show you more fully how, from the beginning, when I first heard and understood that God existed, I always, and with fear, was concerned about my salvation and my observance of his commandments. But when I learned more about God - that he was my Creator and the judge of all my actions - I loved him more dearly, and I was constantly fearful and watchful so as to not offend him by word or deed.

Later, when I heard that he had given the Law and the commandments to the people and worked such great miracles through them, I made a firm decision in my soul to never love anything but him, and all worldly things became most bitter to me. When still later I heard that God himself would redeem the world and be born of a Virgin, I was seized by such great love for him that I thought of nothing but God and desired nothing but him. I withdrew myself, as much as I was able, from the conversation and presence of parents and friends, and I gave away all my possessions to the poor, and kept nothing for myself but meager food and clothing.

Nothing was pleasing to me but God! I always wished in my heart to live until the time of his birth, and perhaps, deserve to become the unworthy handmaid of the Mother of God. I also promised in my heart to keep my virginity, if this was acceptable to him, and to have no possessions in the world. However, if God wanted otherwise, my will was that his will, not mine, be done; for I believed that he could do all things and wanted nothing but what was beneficial and best for me. Therefore, I entrusted all my will to him.

When the time approached for the virgins to be presented in the temple of the Lord, I was also among them due to the devout compliance of my parents to the Law. I thought to myself that nothing was impossible for God, and since he knew that I wanted and desired nothing but him, I knew that he could protect my virginity, if it pleased him. However, if not, I wanted his will to be done. After I had heard all the commandments in the temple, I returned home, burning even more now than ever before with the love of God, being inflamed daily with new fires and desires of love.

For this reason, I withdrew myself even more from everyone, and was alone day and night, fearing greatly, and most of all, that my mouth should say anything, or my ears hear anything against the will of my God, or that my eyes see anything alluring or harmful. I was also afraid in the silence, and very worried that I might be silent about things of which I should, instead, have spoken.

While I was worried in my heart like this, alone by myself and placing all my hope in God, an inspiration about God's great power came over me, and I recalled how the angels and everything created serve him, and how his glory is indescribable and unlimited. While I was thus fascinated by this thought, I saw three wonderful things: I saw a star, but not the kind that shines in the sky; I saw a light, but not the kind that shines in this world; I smelled a fragrance, but not of herbs or anything else of this world. It was most delightful and truly indescribable, and it filled me up so completely that I jubilated with joy!

After this, I immediately heard a voice - but not from a human mouth - and when I heard it, I shuddered with the great fear that it might be an illusion, or a mockery by an evil spirit. But shortly after this, an angel of God appeared before me; he was like the most handsome of men, but not in the flesh as is the body of a created man, and he said to me: 'Hail, full of grace, the Lord is with thee!' When I heard this, I wondered what he meant and why he had come to me with such a greeting, for I knew and believed that I was unworthy of any such thing - or any good thing! However, I also knew that nothing is impossible for God, if he desires it.

Then the angel spoke again: 'The child to be born in you is holy and will be called the Son of God. May his will be done as it pleases him.' But, not even then did I consider myself worthy, and I did not ask the angel why, or when, this would happen. Instead I asked him how it could be that I, an unworthy maiden, who did not know any man, should become the Mother of God. The angel answered me (as I have just said): 'Nothing is impossible for God, for whatever he wants to do will be done.'

When I had heard these words of the angel, I felt the most fervent desire to become the Mother of God, and my soul spoke out of love and desire, saying: 'See, here I am; your will be done in me!' With these words, my Son was conceived in my womb to the indescribable joy of my soul and my every limb! While I had him in my womb, I bore him without any pain, without any heaviness or discomfort. I humbled myself in all things, knowing that he whom I bore was the Almighty!

When I gave birth to him, it was also without any pain or sin, just as I had conceived him, but with such exaltation and joy of soul and body that my feet did not feel the ground where they had been standing because of this indescribable joy! Just as he had entered my limbs to the joy of all my soul, he left my body, leaving my virginity intact, and my soul and whole body in a state of indescribable joy and jubilation.

When I gazed upon and contemplated his beauty, joy seeped through my soul like dewdrops and I knew myself to be unworthy of such a son. But when I considered the places where (as I had learned from the predictions of the prophets) nails would be pierced through his hands and feet at the crucifixion, my eyes filled with tears and my heart was almost torn apart by sorrow.

When my Son saw my weeping eyes, he became almost deathly saddened. However, when I considered his divine power, I was consoled again in knowing that this was what he wanted and that it should happen in this way, and I joined all my will to his. So my joy was always mixed with sorrow.

When the time of my Son's suffering arrived, his enemies seized him and struck him on the cheek and neck, spat at him and ridiculed him. Then he was led to the pillar of torture where he voluntarily removed his clothes and placed his hands around the pillar, and his enemies then mercilessly bound them. When he stood bound at the pillar, he had no covering at all, but stood naked as he had been born, suffering the shame of his nakedness.

Then all my Son's friends fled from him, and his enemies came together from all directions and stood there, scourging his body, which was pure from every stain and sin. I was standing nearby, and at the very first lashing, I fell down as if I were dead. When I regained consciousness, I saw his body whipped and scourged so badly that the ribs were visible! What was even more terrible – when the whip was pulled out, his flesh was furrowed and torn by it, just as the earth is by a plough! As my Son was standing there, all bloody and wounded, so that no place could be found on him that was still intact and no sound spot could be scourged, then someone present there, aroused in spirit, asked: 'Are you going to kill him before he is even judged?' And he cut off his bonds immediately.

Then my Son put his clothes back on, and I saw that the place where he had been standing was filled with blood! By observing my Son's footprints, I could see where he had walked because the ground was bloody there as well. They did not even wait for him to get dressed, but pushed and dragged him to make him hurry up. While my Son was being led away like a robber, he wiped the blood from his eyes. When he had been sentenced to death, they placed the cross on him so that he could carry it to the place of suffering. When he had carried it for a while, a man came along and took the cross to carry it for him. As my Son was going to the place of suffering, some people hit him on the neck, while others hit him in the face. He was so brutally and forcefully beaten that, although I did not see who hit him, I heard the sound of the blow clearly. When I reached the place of suffering with him, I saw all the instruments of his death lying there ready. When my Son got there, he took off his clothes by himself.

The executioners and the crucifiers said to each other: 'These are our clothes! He will not get them back because he is condemned to death!' As my Son was standing there, naked as he had been born, a man came running up and handed him a cloth with which he joyfully covered his private parts. Then the cruel executioners seized him and stretched him out on the cross. First, they fastened his right hand to the wooden beam (which was fashioned with holes for the nails), piercing the hand at the place where the bone was most solid and firm. Then they pulled out his other hand with a rope and fastened it, in a similar way, to the beam. Next they crucified the right foot - with the left foot on top of it - with two nails, so that all his sinews and veins were stretched so much that they burst. After they had done this, they put the crown of thorns [1] on his head. It cut into my Son's venerable head so deeply that his eyes were filled with blood as it flowed down, his ears were blocked by it, and his beard was totally soaked with it. As he stood there, so bloody and pierced, he felt sorry for me, for I was standing nearby and crying. Looking with his blood-filled eyes upon my nephew, John, he commended me to his care. At that moment I heard some people saying that my Son was a robber! Others said that he was a liar, and others that no one deserved to die more than did my Son!

My sorrow was renewed from hearing all this. And, as I said before, when the first nail was driven into him, I became overwhelmed by the sound of the first strike and fell down as if dead with darkened eyes, trembling hands, and faltering legs. In my bitter pain and great sorrow, I was not able to look up again until he had been completely nailed to the cross. But when I got up, I saw my Son hanging pitifully, and I, his most sorrowful Mother, was so grieved and heartbroken that I could barely stand up because of my great and bitter sorrow. When my Son saw me and his friends in inconsolable tears, he called out with a loud and sorrowful voice to his Father, saying: 'Father, why have you forsaken me?' It was as if he wanted to say: 'There is no one who pities me but you, Father.'

By this time, his eyes seemed half-dead. His cheeks were sunken, his face was sorrowful, his mouth open, and his tongue was bloody. His stomach was pressed in towards his back because of all the liquid that had been lost. It was as if he had no intestines. All of his body was pale and languid because of the loss of blood. His hands and feet were very rigidly outstretched, for they had been extended and made to conform to the shape of the cross. His beard and hair were completely soaked with blood. When my Son stood there so bruised and pale blue, only his heart was still vigorous, for it was of the best and strongest nature. He had taken from my flesh the most pure and well-wrought body. His skin was so thin and tender that blood flowed out of it instantly if he was scourged even slightly. His blood was so fresh that it could be seen inside the pure skin. And

---

[1]   Explanation from Book 7 -Chapter 15: "Then the crown of thorns, which they had removed from his head when he was being crucified, they now put back, fitting it onto his most holy head. It pricked his awesome head with such force that then and there his eyes were filled with flowing blood and his ears were obstructed."

because he had the very best constitution, life contended with death in his pierced body. Sometimes the pain from his pierced limbs and sinews rose up to his heart, which was still completely vigorous and unhurt and tormented it with the most unendurable pain and suffering. Sometimes the pain descended from his heart into his wounded limbs and, in so doing, prolonged his bitter death.

Surrounded by these pains, my Son beheld his weeping friends who, with his help, would rather have suffered his pain themselves or have burned in hell for all time than to see him tortured in this way. His sorrow over his friends' sorrow exceeded all the bitterness and grief which he had endured in body and heart, for he loved them so tenderly. Then, out of the exceedingly great suffering and anguish of his body, he cried out on account of his Manhood to the Father: 'Father, into your hands I commend my spirit.' When I, his most sorrowful Mother heard his voice, my whole body trembled in the bitter pain of my heart. As often as I later thought on this cry, it was as if still present and fresh in my ears.

When his death drew near, his heart burst because of the violence of the pain. His whole body convulsed, and his head raised itself a little, and then dropped down again. His mouth was open and his tongue was completely bloody. His hands retracted a little from the place of the nail holes, and his feet were made to bear more of the weight of his body. His fingers and arms were stretched out somewhat, and his back was tightly pressed against the cross.

Then some people said to me: 'Your Son is dead, Mary!' But others said: 'He is dead, but he will rise again.' When everyone was going away, a man came and thrust his spear into his side so forcefully that it almost went out the other side! When the spear was pulled out, its point appeared to be red with blood. It seemed to me then, when I saw my beloved Son's heart pierced, that my own heart had been pierced as well!

Then he was taken down from the cross and I received his body onto my lap. He looked like a leper, and was completely covered with bruises and blood. His eyes were lifeless and filled with blood, his mouth as cold as ice, his beard like string, his face paralyzed, and his hands were so stiffened that they could not be bent over his chest, but only over his stomach, near the navel. I had him on my knee just as he had been on the cross: stiffened in all his limbs.

After this, they laid him in a clean linen cloth and I dried his limbs with my own linen cloth and closed his eyes and mouth, which he had opened when he died. Then they laid him in the grave. I would willingly have been placed alive in the grave with my Son if it had been his will! When these things were done, good John came and brought me home. Behold, my daughter, what my Son has endured for you, and love him with all your heart!

Our Lord Jesus Christ's words to His bride about how He willingly delivered himself up to be crucified by His enemies, and about the way to be abstinent in all members of the body from all illicit movements after His most sweet example of suffering.

# Chapter 11

The Son of God spoke to his bride, saying: "I am the Creator of the heavens and the earth and all the things that are in them, and it is my true body that is consecrated on the altar. Love me with all your heart, for I have loved you, and I delivered myself up to my enemies willingly, while my friends and my Mother remained in the most bitter sorrow and weeping. When I saw the spear, the nails, the whips, and the other instruments of torture there ready, I still went on, no less joyful, to suffer. And when my head was bleeding on all sides from the crown of thorns, and the blood was flowing on all sides, then, even if my enemies had gotten hold of my heart, I would have, still, rather allowed it to be wounded and torn asunder than lose you. For that reason, you are extremely ungrateful, if you do not love me for such a great love.

For if my head was pierced and bent down on the cross for your sake, your head should be bent down toward humility. Since my eyes were filled with blood and tears, your eyes should abstain from pleasurable sights. Since my ears were filled with blood and had to hear blasphemous and scornful words, your ears should be turned away from frivolous and foolish talk. Since my mouth was given the most bitter drink and was denied the good one, you should keep closed your mouth from all evil and open it for good. Since my hands were outstretched and pierced by nails, your deeds, which are symbolized by the hands, should be stretched out to the poor and to my commandments. Your feet, in other words, the desire with which you should walk to me, should be crucified and abstain from all evil lusts. As I have suffered in all my limbs, so may all your limbs be ready for my service. For I demand more service of you than of other people, since I have granted more mercy to you."

About how an angel prays for the bride of God, and how Christ asks the angel what it is that he prays for the bride and what is good for her.

# Chapter 12

The good angel that was the guardian of the bride appeared praying to Christ for her. Our Lord answered the angel and said: "One who wants to pray for another should pray for the other's health and salvation. You are like a fire that is never extinguished, constantly burning with my love. You see and know all things when you see me. You want nothing but what I want. Therefore tell me, what is good for this new bride of mine?" The angel answered: "Lord, you know all things." The Lord said to him: "In truth, all that has been or will be is eternally in me. I know and understand all things in heaven and on earth and there is no change in me. But so that the bride may understand my will, tell me now while she is listening what is good for her." The angel said: "She has a proud and arrogant heart and therefore a cane is needed for her so that she may be tamed." Then our Lord said: "What then do you ask for her, my friend?" The angel said: "My Lord, I beg for your mercy with the rod." Our Lord said: "For your sake, I will do so with her, that I never practice justice without mercy. Therefore, my bride should love me with all her heart and with a good will."

About how the enemy of God has three devils in himself and about the terrifying judgment passed on him by Christ.

# Chapter 13

"My enemy has three devils in himself. The first sits in his sexual organ, the second in his heart, the third in his mouth. The first is like a skipper who lets water in through the keel; the water, rises by increasing gradually, and then fills up all of the ship. Then the water floods over and the ship sinks down. This ship is his body that is harassed by the temptations of devils and by his own lusts as though by tempestuous waves.

First, the evil lust entered into his body through the keel, that is, through the evil desire with which he took delight in bad thoughts. And since he did not resist through repentance and penance and did not repair his body's ship with the nails of abstinence, the water of lust increased daily while he gave his consent to evil. Then the belly of the ship filled with evil desires, and the water flooded over and drowned the ship with lust so that it was unable to reach the haven of salvation.

The second devil sits in his heart and is like a worm lying inside an apple. The worm first eats the core of the apple and then leaves its filth there and crawls around inside the whole apple until it is completely useless. This is what the devil does: First, he destroys the man's will and good desires, which are like the core where all the soul's strength and all goodness reside, and when the heart has been emptied of these goods, the devil then leaves in their place in his heart worldly thoughts and desires that he had loved more. The devil now drives his body to what pleases him, and for this reason, his strength and understanding are diminished and he begins to hate life. This man is indeed an apple without a core, that is to say, a man without a heart, for he enters my church without a heart since he has no love of God.

The third devil is like an archer who looks out through the windows and shoots at the careless. How can the devil not be in him who never speaks without mentioning the devil? That which is loved more is mentioned more often. His bitter words, with which he hurts others, are like arrows shot through as many windows as the number of times the devil is mentioned, and innocent people take offense at his words.

Therefore do I, who am the Truth, swear by my truth that I shall condemn him like a whore to the sulfurous fire, like a deceitful traitor to the mutilation of all his limbs and like a scoffer of the Lord to eternal shame! However, as long as his soul and body are united, my mercy stands ready for him. What I demand of him is that he should attend the divine services and prayers more often, not to fear any humiliation or desire any honor, and that evil or bad words will never be mentioned by his mouth.

## Explanation

This man was an abbot of the Cistercian order. He buried an excommunicated person. When he had read the last funeral prayer over him, Saint Bridget heard in ecstasy of spirit the following words of our Lord: "This man did as he should not have done and buried an excommunicated man. But now you should know and be sure that he is the one that is going to be buried first after the departed. For he sinned against the Father, who told us to never show respect to persons against justice or to honor the rich unjustly. But he honored the unworthy for a small perishable thing and laid him among the worthy, as he should not have done. He also sinned against the Holy Ghost, who is the communion and fellowship of the righteous, when he buried an unrighteous man with the good and righteous. He also sinned against me, the Son, for I have said: "The one who rejects me shall be rejected." But this man honored and exalted the one whom my church and my Vicar had rejected." When the abbot heard these words, he was stricken with remorse and repented from his sins and then died on the fourth day.

The words of Christ to his bride about the method and the veneration she should maintain in prayer, and about the three kinds of people who serve God in this world.

# Chapter 14

"I am your God who was crucified on the cross; true God and true man in one person who is present everyday in the hands of the priest. When you pray any prayer to me, always end your prayer with the intention that my will always shall be done and not yours. For when you pray for the already condemned, I do not hear you. Sometimes you also pray for some things that are against your own welfare and that is why it is necessary for you to entrust your will to me, for I know all things and do not provide you with anything but what is beneficial. Many pray without the right intention and that is why they do not deserve to be heard.

There are three kinds of people who serve me in this world: The first are those who believe me to be God, the Creator and giver of all things and mighty ruler over everything. They serve me with the intention of gaining honor and worldly things, but the things of heaven are considered as nothing to them so that they would gladly do without it if they, instead, could gain the perishable and present things. According to their desire, worldly pleasure falls to them in everything and so they lose the eternal things, but I recompense them with worldly benefits for all the good things they have done for my sake right down to the last farthing and the very last moment.

The second are those who believe me to be God almighty and a strict judge, and these serve me because of fear of punishment but not out of love for the heavenly glory. If they were not afraid of suffering, they would not serve me.

The third are those who believe me to be the Creator of all things and true God and who believe me to be just and merciful. These do not serve me because of any fear of punishment but because of divine love and charity. Rather, they would prefer and endure every punishment, if they could bear it, than to even once provoke me to wrath. These truly deserve to be heard in their prayers, for their will is according to my will.

But the ones who belong to the first kind shall never escape from the place of punishment and torment or get to see my face. The ones who belong to the second kind shall not be punished and tormented as much, but will still be unable to see my face, unless he corrects his fear through penitence and amendment.

The words of Christ to his bride wherein he describes himself as a great king, and about the two treasuries symbolizing the love of God and the love of the world, and a teaching about how to proceed and improve in this life.

# Chapter 15

"I am like a great and mighty king. Four things belong to a king: First, he must be rich; second, generous; third, wise and fourth, charitable. I am in truth the King of the angels and of all Humanity. I also have those four qualities that I mentioned: First, I am the richest of all, for I give to everyone according to their needs but possess after this donation not less than before. Second, I am the most generous, since I am ready to give to anyone who prays with love for my mercy. Third, I am the wisest of all, since I know what is best for each and everyone. And fourth, I am charitable, since I am more ready to give than anyone is to ask.

I have, as it were, two treasuries. The first treasury stores heavy things as lead, and the house where they are stored is surrounded with sharp and stinging spikes. But to the one who first begins to turn and roll these heavy things, and then learns how to carry them, they seem as light as feathers. And so the things that before looked heavy, become very light, and the things that before were thought to be bitter and stinging, become sweet. The second treasury stores things that seem to be like shining gold with precious stones and delicious drinks. But the gold is really filth and the drinks are poison. There are two ways into these treasuries, even though there used to be only one way.

At the crossroads, that is, at the beginning of these two ways, there stood a man who cried out to three men who were walking on a different way, and he said: 'Hear, hear my words! But if you do not want to hear with your ears, then at least see with your eyes that what I say is true. But if you do not want hear or see, then at least use your hands to touch and prove that my words are true and not false.' Then the first of them said: 'Let us hear and see if his words are true.' The second man said: 'All he says is false.' The third said: 'I know that everything he says is true, but I do not care about what he says.'

What are these two treasuries if not my love and the love of the world? There are two ways into these two treasuries: privation and a complete denial of one's own will lead to my love, while the fleshly lust and a man's own will lead to the love of the world. To some people, my love appears to be a heavy burden of lead, for when they should be fasting or keeping vigil in my service or restrain their flesh from sinful desires, they feel as if they are carrying heavy lead. And if they have to hear words or insults, they think it is heavy and hard, or if they must spend time in purity or prayer, it is as if they were sitting between spikes or thorns and they worry every moment.

The one who wants to remain in my love should first begin to lift and turn the burden over, that is, he should attempt to do the good through his good will and constant desire. Then he should gradually lift the burden a little, that is, do the good he can do, thinking thus to himself: 'This I can do well if God gives me his help and grace.' Then he may persevere in the undertaken task and with great joy bear that which before seemed heavy to him so that every trouble in fasts and vigils or any other trouble will seem to be as light as feathers to him.

My friends rest in such a place, which, to the wicked and lazy, seems to be surrounded with things like spikes and thorns, but to my friends it is as the highest peace and soft as roses. The right way into this treasury is to deny and despise your own will, which happens when a man contemplates my suffering and my love, and does not care about his own will or lust but resists it with all his power and might and constantly strives for the things that are higher and better. And although this way is somewhat heavy in the beginning, it pleases so much in the continuation of it that the things that before seemed impossible to bear later become very light, so that he can rightfully say to himself: 'The yoke and work of God is good and sweet.'

The second treasury is the world. In it there are gold, precious stones, and drinks that seem delicious and pleasant-smelling but are bitter as poison when they are tasted. Each and everyone who carries and owns this gold, must - when his body is weakened and his limbs lose their strength, when his marrow is wasted and his body falls dead to the ground - leave the gold and the precious stones behind for they are of no more use to him than filth. And the drinks of the world, that is, her delights, seem delicious, but once in the stomach, they make the heart heavy and the head weak and ruin the body, and then man dries and withers away like grass, and when the pangs of death approach, all these pleasures become as bitter as poison. The way leading to this treasury is his self-will and lust, whenever a man does not care about resisting his evil desires and does not contemplate on what I have commanded or done, but immediately does whatever comes to mind, whether it may be licit or not.

Three men are walking on this way, and by these I mean all evil and unrighteous men who love the world and all their self-will. I cried out to these three men as I stood at the crossroads or the beginning of the ways, for when I came to the world in human flesh and body, I showed mankind two ways, as it were, namely, the one to follow and the one to avoid, in other words, the way leading to life and the one to death. For before my coming in the flesh, there was only one way, and on it, all men - good and bad - wandered toward hell.

I am the one who cried out, and my cry was this: 'People, hear my words that lead to the way of life, for they are true! Use your senses to understand that what I say is true. If you do not want to hear my words or cannot listen to them, then at least see them, that is, with faith and reason, see that my words are true. For just as something visible can be discerned with the eyes of the flesh, so too can invisible things be discerned and believed by the eyes of faith. There are many simple men in the Church and Christendom who do few good deeds but still are saved through their faith wherein they believe me to be the Creator of all things and the Redeemer of souls. There is no one who cannot understand and believe that I am God, if he considers how the earth bears fruit and how the heavens give rain, how the trees bloom, how each and every animal exists in its own kind, how the stars serve man, and how troubles and sorrows come and often happen against the will of man. From all these things, man can see that he is mortal and that it is God who arranges and directs all these things. For if God did not exist, everything would be disorganized. Thus, all things are of God, and everything is rationally arranged for the use and knowledge of mankind. And there is not the least little thing that is created or exists in the world without reasonable cause.

So, if a man cannot understand or comprehend my virtues and powers as they are because of his weakness, he can still see them with faith and believe. But if you people in the world do not want to use your reason to consider my power, you can still use your hands to touch and sense the deeds that I and my saints have done. They are namely so obvious that no one can doubt them to be the deeds of God. Who raised the dead and gave sight to the blind if not God? Who cast out the evil devils from men if not God? What have I taught if not things beneficial for the prosperity of soul and body and easy to bear?

But what the first man said means that some people say: 'Let us listen and test if what he says is true!' They stand a while in my service, not for the sake of love or charity but as an experiment and to imitate others; and they do not give up their own will but exercise it along with my will. They are in a dangerous position, for they want to serve two masters, even though they can serve neither one well. When they are called, they shall be rewarded by the master that they have loved the most.

What the second man said means that some people say: 'All his words are false and the Scripture is false.' I am God and the Creator of all things and without me nothing has been made. I laid down the New and the Old Laws; they came out of my mouth, and there is no falsehood in them because I am the Truth. Therefore, those who say that I have spoken falsely and that the Holy Scripture is false shall never see my face; for their conscience tells them that I am truly God, since all things happen according to my will and ordination. The sky gives them light, nor can they give any light to themselves. The earth bears fruit, the air makes the earth fertile, all the animals have a specific ordinance, the devils fear and confess me to be God and righteous men suffer incredible things for their love of me. All these things they see, and yet they do not see me. They could also see me and understand my justice, if they considered and thought on how the earth swallowed the ungodly and how the fire consumed the unrighteous. So could they likewise see me in my mercy when the water flowed for the righteous out of the rock or the water of the ocean parted for them, when the fire avoided harming them or when heaven gave them food like the earth. Because they see all these things and still say I am a liar, they shall never see my face.

What the third man said means that some people say: 'We know full well that he is the true God, but we do not care about it.' These people will suffer and be tormented for all eternity, because they despise me, who am their God and Lord. Is it not a great contempt of them to use my good gifts but nonetheless refuse to serve me? For if they had earned these things by their own diligence and not wholly and entirely from me, their contempt would be small.

But I will give my grace to those who begin to turn over my burden, that is, to those who voluntarily and with a passionate desire attempt to do the little good they can. I will work with the people who lift my weights, that is, those who advance in good deeds day by day for the sake of my love, and I will be their strength and enlighten them so that they will want to do more good. But those who sit in the place that seems to sting them, but really is most peaceful, they work patiently day and night without tiring, increasing more and more in the ardent fire for my honor, thinking that what they do for my sake is very little. These are my most dear friends, and they are very few, since the drinks found in the other treasury are more pleasing to the others.

About how the bride perceived a saint speaking to God about a woman who was being horribly tormented by the devil and who was later delivered from him through the prayers of the glorious Virgin Mary.

# Chapter 16

The bride saw a saint speaking to God, saying: "Why is the soul of this woman so afflicted by the devil when you have redeemed her by your blood?" The devil replied instantly and said: "Because she is mine by right." Then our Lord said: "With what right is she yours?" The devil answered: "There are two ways; one leads to the kingdom of Heaven and the other to hell. When she saw these two ways, her conscience and reason told her that she should choose my way. And since she had a free will for choosing the way that she wanted, it seemed to her more beneficial to turn her will toward committing sin, and so she began to walk on my way.

Thereafter, I deceived her with three sins: namely, gluttony, love of money, and sensuality. Consequently, I now dwell in her belly and in her nature, and I hold her with five hands. With the first hand I hold her eyes, so she will not see spiritual things. With my second hand I hold her hands, so she will not do any good deeds. With the third hand I hold her feet, so she will not walk to that which is good. With the fourth hand I hold her reason and understanding, so she will not be ashamed to sin. And with the fifth hand I hold her heart, so she will not return to the right way through remorse and penance."

Then the Blessed Virgin Mary said to her dear Son: "My beloved Son, compel him to tell the truth about the things I want to ask him." The Son said: "You are my Mother, you are the Queen of Heaven and the Mother of mercy, you are the consolation of the souls in purgatory and the joy of those who make their way in the world; you are the Mistress of the angels and the most Holy before God, and you are also in authority over the devil. Therefore, command this devil what you want, and he will answer you."

Then the Holy Virgin Mary asked the devil, saying: "Tell me, devil, what intention had this woman before she entered the church?" The devil answered her: "She had an intention to abstain from sin." Then the Virgin Mary said to the devil: "Since the will that she previously had led her to hell, tell me now, where does the will that she presently has lead her - namely, her will to abstain from sin?" The devil answered reluctantly: "This will of abstaining from sin leads her toward Heaven."

Then the Virgin Mary said: "Because you accepted that it was your just right to lead her away from the way of the Holy Church because of her former will to sin, then it is now right and just that her present will shall lead her back to the Church and to the mercy of God. But now, devil, I will ask you another question. Tell me, what intention does she have in her present state of conscience?" The devil answered: "She has remorse in her mind for the things she has done, and great sadness, and resolves to never again commit such sins but wants to amend as much as she is able."

Then the Virgin Mary asked the devil: "Tell me, could these three sins, namely, sensuality, gluttony, and greed, exist together in a heart at the same time as the three good deeds of remorse, sorrow, and the resolution to improve oneself?" The devil answered: "No." The Holy Virgin Mary then said: "Therefore, tell me, which of these should flee and vanish from her heart, the three virtues or the three vices and sins; for you are saying that they cannot occupy the same heart or place together." The devil said: "I say that the sins must give way."

Then the Virgin Mary answered: "Therefore, the way to hell is closed to her and the way to the kingdom of Heaven is open." Now the Holy Virgin Mary asked the devil further: "Tell me, if a robber was waiting outside the house of the bride and wanted to rob and rape her, what should the bridegroom do?" The devil answered: "If the bridegroom is good and noble-minded, he should defend her and risk his life for her life." The Virgin Mary then said: "You are the wicked robber, and the soul is my Son's bride, for he redeemed her with his own blood. You violated and seized her by force. But since my Son is the Bridegroom of the soul and Lord over you, then it is right for you to flee from him."

# Explanation

This woman was a harlot. She wanted to return to the world because the devil tormented her day and night, so much so that he visibly pressed down her eyes, and in the sight of many, dragged her out of bed. Saint Bridget then said openly in the presence and hearing of many trustworthy men: "Move away, devil, for you have troubled and occupied this creature of God enough!" After she had said this, the woman laid a half hour as if dead with her eyes to the ground, and then she got up and said: "In truth, I saw the devil going out through the window in the most hideous of shapes, and I heard a voice saying to me: 'You are in truth liberated from the devil, woman!'" From that moment on, this woman was delivered from all impatience and suffering and was no longer tormented by impure thoughts, and then she died a good death.

The words of our Lord Jesus Christ to his bride wherein he compares a sinner to three things: namely, an eagle, a fowler, and a fighting man.

# Chapter 17

"I am Jesus Christ who am speaking with you. I was in the womb of the Virgin as true God and true man but was, nonetheless, with the Father and controlled and ruled all things, although I was in the Virgin. This most wretched enemy of mine is like three things: First, he is like an eagle that flies in the air while other birds fly under it. Second, he is like a fowler that gently blows and plays on a pipe plastered with glue, causing the birds to be enchanted by his tunes so that they fly toward the pipe and get stuck in the glue. Third, he is like a fighting man who is first in every battle.

He is like an eagle, because in his pride he cannot tolerate anyone being over him, and he injures everyone he can reach with his claws of malice. Therefore, I will cut off the wings of his violence and pride. I will remove his malice from the earth and give him over to the unquenchable boiling kettle, which is the suffering of hell, where he will be tormented without end, if he does not better himself.

He is also like a fowler because he attracts everyone to himself with sweet words and promises, so that anyone who comes to him gets caught in damnation and perdition and can never escape from it. Therefore, the birds of hell shall destroy his eyes so that he will never see my glory but only the eternal darkness of hell. They shall cut off his ears so that he will not hear the words of my mouth. They shall inflict him with pain and bitterness from the feet to the head so that he will endure as many torments as the number of men he led to damnation.

He is also like a fighting man who is first in all evil, not willing to give way to anybody but determined to press everyone down. Therefore, he shall be first in every torment; his suffering shall always be renewed and his lament will never end. However, my mercy stands ready for him as long as his soul is with the body.

# Explanation

This man was a very powerful knight who hated the church and the priesthood greatly and inflicted it with insulting words. The previous revelation is about him as well as the following. The Son of God says: "O worldly knight, ask the wise about what happened to prideful Haman who despised my people. Did he not die shamefully and with great disgrace? Likewise does this man scoff at me and my friends. Just as the people of Israel did not mourn Haman's death, so will my friends not mourn this man's death, but he will die a most bitter death if he does not better himself." This is what happened to him.

The words of Christ to his bride about how there should be humility in the house of God, and about how such a house signifies purity of life, and about how buildings and alms should be donated only from goods that are righteously acquired, and about how to restore wrongly acquired goods.

# Chapter 18

"In my house should all humility be, which now is completely rejected. There should be a strong wall between the men and the women, because even though I am able to defend everyone and hold them all without a wall, still, for the sake of precaution and because of the devil's cunning, I want that a wall should separate the two dwelling-houses. It should be strong, and not very high but moderate. The windows should be very simple and clear, and the roof moderately high, so that nothing can be seen there that does not belong to humility. For those who now build houses for me are like master builders, who, when the lord or the master of the house enters into them, grab him by the hair and trample him under their feet; they raise the filth up high and trample the gold underfoot. This is what many do to me now.

They build up the filth, that is, they build up perishable and worldly things to the sky, but the souls that are more precious than all gold, they could not care any less about. If I want to go in to them through my preachers or through good thoughts, they grab me by the hair and trample me under their feet, that is, they insult me and consider my deeds and my words to be as despicable as filth. They consider themselves to be much wiser. But if they wanted to build up things for me and for my honor, they should first build up the souls to the kingdom of Heaven.

The one who wants to build my house should, with the utmost precision, take care about not letting a penny that has not been properly and justly acquired, go to the building. There are indeed many who know full well that they have wrongly acquired goods and yet are not sorry for it nor have the will of making restitution or giving it back to the people they have cheated and plundered, although they could give it back and make restitution for the injustice if they wanted. But since they know and think to themselves that they cannot keep these things forever, they give a part of their wrongly acquired goods to the churches or monasteries, as if they wanted to appease me by their gift. But the other goods that are properly acquired, they keep for their descendants. In truth, this does not please me.

The one who wants to please me with his gifts should first have the will to better and correct himself and then do the good deeds he is able to do. He should also cry and mourn over the evil things and deeds he has done and then make restitution if he can; and if he cannot, he should have the will of making restitution for the deceitfully acquired goods. Thereafter, he should take great care to never again commit such things. But if it is not possible to find anyone to give back the unlawfully acquired goods to, then he could give it to me, for I am able to pay back everyone what is theirs. If he cannot give it back but has the intention of humbling and improving himself before me with a broken heart, then I am rich enough to give it back and I can restore the property of all those who have been cheated, either now in this world or in the next to come.

I want to explain to you the meaning of the house that I want to build. This house is the life of purity, and I myself, who created all things and through whom all has been made and exists, am its foundation. There are four walls in this house. The first is my justice, by which I will judge those who are adversarial to this house. The second wall is the wisdom by which I will enlighten the builders of this house with my knowledge and understanding. The third wall is my power, by which I will strengthen them against the temptations of the devil. The fourth wall is my mercy, which receives everyone who prays for it. In this wall is the door of grace through which all, who pray for it, are accepted in. The roof of this house is the love with which I cover the sins of those who love me so that they will not be judged for their sins. The window of the roof, whereby the sun enters, is the thought and consideration of my mercy, and through it the warmth of my Divinity is let in to the builders of the house. But that the wall should be strong and big means that no one is able to undermine my words or overthrow them. That the wall should be moderately high means that my wisdom can be understood and perceived in part, but never fully. The simple but clear windows mean that my words are simple, yet through them the light of divine knowledge is let into the world. The moderately high roof means that my words shall be revealed, not in an incomprehensible way, but in an understandable way that one may easily perceive and comprehend.

The words of our God and Creator to his bride about the splendor of his power, wisdom, and virtue, and about how those who are now called powerful and wise, sin the most against him.

# Chapter 19

"I am the Creator of the heavens and the earth. I have three qualities: I am most mighty, most wise, and most virtuous. I am namely so mighty that all the angels in Heaven honor me, the demons in hell dare not look upon me, and all the elements obey my command. I am also so wise that no one can fathom or understand my wisdom, and I have so great insight that I know all that has been and will come to be. I am thereto so rational that not the least little worm or any other animal, no matter how ugly it may seem, has been made without a cause. I am also so virtuous that all good flows from me as from a good spring, and all sweetness emanates from me as from a good wine. Therefore, no one can be mighty, wise, or virtuous without me.

And therefore do the mighty men of the world sin against me very much, for I gave them strength and power so they could honor and glorify me; but they awarded the honor to themselves, as if they had it from themselves. These miserable wretches do not realize their own powerlessness: for if I were to send them the least sickness, they would immediately wither away and everything would become worthless to them. How then could they be able to withstand my strength and power or the eternal torments? But even more do those, who are now said to be wiser than others, sin against me. For I gave them mental powers, understanding, and wisdom so they would love me, but they do not want to understand anything other than that which is to their own temporal benefit and greed. They have their eyes in the back of their head and look only to their own lusts and pleasures, and they are so blind in serving me that they do not give thanks to me, who gave them everything. For no one, neither good nor bad, could feel and understand anything without me, although I allow the wicked to turn their will to their desires. Moreover, no one can be virtuous without me.

Therefore, I could now use the words of the proverb that everyone commonly cites: 'The patient man is despised by everyone.' So am I now considered by mankind to be utterly foolish for my patience, and that is why I am despised by everyone. But woe to them, when my time of patience is over and they will come to know my judgment! They will then be like mud before me that falls down to the deepest depths and does not stop until it comes down to the lowest part of hell.

The Virgin Mother's and the Son's pleasant dialogue with each other and with the bride, and about how the bride should prepare herself for the wedding.

# Chapter 20

The Mother of God, the Virgin Mary appeared saying to her Son: "O my Son, you are the King of glory. You are Lord over all lords. You created heaven and earth and all the things in them. Therefore, may your every desire be done, may all your will be done!"

The Son answered: "It is an ancient proverb that says that what a youth learns in his youth, he preserves in his old age. So have also you, my dear Mother, from your youth learned to follow my will and to surrender all your will for my sake. Therefore you did well to say: 'May your will be done.' You are like precious gold that is laid on a hard anvil and hammered, for you were hammered with every kind of tribulation, and through my suffering you endured more pain than anyone before. For when my heart burst from the violent pain and bitterness on the cross, your heart was also wounded as if by the sharpest steel, and you would have willingly let it be cut into pieces, had that been my will. But even if you had been able to stop my suffering and wished for my life, still you did not want to if it was not my will. Therefore you did well to say: 'Your will be done.'

Thereafter, the Virgin Mary said to the bride of God: "My Son's bride, love my Son, for he loves you, and honor his saints who stand in his presence, for they are like countless stars whose light and brilliance cannot be compared to any worldly light. Just like the light of the world differs from darkness, yet even more does the light of the saints differ from the light of this world. In truth, I tell you that if the saints were seen in their brightness as they really are, no human eye could set eyes on them or endure it without losing their sight and life."

Thereafter, the Son of God spoke to his bride and said: "My bride, you should have four qualities: First, you should be ready for the wedding of my Divinity wherein no fleshly lusts are found, but only the most sweet spiritual desire, the one that is becoming for God to have with a chaste soul. The love for your children, your friends, or your temporal belongings should not draw you away from my love. May it not happen to you what happened to those foolish virgins who were not ready when the Lord wanted to call them to the wedding and were therefore excluded.

Second, you should believe my words, for I am the Truth, and from my mouth has never anything come but truth, and nobody can find anything other than truth in my words. Sometimes I have a spiritual meaning with what I am saying, and sometimes I expressly mean what the words say, and my words should then be understood as they are, without any interpretation. Therefore, no one can justly accuse me of lying.

Third, you should be obedient in order for you to do righteous penance and reparation in all the limbs with which you sinned; for even though I am merciful, I do not forego justice. Therefore, obey with humility and gladness those whom you are charged to obey, so that you do not do even the things which seem beneficial and reasonable to you if it goes against obedience. For it is better to surrender your own will for the sake of obedience, even if it is good, and to follow the will of your superior, as long as it does not go against the salvation of the soul or is unreasonable in any other way.

Fourth, you should be humble, for you are united in a spiritual marriage. Thus, you should be humble and modest at the arrival of your bridegroom. Your handmaid should be sober and restrained, which means that your body should be abstinent from all superfluous things and well disciplined. For you will become fruitful with spiritual offspring for the benefit and good of many, just as a shoot is grafted onto a dry stem and makes the stem begin to blossom; so through my grace you shall bear fruit and blossom. My grace will gladden and intoxicate you, and the whole host of Heaven will rejoice because of the sweet wine I will give you. You must not lack trust in my goodness.

I assure you that just as Zechariah and Elizabeth rejoiced in their souls with an unspeakable joy over the promise of a future child, you too, shall rejoice over my grace that I want to give you, and thereto, others will rejoice through you. With these two, Zechariah and Elizabeth, an angel spoke; but I, the God and Creator of the angels, want to speak to you. These two, Zechariah and Elizabeth, gave birth to my most dear friend John, but I want many sons to be born to me through you, not of the flesh but of the spirit. In truth, I tell you, John was like a tube or flower full of sweetness and honey, for never did anything unclean or superfluous enter his mouth, and he never received the necessities of life over the limits of what he needed. And semen never went out of his body and that is why he can rightly be called an angel and a virgin for the divine life that he lived."

The Bridegroom's words to his bride found in the most delightful parable about a sorcerer by which the devil is ingeniously signified and described.

# Chapter 21

The Bridegroom of the kingdom of Heaven, Jesus, spoke to his bride in a parable presenting the example of a frog and said: "Once there was a sorcerer who had the most shining gold. A simple and mild man came to him and wanted to buy this gold from him. The sorcerer said to the simple man: 'You will not receive this gold, unless you give me better gold and in larger quantity.' The man said: 'I have such a great desire for your gold that I will give you what you want rather than losing it.' He then gave the sorcerer better gold and in larger quantity and received the shining gold from him and put it in a casket, thinking of making himself a ring from it for his finger.

After a short time, the sorcerer approached that simple man and said: 'The gold you bought from me and laid in your casket is not gold, as you thought, but the most ugly frog. It has been fostered in my chest and fed with my food. And in order for you to test and know that this is true, you may open the casket and you will see how the frog will jump to my chest where it was fostered.' When the man wanted to open it and find out if it was true, the frog appeared in the casket. The cover of the casket was hanging on four hinges that were about to break and fall off soon. Immediately when the cover of the casket was opened, the frog saw the sorcerer and jumped into his chest.

When the servants and friends of the simple man saw this, they said to him: 'Lord, this most fine gold is in the frog, and if you want, you can easily get the gold.' The man said: 'How can I get it?' They replied: 'If someone took a sharp and heated spear and thrust it into the hollow part of the frog's back, he would quickly get the gold out. But if he cannot find any hollow in the frog, he should then, with the greatest force and effort, thrust his spear into it, and this is how you will get back the gold you bought.'

Who is this sorcerer if not the devil, inciting and counseling mankind to fleshly lusts and honor, which are nothing else but vanity and destruction? He promises that what is false is true and makes what is true seem to be false. He possesses this most precious gold, namely, the soul, who I, through my divine power, created more precious than all the stars and planets. I created it immortal and imperishable and more pleasing to me than everything else and I prepared for her an eternal resting place with me. I bought her from the violence of the devil with better and more valuable gold when I gave my own flesh for her, spotless from every sin, and suffered such a bitter torment that none of my limbs were without wounds or pain. I placed the redeemed soul in the body as in a casket, until the time when I would place her in the presence of my divine honor and glory in the kingdom of Heaven. But now, the redeemed soul of man has become like the most ugly and shameless frog, jumping in its arrogance and living in filth through its sensuality. She has taken my gold away from me, that is, all my justice.

That is why the devil rightly can say to me: 'The gold you bought is not gold but a frog, fostered in the chest of my lust. Separate therefore the body from the soul and you shall see that she will jump directly to the chest of my lust where it was fostered.' My answer is this: 'Since the frog is hideous to look at, frightful to hear, and poisonous to touch, and does not bring me any good nor any pleasure or comfort but only does so for you, in whose chest she was fostered, you can have it, since she is yours by right. And when the door is opened, that is, when the soul is separated from the body, she will fly directly to you to remain with you for all eternity.'

Such is the soul of the man I am talking about to you. She is namely like the most vile frog, full of filthiness and lust, fostered in the chest of the devil. To the casket, that is, to his body, I am now coming closer through his coming death. The casket is hanging by four hinges that are about to fall off, for his body is supported by four things: namely, strength, beauty, wisdom, and sight, which are all now beginning to perish and fade for him. When his soul begins to separate from the body, she flies straightaway to the devil on whose milk it was fostered, that is, his lust, since she has forgotten my love with which I took upon myself the suffering and pain she deserved. She does not repay my love with love, and deprives me of my rightful possession, because she should love me more than anyone else since I redeemed her. But she finds a greater pleasure in the devil. The voice of her prayer is like the voice of the frog, and her appearance is abominable and hideous in my sight. Her ears will never hear my joy, and her poisoned senses will never feel my Divinity.

But, I am still merciful, and if anyone were to touch his soul, even though she is unclean, and examine her to see if there is any remorse or good will in it, and thrust a sharp and burning spear into his mind, which means the fear of my severe judgment, then he could still find my mercy, if he only would obey me. And if there is no remorse and love in him, still there is hope, if someone were to pierce him with a sharp and bitter correction and rebuked him strictly. For as long as the soul lives with the body, my mercy is open and ready for everyone.

Consider therefore how I died because of my love, and yet nobody repays me with love, but they even take from me what is mine by right; for it would be true justice if men improved their lives in proportion to the pain and suffering of their redemption. But now they want to live all the worse in proportion to the bitter pain and death I suffered when redeeming them; and the more I show them the hatefulness and ugliness of sin, the more boldly they want to sin. Behold, therefore, and consider that I do not get angry without cause, for they have changed my mercy into wrath. I redeemed them from sin, and they entangle themselves even more in sin.

But you, my bride, give me what you are obliged to give me, that is, may you keep your soul pure for me, because I died for you in order that you might keep her pure for me."

The Mother's most lovely question to the bride, the humble answer of the bride to the Mother, and the Mother's useful answer to the bride, and about the improvement of good people among the evil.

# Chapter 22

The Mother of God spoke to her Son's bride, saying: "You are my Son's bride. Tell me what is on your mind and what you are praying for." The bride answered: "My Lady, you know it very well, for you know all things." Then the Holy Virgin said: "Even though I know all things, I would still like to hear you tell me while those standing here present are listening." The bride said: "My Lady, I fear two things: First, for my sins, for which I do not cry and make amends for as I would like. Second, I am sad because your Son's enemies are so many."

Then the Virgin Mary answered: "In regard to the first one, I give you three cures: First, think about how all things that have spirit, such as frogs and other animals, have troubles sometimes, and yet their spirits do not live eternally but die with the body. But your soul and every human soul does live forever. Second, think about the mercy of God, because there is no man who is so sinful that his sin is not immediately forgiven, if he only prays for God's forgiveness with an intention to better himself and with true repentance for his former sins. Third, think and visualize about how great the glory of the soul is when she lives forever with God and in God.

And regarding the second, namely, that the enemies of God are so many, I give you three cures also: First, consider that your God and your Creator and theirs is judge over them, and they will never judge him again, even though he patiently bears their malice for a time. Second, consider that they are the sons of damnation and how heavy and intolerable it will be for them to burn for all eternity in hell. They are like the most wicked servants who will lose the inheritance of the kingdom of Heaven, while the sons will partake of the inheritance. But now maybe you will say: 'Should not one preach to them?' Yes, of course one should preach to them! Consider how good people are often found among the evil, and that the sons of evil sometimes turn away from the good, just like the prodigal son who demanded his inheritance from his father and went away to a faraway kingdom and lived an evil life. But sometimes they are seized by remorse through the preaching and return to the Father, and they are more welcome to him then as if they had never been sinful before. Therefore, one should preach especially to them, because, even though the preacher almost only sees evil people, he, nonetheless, thinks to himself: 'Perhaps there are some among them who will become the sons of my Lord; I will therefore preach to them.' This kind of preacher will receive the greatest reward. Third, consider that the wicked are allowed to live as a trial for the good, so that, if they are sorrowful for the behavior of the wicked, they might be rewarded with the fruit of patience, as you will understand better by the following parable.

The rose smells sweet, is beautiful to look upon, is soft to the touch, and yet it only grows among thorns that are sharp to the touch, hideous to look upon, and do not have a pleasant scent. Similarly, good and righteous men, even though they are soft in their patience, beautiful in their virtues, and sweet smelling in their good example, still cannot become perfected or be put to the test except among the evil. Sometimes the thorn also protects the rose so that it will not be picked before it has bloomed; likewise, the evil give the good an occasion and a reason not to fall into sin, and sometimes the good are restrained by their malice so that they do not fall into immoderate cheerfulness or lust or any other sin. A wine will never become good unless it is stored in the dreg, and neither can the good and righteous remain and improve in virtues if they are not tested through afflictions and persecutions by the unrighteous. So tolerate willingly the enemies of my Son, and remember that he is their judge, and that he, if justice demanded to destroy them all, could easily exterminate them in a moment. Therefore, may you tolerate them as long as he tolerates them."

The words of Christ to his bride about a false man, who is called an enemy of God, and about his hypocrisy and all his characteristics.

# Chapter 23

"This man appears to the people to be a well-dressed, strong, and attractive man, who is brave in his Lord's battle, but when his helmet is removed from his head, he is ugly and disgusting to look at and is useless for work. His brain is seen to be bare. His ears are on his forehead and his eyes are in his neck. His nose is dissevered and his cheeks are altogether sunken like those of a dead man. On the right side, his chin and half of his lips have all fallen off, so that nothing is left on the right side except his throat which is seen to be all uncovered. His chest is full of swarming worms and his arms are like two snakes. The most poisonous scorpion lives in his heart. His back is like burnt coal. His intestines are stinking and rotting like pus-filled, unclean flesh. His feet are dead and useless to walk with.

I will tell you what all this signifies. On the outside he appears to people to be decorated with good habits, wisdom and bravery in the service and honor of me, but he is by no means like that. For if the helmet were removed from his head, that is, if it were shown to people how he really is spiritually in his soul, he would be uglier than all men. His brain is bare because his foolish customs and frivolity clearly demonstrate to good men that he is unworthy of such an honor. For if my wisdom pleased him, he would understand how much his honor is greater than others, thereby clothing himself in the most rigorous of conduct and divine virtues as compared to others.

The ears are on his forehead because, instead of having the humility due to his high dignity in being a light for others to teach them good things, he only wants to hear about his own praise and glory, thereby becoming so prideful that he only wants to be called great and good by everyone. He has eyes in his neck, because all his thoughts are turned to the present instead of the eternal. He thinks about how to please men and about the requirements for the needs of the flesh, but not about how he may please me and benefit souls. His nose is dissevered, since he has lost all rational discretion whereby he might see and distinguish between sin and virtue, between worldly honor and eternal honor, between worldly and eternal riches, between the short pleasures of the world and the eternal pleasures.

His cheeks are sunken, that is, all the veneration he should have for me, with the beauty of the virtues whereby he might please me, are entirely dead in the service of me: for he is ashamed to sin in front of men but not in front of me. One part of his cheekbone and lips has fallen off so that nothing remains except for his throat, for the imitation of my works and the preaching of my words, in Addition to a divine and fervent prayer, have totally fallen off from him so that nothing remains in him except his gluttonous throat. But to imitate the wicked and to be involved in worldly affairs seems altogether healthy and beautiful to him.

His chest is full of worms, because in his chest, where the remembrance of my suffering and the thought and consideration of my deeds and commandments should be, there is only a care for the things of the world with the desire and greed of the world, which are like worms devouring his conscience so that he does not think of spiritual or divine things. In his heart, where I would wish to dwell and my love should be, there now sits the most evil scorpion with a stinging tail and an enticing face and tongue; because pleasing and reasonable words proceed from his mouth, but his heart is full of injustice and deceit, because he does not care if the church he is supervising gets destroyed, as long as he can fulfill his own will.

His arms are like two snakes, because in his malice he reaches out his arms to the simple-minded and calls them to himself with simplicity, but, when he gets a suitable opportunity, he causes them to fall pitifully. Like a snake, he coils himself into a ring, because he hides his malice and unrighteousness, so that barely anyone can understand his treacherous plans. He is like the most vile snake in my sight, for just as the snake is more detestable than any other animal, so is he more ugly in my sight than any other man, since he counts my justice as nothing and holds me to be as a man who is unwilling to judge righteously.

His back is like coal, but it should be like ivory since his deeds should be more mighty and pure than others in order to be able to better carry the weak through his patience and his example of a good life. But now he is like coal, because he is too impatient to endure a single word for my honor, unless he benefits from it. Yet he seems to be mighty to the world. Therefore, when he thinks he stands, he will fall, since he is as hideous and lifeless as coal before me and my saints.

His intestines stink, because his thoughts and desires smell like rotting flesh before me with a stench that no one can tolerate. Neither can any of my saints tolerate him, but everyone turns his face away from him and demands a judgment over him. His feet are dead. His two feet are his two dispositions towards me, that is, his will to make amends for the sins he has done and his will to do good deeds. But these feet are altogether dead in him, because all the marrow of love is consumed in him and nothing is left in him except the hardened bones. And in this way he stands before me. However, as long as the soul is with the body, he can find my mercy.

## Explanation

Saint Lawrence appeared and said: "When I was in the world, I had three things: self-purity, mercy to my neighbor, and love of God. Therefore I preached the word of God fervently, distributed the goods of the Church wisely, and suffered the scourging, fire, and death gladly. But this bishop tolerates and pretends not to notice the incontinence of the clergy, and he liberally distributes the goods of the Church to the rich and shows love only toward himself and his own friends. Therefore, I declare to him that the lightest cloud now has ascended into heaven, but dark smoke of fire overshadows it so that it cannot be seen by many. This cloud is the prayer of the Mother of God for the Holy Church. The fire of greed, ungodliness, and unrighteousness darken it so much that the mercy of the Mother of God cannot easily enter the hearts of the wretched. Therefore, let the bishop quickly turn to the divine love by correcting himself and his subordinates, admonishing them with his good example and word, and leading them to a better life. Otherwise, he will feel the hand of the judge which is his vengeance and justice, and his church will be purged by fire and the sword and afflicted by plundering and tribulation so that it will be a long time before anyone consoles her."

God the Father's words before the host of the kingdom of Heaven, and the answer of the Son and Mother to the Father asking for mercy for the daughter, that is, the Church.

# Chapter 24

God the Father spoke while the whole host of heaven was listening, and said: "Before you all, I complain over giving my daughter to a man who tortures her greatly and without measure, crushing her feet in the stocks so severely that all the marrow has gone out of her feet." The Son answered him: "Father, she is the one I redeemed with my blood and espoused to myself, but now she has been brutally violated." Then the Mother of God spoke and said: "You are my God and my Lord, and your blessed Son's limbs were enclosed within my body, who is your true Son and my true Son. I refused you nothing on earth. Have mercy on your daughter for the sake of my prayers."

Thereafter the angels spoke, saying: "You are our Lord and Creator; in you we possess every good thing, and we need nothing but you. We all rejoiced when your bride went forth from you, but now we are rightly sad, because she has been given into the hands of the worst man who insults her with all kinds of mocking and abuse. Have mercy on her for the sake of your great mercy, for her misery is very great, and there is no one to console and save her but you Lord, God Almighty."

Then God the Father answered the Son, saying: "O my Son, your grievance is my grievance, your word my word, your deeds my deeds. You are in me and I am in you inseparably. Your will be done!" Then he said to the Mother of the Son: "Since you did not refuse me anything on earth, I will not refuse you anything in heaven, and your will shall be fulfilled." Then he said to the angels: "You are my friends, and the flame of your love burns in my heart. Therefore, I shall have mercy on my daughter for the sake of your prayers."

The words of the Creator to his bride about how His justice endures evil men for a threefold reason, and how His mercy spares the evil for a threefold reason.

# Chapter 25

"I am the Creator of the heavens and the earth. You wondered, my bride, why I am so patient with the evil. That is because I am merciful: for my justice endures and spares them for a threefold reason and my mercy spares them for a threefold reason. First, my justice endures them so that their time may be fully completed. For just as a righteous king might be asked, if he holds someone imprisoned, why he does not put them to death, and he answers: 'Because it is not yet time for the inquisition of the court where they may be heard so that those who hear it can take greater warning.' In this way do I tolerate the evil until the time comes for their malice to be made known to others as well. Did I not foretell the rejection of Saul and that he would be expelled from his kingdom and dethroned long before it was made known to men? And I tolerated him for a long time so that his malice would be shown and proven to others. Second, because of the few good deeds that the evil do for which they should be rewarded even down to the last farthing, there shall not be the least little good they have done for me that will go unrewarded; herein they will receive their wage for the good they have done. Third, in order to reveal God's glory and patience. It was for this reason that I tolerated Pilate, Herod, and Judas, even though they were evil and damned. And if anyone questions why I tolerate this or that person, let him regard Judas and Pilate.

My mercy also spares the evil for a threefold reason: First, because of my great love, for their eternal torment will be long. For that reason, because of my great love, I tolerate them until the last moment so that their torment will be delayed by the long extension of time here in the world. Second, so that their nature will be consumed by the sins, because the human nature gets consumed by sin so that they would experience the bodily death more bitterly if their nature was healthier and stronger. For a healthy nature dies a more prolonged and bitter death. Third, for the improvement and strength of good people and the conversion of some of the evil. For when good and righteous people are tormented by the evil, it benefits the good and righteous since it helps them to abstain from sin or to gain greater merit.

Likewise, the evil sometimes live for the good of other evil persons. For when the evil reflect on the fall, wickedness, and heinous deeds of some people, they think to themselves and say: 'What good does it do us to follow them or to live like them? While our Lord is so patient, it is better for us to repent.' And in this way they sometimes return to me, because they fear to do the things those evil men did, and their conscience tells them they should not do these things. Therefore, it is said, that if someone has been stung by a scorpion, he can be cured by being anointed with the oil wherein another reptile has died. In the same way, sometimes an evil man, who sees another person who is also evil fall and beholds his unrighteousness and vanity, is struck by remorse for his sins and is cured by the mercy and grace of God.

The angelic host's words of praise to God, and about how children would have been born if the first parents had not sinned, and about how God showed miracles to the people through Moses and also later through himself to us on his own coming; and about the breakdown of the bodily marriage in this time, and the conditions of a spiritual marriage.

# Chapter 26

The angelic host was seen standing before God, and the entire host said: "Praised and honored be you, Lord God, who are and were without end! We are your servants and we praise and honor you for a threefold reason: First, because you created us to rejoice with you and gave us an indescribable light in which to rejoice forever. Second, because all things are created and maintained by your goodness and constancy, and all things stand according to your will and remain through your word. Third, because you created mankind and took Manhood for their sake! We rejoice greatly for this Manhood, and also for your most chaste Mother who was worthy to bear you whom the heavens cannot comprehend and enclose. Therefore, your honor and blessing are above all things for the dignity of the angels that you have exalted greatly in honor. May your everlasting eternity and constancy be over all things that are and can be constant! May your love be over mankind whom you created! O Lord God, you alone should be feared for your great power, you alone should be desired for your great love, you alone should be loved for your constancy. May all praise and honor be to you forever without end. Amen!"

Then our Lord answered: "You honor me worthily for every created creature. But, tell me, why do you praise me for mankind which has provoked me to wrath more than any other creature? I created him more superior and dignified than all the lower creatures under the sky, and for none else did I suffer such indignities as for mankind and none was redeemed at so great a cost. Or what creature does not abide by its created order other than man? He inflicts me more with sorrow than any other creature. For just as I created you to praise and honor me, so I made man to honor me. I gave him a body like a spiritual temple, and I made and placed the soul in it like a beautiful angel, for the human soul has power and strength like an angel. In this temple, I, the God and Creator of mankind, wished to be like the third so that he would enjoy me and find delight in me. Then I made him another temple, similar to himself, out of his rib.

But now, my bride, for whose sake all these things are being said and shown, you might ask, how children would have been born by them if they had not sinned? I shall answer you: In truth, by the love of God and the mutual devotion and union of the flesh wherein they both would have been set on fire internally, love's blood would have sown its seed in the woman's body without any shameful lust, and so the woman would have become fertile. Once the child was conceived without sin and lustful desire, I would have sent a soul into the child from my divinity, and the woman would have carried the child and given birth to it without pain. When the child was born, it would have been perfect like Adam when he was first created. But this honor was despised by man when he obeyed the devil and coveted a greater honor than I had given to him. After the disobedience was enacted, my angel came over them and they were ashamed over their nakedness, and they immediately experienced the lust and desire of the flesh and suffered hunger and thirst. Then they also lost me, for when they had me, they did not feel any hunger or sinful fleshly lust or shame, but I alone was all their good and pleasure and perfect delight.

But when the devil rejoiced over their perdition and fall, I was moved with compassion for them and did not abandon them but showed them a threefold mercy: I clothed them when they were naked and gave them bread from the earth. And for the sensuality the devil had aroused in them after their disobedience, I gave and created souls in their seed through my Divinity. And all the evil the devil tempted them with, I turned to good for them entirely.

Thereafter, I showed them how to live and worship me, and I gave them permission to have relations, because before my permission and the enunciation of my will they were stricken with fear and were afraid to unite and have relations. Likewise, when Abel was killed and they were in mourning for a long time and observing abstinence, I was moved with compassion and comforted them. And when they understood my will, they began again to have relations and to procreate children, from which family I, their Creator, promised to be born. When the wickedness of the children of Adam grew, I showed my justice to the sinful, but mercy to my elect; of these I was appeased so that I kept them from destruction and raised them up, because they kept my commandments and believed in my promises.

When the time of mercy came, I showed my mighty miracles and works through Moses and saved my people according to my promise. I fed them with angel manna and went before them in a pillar of cloud and fire. I gave them my Law and revealed to them my secrets and the future through my prophets. Thereafter, I, the Creator of all things, chose for myself a virgin born of a father and mother; and from her did I take human nature and condescended to be born of her without sin. Just like the first children would have been born in paradise through the divine love of their father's and mother's mutual love and affection without any shameful lust, so my Divinity took Manhood from a virgin without any shameful lust and without hindering or damaging her virginity.

I came in the flesh as true God and man and fulfilled the Old Law and all the scriptures just as it earlier had been prophesied about me, and I initiated the New Law, for the Old Law was narrow and hard to bear and was nothing but a figure of future things to come. For in the Old Law it had been allowed for a man to have several wives, so that the people would not be left without any offspring or would have to intermarry with the gentiles. But in my New Law it is permitted for one man to have one wife, and it is forbidden for him during her lifetime to have several wives. Those who unite with divine love and fear for the sake of procreation and to raise children for the honor of God are my spiritual temple where I wish to dwell as the third with them.

But people in this age are joined in marriage for seven reasons: First, because of facial beauty. Second, because of wealth. Third, because of the despicable pleasure and indecent joy they get out of their impure intercourse. Fourth, because of feasts with friends and uncontrolled gluttony. Fifth, because of vanity in clothing and eating, in joking and entertainment and games and other vanities. Sixth, for the sake of procreating children but not to raise them for the honor of God or good works but for worldly riches and honor. Seventh, they come together for the sake of lust and they are like brute beasts in their lustful desires.

They come to the doors of my church with one mind and consent, but all their desires and inner thoughts are completely against me. They prefer their own will, which aims at pleasing the world, instead of my will. If all their thoughts and wishes were directed toward me, and if they entrusted their will into my hands and entered into wedlock in fear of me, then I would give them my consent and be as the third with them. But now is my consent, which should be their most precious thing, gone from them, because they have lust in their heart and not my love. Thereafter, they go up to my altar where they hear that they should be one heart and one soul, but then my heart flees from them because they have not the warmth of my heart and know not the taste of my body.

They seek the warmth and sexual lust that will perish and love the flesh that will be eaten by worms. Therefore do such people join in marriage without the bond and union of God the Father and without the Son's love and without the Holy Ghost's consolation. When the couple comes to the bed, my Spirit leaves them immediately and the spirit of impurity approaches instead because they only come together for the sake of lust and do not discuss or think about anything else with each other. But my mercy is still with them if they will be converted to me. Because of my great love, I place a living soul created by my power into their seed. Sometimes I let evil parents give birth to good children, but more often, evil children are born of evil parents, since these children imitate the evil and unrighteous deeds of their parents as much as they are able and would imitate it even more if my patience allowed them. Such a married couple will never see my face unless they repent. For there is no sin so heavy or grave that penitence and repentance does not wash it away.

For that reason, I wish to turn to the spiritual marriage, the kind that is appropriate for God to have with a chaste soul and chaste body. There are seven good things in it opposed to the evils mentioned above: First, there is no desire for beauty of form or bodily beauty or lustful sights, but only for the sight and love of God. Second, there is no desire to possess anything else than what is needed to survive, and just the necessities with nothing in excess. Third, they avoid vain and frivolous talk. Fourth, they do not care about seeing friends or relatives, but I am their love and desire. Fifth, they desire to keep the humility inwardly in their conscience and outwardly in the way they dress. Sixth, they never have any will of leading lustful lives. Seventh, they beget sons and daughters for their God through their good behavior and good example and through the preaching of spiritual words.

They preserve their faith undefiled when they stand outside the doors of my church where they give me their consent and I give them mine. They go up to my altar when they enjoy the spiritual delight of my Body and Blood in which delight they wish to be of one heart and one body and one will with me, and I, true God and man, mighty in heaven and on earth, shall be as the third with them and will fill their heart. The worldly spouses begin their marriage in lustful desires like brute beasts, and even worse than brute beasts! But these spiritual spouses begin in love and fear of God and do not bother to please anyone but me. The evil spirit fills and incites those in the worldly marriage to carnal lust where there is nothing but unclean stench, but those in the spiritual marriage are filled with my Spirit and inflamed with the fire of my love that will never fail them.

I am one God in three Persons, and one in Divinity with the Father and the Holy Ghost. Just as it is impossible for the Father to be separated from the Son and the Holy Ghost to be separated from them both, and as it is impossible for warmth to be separated from fire, so it is impossible for these spiritual spouses to be separated from me; I am always as the third with them. Once my body was ravaged and died in torments, but it will never more be hurt or die. Likewise, those who are incorporated into me with a true faith and a perfect will shall never die away from me; for wherever they stand or sit or walk, I am always as the third with them."

The Virgin Mary's words to the bride about how there are three things in the dance and company of the world, and about how this world is symbolized by the dance, and about Mary's suffering at her Son's death.

# Chapter 27

The Virgin Mary, the Mother of God spoke to the bride and said: "My daughter, I want you to know that where there is a dance, there are three things: namely, empty joy, loud shouting, and useless and vain work. But when someone enters the dance house sorrowful or sad, then his friend, who attends in the joy of the dance sees his friend coming there sad and sorrowful, immediately leaves the joy of the dance and separates himself from the dance and mourns with his sorrowing friend.

This dance is this world that is always caught up in trouble, even though it seems like joy to foolish men. In this world there are three things: empty joy, frivolous words, and useless work, because everything that a man gathers by his work he must leave behind himself. The one who joins in this worldly dance should consider my labor and sorrow and then mourn with me, who was separated from all worldly joy, and then separate himself from the world.

At my Son's death I was like a woman whose heart had been pierced by five spears. The first spear was his shameful and blameworthy nakedness, for I saw my most beloved and mighty Son stand naked at the pillar without any clothing to cover him at all. The second spear was the accusation against him, for they accused him of being a traitorous betrayer and liar, him, whom I knew to be righteous and true and never to have offended or wished to offend or injure anyone. The third spear was his crown of thorns that pierced his sacred head so violently that the blood flowed down into his mouth and his beard and ears. The fourth spear was his sorrowful voice on the cross with which he cried out to the Father, saying: 'O Father, why have you abandoned me?' It was as if he wanted to say: 'O Father, there is no one who pities me but you.' The fifth spear which pierced my heart, was his most bitter and cruel death. My heart was pierced with as many spears as the arteries from which his most precious blood flowed out of him. In truth, the pain in his pierced sinews, arteries, feet, hands and body went mercilessly to his heart and from the heart back to his sinews; for his heart was healthy and strong and of the finest nature, and life contended long with death; and thus his life was prolonged in the midst of the most bitter pain.

But when his death drew near and his heart burst from the unendurable pain, then his whole body shook and his head, which was bent backwards, raised itself a little. His half-closed eyes opened, and likewise his mouth was opened so that his bloodied tongue was seen. His fingers and arms, which were as if paralyzed, stretched themselves out. But when he had given up his spirit, his head sank toward his chest, his hands lowered themselves a little from the place of the wounds and his feet had to bear most of the weight of the body.

Then my hands became numb, my eyes were darkened, and my face became pale as a dead man. My ears could hear nothing, my mouth could not speak, my feet trembled, and my body fell to the ground. When I got up from the ground and saw my Son looking horribly disfigured and more miserable than a leper, I submitted my entire will to his knowing with certainty that everything had happened according to his will and could not have happened unless he had allowed it. I therefore thanked him for everything, and so there was always some joy mixed with my sadness, because I saw that he, who had never sinned, had, in his great love, wanted to suffer this much for the sins of mankind. Therefore, may all those who are in the world contemplate how I suffered when my Son died and always have it in front of their eyes and in their thoughts!"

The words of the Lord to the bride about how a man came to be judged before God's tribunal, and about the fearsome and horrendous judgment passed on him by God and all the saints.

# Chapter 28

The bride of Christ saw God looking angry, and he said: "I am without beginning and without end. There is no change in me either of year or day, but all time in this world is like a single second or moment to me. Everyone who sees me, sees and knows and understands everything that is in me in a moment. But since you, my bride, are in a material body, you cannot perceive and understand like a spirit, and therefore, for your sake, I will explain to you what has happened.

I was seated as a judge, for all judgment has been given to me, and a man came before my judgment seat to be judged. The voice of the Father thundered and said to him: 'Woe unto you that you ever were born!' God did not say this because he had repented of having created him, but it was just like anyone mourning for another and feeling compassion for him. Thereafter, the voice of the Son answered saying: 'I shed my blood for you and suffered the most bitter and harsh pain for you, but you have separated yourself entirely from it and will have nothing to do with it.'

The voice of the Holy Ghost said: 'I have searched all the corners of his heart to see if I might find some tenderness or love in his heart, but he is as cold as ice and as hard as stone, and I have nothing to do with him.' These three voices have not been heard audibly as if there were three gods, but they were heard for your sake, my bride, because you would not be able to understand these spiritual mysteries otherwise.

Thereafter, the three voices of the Father, Son and Holy Ghost were immediately transformed into a single voice, and this voice thundered and said: 'By no means shall the kingdom of Heaven be given to you!' The Mother of mercy, the Virgin Mary, was silent and did not open up her mercy, for he who was to be judged was unworthy to receive or enjoy her mercy; and all the saints cried out with one voice saying: 'It is divine justice for him to be eternally exiled and separated from your kingdom and from your joy.'

All those who were in the fires of purgatory said: 'No pain here is so bitter or harsh that it is enough to punish your sins; you deserve to endure much greater torments and you will therefore be severed from us.' But then the wretched man himself cried out in a fearsome voice, saying: 'Woe, woe for the seed that came together in my mother's womb and from which I received my body!' He called out a second time, saying: 'Accursed be the moment when my soul was joined to my body and accursed be he who gave me a body and soul!' He called out a third time: 'Accursed be the moment when I came forth alive from the womb of my mother!'

Then came three horrendous voices against him from hell saying: 'Come to us, accursed soul, like liquid copper draining down, to eternal death and life everlasting!' They called out a second time: 'Come, accursed soul, empty of all goodness, and receive our malice! For there will be none of us who will not fill you with his own malice and pain.' They called out a third time: 'Come, accursed soul, heavy like the stone that sinks down perpetually and never reaches the bottom where it can rest! You will sink deeper into the deep than we, so that you will not stop until you have reached the lowest part of hell.'

Then our Lord said: 'Just like the man who had several wives who sees one of them fall away from him and turns away from her, and turns to the others who remain steadfast in his will and rejoices with them, so too have I turned my face and my mercy away from him, and I turn to my servants and rejoice with them. Therefore, when you have heard of his fall and misery, you shall serve me with so much greater sincerity and purity in proportion to the greater mercy I have shown to you. Flee the world and her desire! I did not accept such a bitter suffering for the sake of worldly glory or because I was unable to fulfill it more quickly or easily, - for I could have – but, justice demanded that because humanity sinned in every limb, so must also satisfaction be made in every limb. This was why the Divinity felt compassion for mankind, and in his burning and great love for the Virgin, assumed Manhood from her through which he would suffer all the punishment mankind was destined to suffer. Since I took your punishment upon me out of love, you should remain in true humility, just like my servants, so that you will not be ashamed before anyone and fear nothing but me. Guard your mouth in such a way that, if such were my will, you would never speak. Do not be saddened about worldly things, for they will perish, and I am able to make whomever I want rich or poor. Therefore, my bride, place all your hope in me and I will help you"

## Explanation

This man whose judgment is here proclaimed was a nobleman, canon and subdeacon, who received a false dispensation and married a rich virgin but was surprised by a sudden death and thus lost what he desired.

The words of the Virgin to the daughter about two wives, one of whom is called Pride and the other Humility (the latter signifying the most sweet Virgin Mary), and about how the Virgin Mary comes to meet those who love her at the moment of their death.

# Chapter 29

The Virgin Mary, the Mother of God spoke to the Son's bride and said: "There are two wives. One of them has no special name, because she is too unworthy to have a name. The other wife is Humility, and she is called Mary. The devil himself is lord over the first wife because he has control over her. This wife's knight said to her: 'O my wife, I am ready to do anything I can for you, if only I can satisfy my sexual lust with you just once. I am mighty and strong and brave of heart, I fear nothing and am ready to go to my death for you.' She answered him: 'My servant, your love for me is great. But I am seated on a high throne, and I have only this one throne, and there are three gates between us.

The first gate is so narrow that all that a man is wearing on his body gets pulled off and torn to pieces if he enters by this gate. The second one is so sharp that it cuts through even to the very sinews of the man. The third gate is burning with such a fire that there is no escape or rest for him from its heat but, instead, anyone entering through this gate is immediately melted down like copper. In Addition, I am seated so high up on my throne that anyone who wants to sit next to me – for I have only one throne – will fall down into the greatest depth under me.' The knight answered her: 'I will give my life for you and the fall does not bother me.'

This wife is Pride and the one who wants to come to her must go, as it were, through three gates. Through the first gate enters the one who gives all he has for human praise and for the sake of pride. And if he does not own anything, he uses all of his will to have a reason to be proud and win praise of men. Through the second gate enters the one who sacrifices all his work and everything he does, all his time and all his thoughts and all his strength so that he may fulfill his pride. And even if he could give his own flesh over to be wounded for the sake of pride and honor and riches, he would do so willingly. Through the third gate enters the one who never rests or has peace but entirely burns like fire with the thought of how he may attain some honor or something he may feel worldly pride over. But when he attains his desire, he cannot stay in the same state but falls painfully and miserably; however, pride still remains in the world."

"But I," Mary said, "am the one who is most humble. I am seated on a spacious throne and above me there is neither sun nor moon nor stars nor even a sky, but a wonderful and unimaginable clear light proceeding from the beauty of God's majesty. Below me there is neither earth nor stone but only an incomparable sweet rest in God's virtue. Around me there is neither barrier nor wall but only the glorious host of angels and holy souls. And although I am seated so high, I still hear my friends who are in the world, daily pouring out their sighs and tears to me. I view their work and their perfection to be greater than that of those who fight for their wife Pride.

I shall therefore visit them with my mercy and help and place them near me on my throne, for it is very spacious and can house everyone. But they cannot come to me or sit with me yet, for there are still two walls between us which I shall lead them securely over so that they may come to my throne. The first wall is the world, and it is narrow. Therefore, my servants in the world shall be consoled by me. The second wall is death. Therefore, I, their most dear Lady and Mother, shall come to meet them and run to them at their death, so that even in death they will feel encouraged and consoled! I will place them together with me on the throne of heavenly joy, so that they, in limitless joy, may rest eternally in the delight of God and in his sweet arms and love of eternal glory and unimaginable joy."

The words of our loving Lord to his bride about how the many false Christians are being multiplied, and about how they are crucifying him again, and about how he is still prepared to suffer death once more for the sake of sinful people, if this were possible.

# Chapter 30

"I am the God who created all things for the benefit of man in order that all things should serve and help him. But mankind misuses all the things I created for his benefit unto his own damnation, and he cares less about God and loves him less than the created world. The Jews prepared three kinds of torture tools for my suffering: First, the wood on which I, scourged and crowned, was crucified. Second, the iron by which they pierced through my hands and feet. Third, the gall that they gave me to drink. Thereafter, they insulted me calling me a fool because of the death I gladly endured, and they called me a liar because of my teachings. Such men are now many in the world and there are very few who console me.

They crucify me on the wood through their will to sin, they scourge me through their impatience (no one can namely endure a single word for my sake) and they crown me with the thorns of their pride when they want to be raised higher and have more honor than I want them to have. They pierce my hands and feet with hardened iron when they praise their sin and harden themselves so that they should not have to fear me. As the drink of gall, they offer me sorrow. They call me a liar and a fool for the suffering which I went to and gladly endured.

I am powerful enough to kill and drown all my enemies and the entire world in one moment for the sake of their sins, if I wanted. But if I did drown them, the ones remaining would serve me out of fear, and that would not be right, because mankind should serve me out of love and not because of fear. If I myself came to them in a visible shape, their eyes would not endure to see me or their ears to hear me. For how could a mortal human endure to look upon an immortal? Truly, in my love, I would gladly die again for the sake of mankind, if it were possible.

Then the Holy Virgin Mary appeared and the Son of God said to her: "What do you wish, my chosen Mother?" And she said: "O my

Son, have mercy on your creation for the sake of my love." He answered: "I will show them my mercy once again, for your sake." Thereafter, our Lord spoke to his bride and said: "I am your God and the Lord of the angels. I am Lord over life and death. I myself want to live in your heart. See what a great love I have for you! The heavens and the earth and all the things in them cannot contain me, and yet I want to live in your heart, which is only a little piece of flesh. Whom could you then fear or what could you need when you have inside you God Almighty in whom all good things are?

There should be three things in the heart where I live: First, there should be a bed where we may rest. Second, there should be a seat where we may sit. Third, there should be a lamp that gives us light. In your heart there should be a bed to rest in so that you can rest from evil thoughts and worldly desires and always remember and contemplate the joy of eternity. The seat should be your will of staying close to me, even if it sometimes happens that you have to go out. For it is against nature to be always standing or sitting. But the one who is always standing is the one who always has the will of being with the world and never to sit with me. The light shall be the faith by which you believe that I am able to do all things and am almighty over all things."

About how the bride saw the most sweet Virgin Mary adorned with a crown and other adornments of indescribable beauty, and about how Saint John the Baptist explains to the bride the meaning of the crown and the other adornments.

# Chapter 31

The bride of God saw the Queen of Heaven, the Mother of God, wearing a priceless and beautiful crown on her head and her wonderfully shining and indescribably beautiful hair hanging down over her shoulders, with a golden tunic shining with an indescribable light, and a blue mantle of the color azure or a clear sky. When the bride of God, Saint Bridget, was full of wonder at such a lovely sight, and in her wonderment was standing there totally enraptured and amazed, then blessed John the Baptist appeared to her and said: "Listen closely to what all this signifies. The crown signifies that she is the Queen and Lady and Mother of the King of angels; the hair hanging down signifies that she is an unstained and pure virgin; the sky colored mantle signifies that all worldly things were as dead in her heart and will; the golden tunic signifies that she was fervent and burning in the love of God, both inwardly and outwardly. Her Son, Jesus Christ, placed seven lilies in her crown, and between the lilies he placed seven gems.

The first lily is her humility; the second lily is her fear; the third, her obedience; the fourth, her patience; the fifth, her steadfastness; the sixth, her kindness, for she is kind and gives to all who beg of her with love and a will to amend; the seventh, her mercy in difficulties, for in whatever difficulty a man may be in, if he calls on her with all his heart, he will receive mercy and help from her because she is full of compassion and mercy.

Between these shining lilies her Son placed seven precious gem stones. The first gem is her incomparable virtue, for there is no virtue in any other spirit or in any other body, which she does not have in a higher fashion. The second gem is her perfect purity, for the Queen of the kingdom of Heaven was so pure that from her first entrance into the world up to the final day of her death, not a single stain of sin was ever to be found in her; and none of all the devils could ever find enough impurity in her to fit on the head of a needle-point. She was truly the most pure, for it was not fitting for the King of glory to lie in any vessel but the purest, chosen before all angels and men and more pure than they. The third gem was her beauty, for God is praised constantly by his saints for his Mother's beauty, and all the holy angels and holy souls are filled with joy over her beauty. The fourth precious gem in the crown is the Virgin Mother's wisdom, for she is filled with all divine wisdom in God and all wisdom is fulfilled and perfected through her. The fifth gem is her power and might, for she is so powerful and strong with God in her that she can subdue anything that has been created. The sixth gem is her clarity, for she shines so clear that she even illuminates the angels, whose eyes are clearer than light, and the devils do not dare to look upon her clarity. The seventh gem is the fullness of every delight and joy and all spiritual sweetness, for her fullness is such that there is no joy that she does not increase, no delight that is not made fuller and more perfect by her and through the blessed vision of her, for she is filled with grace and mercy above all the holy saints. She is the most pure vessel in which the Bread of angels laid and in which all sweetness and all beauty is found.

Between the seven lilies in her crown, her Son placed these seven gemstones. Therefore may you, her Son's bride, honor and praise her with all your heart, for she is in truth worthy of all praise and all honor with her Son!"

About how, on God's exhortation, the bride of Christ chose poverty for herself and renounced riches and carnal behavior, and about the truth of the things revealed to her, and about three remarkable things that Christ showed her.

# Chapter 32

Our Lord said to his bride: "You should be like a person who leaves and like one who gathers. For you should leave riches and gather virtues, leave perishable things and gather eternal things, leave visible things and gather invisible. I shall namely give you the exultation of the soul instead of the pleasures of the flesh, the joy of heaven instead of the joy of the world, the honor of the angels instead of the honor of the world, the sight of God instead of the sight of your friends; I, the giver and Creator of all good things, will give you myself, instead of the possession of worldly goods.

Answer me on the three things I am going to ask you. First, do you want to be rich or poor in this world?" She answered: "O my Lord, I would rather be poor since riches do me no good; instead they bother and distract me very much and draw me away from serving you." "Tell me, second, do you find anything reprehensible or false according to your conscience and heart in the words that you heard from my mouth?" She answered: "Certainly not, all your words are reasonable." Our Lord said for the third time: "What delights you more, the sensual lust of the flesh you earlier had or the spiritual consolation and delight that you now have?" She answered: "I feel ashamed and disgraced in my heart to think of my earlier fleshly lust and it is now to me like poison and tastes all the more bitter in proportion to my earlier ardent love for it. I would rather die than ever return to such a lust; it cannot be compared to this spiritual delight and happiness."

"Thus," our Lord said, "you confess in your mind that all the things I have told you are true. Why then are you afraid and worried that I am delaying the things I told you would happen? Behold the prophets and remember the apostles and the holy teachers of the Church. Did they find anything in me except the truth? That is why they did not care about the world or the desire for it. Why else did the prophets foretell the future things so far in advance unless it was because God wanted them first to proclaim the words with the deeds coming after so that the ignorant should be taught in the faith? In truth, all the mysteries of my Holy Incarnation were proclaimed to the prophets before I assumed manhood and became man, even the star that went before the three kings. They believed the words of the prophet and deserved to see what they believed in, and they were made certain immediately after they saw the star. In the same way now, my words should first be announced so that, when the deeds come later, they will be believed more surely.

I showed you three things. First, the conscience of a man whose sin I revealed and proved to you by the most clear and evident signs. But why did I do so? Could I not have killed him myself? Or could I not have drowned him in a moment, if I wanted? Of course I could have. But, so that others may be instructed and my words revealed showing how just and patient I am and how unhappy this man is whom the devil rules, I endure him still. Because of his evil will of remaining in sin and through his sinful lust in it, the devil's power over him has increased so much that neither gentle words nor harsh threats nor the fear of hell can make him turn back from his sin. And this is true justice too, because, since he always had the will of sinning, even though he did not fulfill his sin by deed, he rightly deserves to be handed over to the devil for all eternity. For the smallest sin, lusted after, is enough to damn anyone from the kingdom of Heaven, who does not repent.

I showed you two others. The devil tormented the body of one but was not in his soul. He darkened the other's conscience through his intrigues and yet did not get into his soul and had no power over him. But now you might ask: 'Is not the soul the same as the conscience? Is the devil not in the soul when he is in the conscience?' By no means! The body has two eyes to see with, and even if they lose their sight, the body can still be healthy. So it is with the soul. For even though the reason and conscience are sometimes distracted and troubled, nevertheless, the soul does not always get hurt by the sin. And thus, the devil had power over his conscience but not over his soul.

I shall show you a third man whose soul and body are completely ruled by the devil, and unless he is forced by my power and by my special grace, he will never be expelled from the man or leave him. From some people, the devil goes out willingly and quickly, but out of others, only reluctantly and by force. For in some people the devil enters because of the sin of their parents or because of some hidden judgment of God; this happens for example with children and witless men. He enters into others because of their infidelity or for the sake of some other sin. From these, the devil goes out willingly if he is exorcised by people who know conjurations or the art on how to exorcise devils. If they undertake such an exorcism for the sake of vainglory or for some worldly gain, then the devil has the power of entering into the one exorcising him, or again, into the same person he got exorcised from, for neither of them had any love of God. From those whose soul and body the devil possesses completely, he never goes out, unless he is forced through my power. Just as vinegar, if mixed with a sweet and good wine, spoils all the sweetness of the wine and can never be separated from it, so too will the devil not go out of the soul whom he possesses, unless he is forced through my divine power.

What is this wine if not the human soul that was sweeter to me above all created beings and so dear to me that I let my sinews be slashed and my body lacerated to the ribs for her sake? I suffered death for her sake rather than lose her. This wine was conserved in dregs, for I placed the soul in a body where it was kept according to my will as in a sealed vessel. But now this sweet wine has been mixed with the worst vinegar, that is, with the malice of the devil, whose evilness is more bitter and abominable to me than any vinegar. By my power, this vinegar shall be separated from this man whose name I will tell you, so that I may show my mercy and wisdom through him, but my judgment and justice through the former man."

## Explanation

The first man was a high-born and proud cantor who, without the pope's permission, went to Jerusalem and was attacked by the devil. About this demon-possessed man more can be read in book III,Chapter 31 and in book IV,Chapter 115. The second demon-possessed man in the sameChapter became a Cistercian monk. The devil tormented him so much that four men could barely hold him down. His outstretched tongue looked like an ox tongue. The shackles on his hands were invisibly broken in pieces. After a month and two days this man was cured by Saint Bridget. The third demon-possessed man was a bailiff of Ostergotland. When he was admonished to do penance, he said to the one advising him: "Cannot the owner of the house sit where he likes? The devil has my heart and my tongue, how can I do penance?" He also cursed the saints of God and died the same night without the sacraments and confession.

Our Lord's words of admonishment to the bride about true and false wisdom, and about how good angels aid the wise who are good while devils aid the wise who are evil.

# Chapter 33

"My friends are like scholars who have three things: First, a reasonable understanding above what is natural to the brain. Second, wisdom without human aid, for I myself teach them inwardly. Third, they are full of the sweetness and divine love with which they defeat the devil. But nowadays people study in a different way. First, they want to be wise out of vainglory in order to be called good clerks and masterly scholars. Second, they want to be wise in order to own and win riches. Third, they want to be wise in order to win honors and privileges.

That is why I leave them when they go to their schools and enter there, since they study because of pride, but I taught them humility. They enter the schools for the sake of greed, but I had no place to rest my head. They enter in order to win privileges, envying those more highly placed than themselves, but I was judged by Pilate and mocked by Herod. That is why I will leave them, because they are not learning my wisdom. But, since I am good and kind, I give each one what he prays for. The one who prays for bread will receive bread. And the one who prays for straw will be given straw.

My friends pray for bread, because they seek and learn the wisdom of God where my love is. But others, however, pray for straw, that is, worldly wisdom. For just as straw is useless for man to eat but, is instead, the food of irrational animals, so too there is neither use for the worldly wisdom that they seek nor nourishment for the soul, but only a small name and useless work. For when a man dies, all his wisdom is eradicated into nothing and he can no longer be seen by those who used to praise him.

I am like a mighty lord with many servants who, on their lord's way, give to the people what they need. In this way the good angels and the evil angels stand in my service. The good angels minister to those who study my wisdom, that is, those who work in my service, nourishing them with consolation and pleasing work. But the worldly wise are assisted by evil angels who inspire them with what they want and form them after their will, inspiring them with thoughts of great speculation with much work. But if they would look to me, I could give them bread and wisdom without any work or trouble and a sufficient amount of the world to satisfy them. But they can never be filled of the world, since they turn that which is sweet into bitterness for themselves.

But you, my bride, should be like cheese, and your body like the mold wherein the cheese is formed until it has received the form of the mold. In this way, your soul, which is as delightful and sweet to me as cheese, must be tried and cleansed in the body, until body and soul united agree to maintain the same form of abstinence, so that the flesh obeys the spirit and the spirit leads the flesh toward all virtues.

The teaching of Christ to his bride about how she should live, and also about how the devil admits to Christ that the bride loves Christ above all things, and about how the devil asks Christ why he loves her so much, and about the love that Christ has for the bride.

# Chapter 34

"I am the Creator of the heavens and the earth. I was true God and true man in the Virgin's womb and I rose from the dead and ascended into heaven. You, my new bride, have come to an unknown place. Therefore, you must do four things: First, you must know the language of the place. Second, you must have proper clothes. Third, you must know how to organize your days and your time according to the custom of the place. Fourth, you must become accustomed to the new food.

So, since you have come from the instability of the world to stability, you must learn a new language, that is, the abstinence from useless and vain words and sometimes even from permissible ones in order to observe the importance and virtue of silence. Second, your clothes should be humble both in the interior and exterior so that you do not extol yourself inwardly as being holier than others nor are outwardly ashamed to be seen as humble before people. Third, your time should be ordered in such a way that, just as you before used to have much time for the needs of the body, so now you should only have time for the soul, that is, to never again want to sin against me. Fourth, your new food is abstinence from gluttony and from delicacies with all prudence, as far as your human nature can endure it. The abstinence that goes beyond the capacity of human nature is not pleasing to me, for I demand the rational and the taming of lusts.

Then the devil appeared in the same moment. Our Lord said to him: "You were created by me and have seen all justice in me. Answer me now whether this new bride of mine is lawfully mine by proven justice. For I allow you to see and understand her heart so that you may know how to answer me. Does she love anything else as much as me or would she take anything in exchange for me?"

The devil answered: "She loves nothing as much as you, and rather than losing you, she would suffer any torment, if only you gave her the virtue of patience. I see like a bond of fire descending from you to her and it ties her heart so much that she thinks of and loves nothing but you." Then our Lord said to the devil: "Tell me how she pleases your heart or how you like this great love I have for her." The devil said: "I have two eyes; one is corporeal, although I am not corporeal, and with this eye I perceive temporal things so clearly that there is nothing so secret or dark that it could hide itself from me. The second eye is spiritual, and I see so clearly with it that there is no pain so small that I cannot see and understand to which sin it belongs. And there is no sin so small or slight that I do not see it, unless it has been purged by repentance and penance. But, although there are no body parts more sensitive and vulnerable than the eyes, I would still much rather desire that two burning torches without end penetrated my eyes than for her to see with the eyes of the spirit.

I also have two ears. One is corporeal, and no one can speak so secretly and silently that I do not immediately hear and know it through this ear. The second ear is spiritual, and no one can have such a secret thought or desire for any sin, that I do not hear it through this ear, unless it has been washed away by penance. And I would gladly prefer that the suffering of hell, surging forward like a stream and spreading the most terrible hot fire without end flowed through my ears than that she should hear anything with the ears of the spirit. I also have a spiritual heart, and I would gladly let it be ceaselessly cut to pieces and constantly renewed to the same suffering in order for her heart to grow cold in your service and love.

But, since you are righteous, I now have a question for you that you may answer. Tell me, why do you love her so much? Why did you not choose someone holier, richer and prettier for yourself?" Our Lord answered: "Because justice demanded this. You were created by me and have seen all justice in me. Tell me, while she is listening, why it was justice that you should have such a bad fall and what you were thinking when you fell!"

The devil answered: "I saw three things in you. I saw your glory and honor being above all things, and I thought about my own glory. For this reason I became proud and decided to not merely become your equal, but to be even higher than you. Second, I saw that you were mightier than all others, and therefore I desired to be more mighty than you. Third, I saw what would happen in the future, and since your glory and honor are without beginning and would be without end, I envied you and thought that I would gladly be tortured forever by the most bitter punishment if, thereby, you would die. And with such thoughts and desires I fell, and immediately hell was created."

Our Lord answered: "You asked me why I love my bride so much. Assuredly, it is because I change all your malice into good. For since you became proud and did not want to have me, your Creator, as your equal, therefore, humiliating myself in all things, I gather sinners to myself and make myself their equal by giving them my glory. Second, since you had such an evil desire that you wanted to be more mighty than I, therefore I make sinners more mighty than you and partakers in my power. Third, because of your envy against me, I am so full of love that I offered myself up and sacrificed myself for the sake of everyone through my death." Thereafter, our Lord said: "Now, devil, your dark heart is enlightened. Tell me, while she is listening, what love I have for her."

The devil answered: "If it were possible, you would gladly suffer the same pain in each and every limb just as you once suffered on the cross in all your limbs, before losing her." Then our Lord answered: "Since I am so merciful that I do not refuse my mercy and forgiveness to anyone asking for it, ask me then humbly for mercy yourself, and I will give it to you." The devil answered: "Never shall I do this. For when I fell, a punishment was established for every sin and for every worthless word and thought. And every spirit or devil that fell will have his punishment. And before I would bend my knee before you, I would rather swallow all the punishments in me, as long as my mouth could be opened and closed in punishment, so that my punishment would be forever renewed."

Then our Lord said to his bride: "See how hardened the lord of the world is and how mighty he is against me because of my hidden justice. I could indeed destroy him in a moment through my power, but I do no more injustice to him than to a good angel in the kingdom of Heaven. But when his time comes, and it is now approaching, I shall judge him with his followers. Therefore, my bride, may you always persevere in good deeds. Love me with all your heart. Fear nothing but me. I am namely the Lord over the devil and over all things created."

The Virgin Mary's words to the bride about her own sorrow at the suffering of Christ, and about how the world was sold through Adam and Eve and bought back as with one heart through Christ and his Virgin Mother.

# Chapter 35

Mary, the Mother of God spoke to the bride of Christ and said: "My daughter, consider the suffering of my Son, for his limbs were like my own limbs and his heart like my own heart. For just as other children use to be carried in the womb of their mother, so was he in me. But he was conceived through the burning charity of God's love. Others, however are conceived through the lust of the flesh. Thus, John the evangelist, his cousin, rightly says: 'The Word was made flesh.' He came through love and was in me. The Word and love created him in me. He was truly for me like my own heart. For when I gave birth to him, I felt as though half my heart was born and went out of me. And when he endured suffering, it felt like my own heart was suffering. Just as when something is half inside and half outside - the half outside feels pain and suffering, but the inside also feels a similar pain - so it was for me when my Son was scourged and wounded; it was as if my own heart was scourged and wounded.

I was also the one closest to him at his suffering and I was never separated from him. I stood very near his cross, and just like that which is closest to the heart stings the worst, so his pain was heavier and worse for me than for others. When he looked at me from the cross and I saw him, then tears flowed from my eyes like blood from veins. And when he saw me so stricken with pain and overwhelming sorrow, he felt such a sorrow over my pain that all the pain of his own wounds became as subsided and dead for the sake of the pain he saw in me. I can therefore boldly say that his pain was my pain since his heart was my heart. For just as Adam and Eve sold the world for an apple, so my Son and I bought back the world as with one heart. Consider therefore, my daughter, how I was at the death of my Son, and it will not be hard for you to give up the world and her cares."

Our Lord's answer to an angel who was praying that sorrow in body and soul should be given to the bride, and about how even greater sorrow should be given to more perfect souls.

# Chapter 36

An angel was praying for his Lord's bride and our Lord answered him: "You are like a knight of the Lord who never took off his helmet for the sake of sloth and who never turned his eyes away from the battle for the sake of fear. You are steadfast as a mountain and burning like a flame. You are so pure that there is no stain in you. You beg me to have mercy on my bride. You know and see all things in me. Nevertheless, while she is listening, tell me what kind of mercy you are asking for her; for mercy is namely threefold.

One is the mercy by which the body is punished and tortured and the soul is spared, as it happened with my servant Job whose flesh had to suffer all kinds of pain and torment but whose soul was protected. The second mercy is the one by which soul and body are spared from torment, as it was in the case of the king who lived in all sorts of lust and worldly pleasure and had no pain either in body or soul while he lived in the world. The third mercy is the one by which soul and body are punished, so that they have distress in their flesh and sorrow in their heart, as it happened with Peter and Paul and other saints.

For there are three states for humans in the world: The first state is that of those who fall into sin and get up again; these do I sometimes allow to suffer in their bodies so that they may be saved. The second state is that of those who would gladly live forever to be able to sin forever and who have all of their will and thought directed to the world, and if they do anything for me at any time, they do it with the intention of their worldly possessions growing and prospering. Neither punishment of the body nor very much pain of the heart is given to these people, but instead they are allowed to follow their own power and will, because they will receive a reward here for the least little good they have done for me to then be tormented for all eternity. For since their will to sin is everlasting, their torment shall also be everlasting. The third state is that of those who are more afraid of sinning against me and offending me than they fear any torment. They would rather endure to be tortured with unbearable pain in eternity than consciously provoke me to wrath. Sorrow of body and heart are given to these men, as with Peter and Paul and other saints, so that they may amend for all their sins in this world, or so that they may be chastised for a time for the sake of their greater glory and as an example to others. I have shown this threefold mercy to three persons in this kingdom whose names are well known to you.

But now, my angel and servant, tell me, for what kind of mercy do you pray for my bride?" He answered: "I pray for the mercy of her soul and body, so that she may amend for all her sins in this world and so that none of her sins may come before your judgment." Our Lord answered: "May it be done according to your will." Then he said to the bride: "You are mine and I will do with you as I please. Love nothing as much as me. Purify yourself constantly from sin every hour according to the advice of those I have entrusted you to. Hide no sin! Leave nothing unexamined! Do not consider any sin to be light or worthy of disregard! For anything you forget, I will remind you of and judge. None of the sins you have done will come before my judgment if they are punished and expiated through your penance while you live. But those sins for which you made no penance will be purged either in purgatory or by some secret judgment of mine, unless you make a full satisfaction and amendment for them here in the world."

The words of the Virgin Mother to the bride about the excellence of her Son, and about how Christ is now being crucified more cruelly by his enemies, the evil Christians, than he once was by the Jews, and about how such people will receive a harder and more bitter punishment.

# Chapter 37

The Queen of Heaven said: "My Son had three good things: The first one was that no one ever had such a beautiful body as he did, since he had two perfect natures, namely, his Divinity and Manhood. His body was so pure that, just as no stain can be found in the clearest of eyes, so not a single defect could be found on his body. The second good was that he never sinned. Other children, however, sometimes bear the sins of their parents and sometimes their own; but he never sinned and yet bore the sins of everyone. The third good was that some men die for the sake of God and to receive a greater reward, but he died just as much for the sake of his enemies as for me and his friends.

When his enemies crucified him, they did four things to him: First, they crowned him with a crown of thorns. Second, they pierced his hands and feet. Third, they gave him gall to drink. Fourth, they pierced his side. But now I complain that the enemies of my Son, who are now in the world, crucify him more cruelly in a spiritual sense than the Jews who crucified his body. For even though the divinity is unable to suffer and die, still they crucify him through their own vices and sins. For if a man insults and injures an image of his enemy, the image does not feel the damage done to it; nevertheless, the perpetrator should be accused and judged for his evil intention to do harm as though it was a deed. In the same way, the vices and sins by which they crucify my Son spiritually are more abominable and heavy to him than the vices of those who crucified his body.

But now you may ask: 'How do they crucify him?' First off, they fasten him on the cross they have prepared for him when they do not heed the commandments of their Creator and Lord, but dishonor him when he warns them through his servants to serve him, and they despise this and instead do what pleases them. Then they crucify his right hand when they hold justice to be as injustice, saying: 'Sin is not so heavy and abominable to God as it is said. God does not punish anyone for all eternity; he only threatens us with these hard things to scare us. Why else would he redeem man if he wanted us to perish?' They do not consider that the least little sin a man finds delight in is enough to damn him to an eternal torment, and that God does not let the least little sin go unpunished, just like he does not let the least little good deed go unrewarded.

Therefore, they shall be tormented for all eternity because of their constant intention of sinning, and my Son, who sees the heart, counts that as a deed. For they would fulfill their will with deeds if my Son tolerated or allowed it. Then they crucify his left hand when they turn virtue into sin and the will to continue in sin until the end, saying: 'If we just once say at the end of our life, "O God, have mercy on me," God's mercy is so great that we will be forgiven.' But this is not virtue - to want to sin without bettering oneself, and wanting to receive a reward without having to work for it, not unless a real contrition is found in the heart that the man wants to change if only he could do so were it not for illness or some other hindrance.

Thereafter, they crucify his feet when they take pleasure in sinning without once thinking of my Son's bitter suffering or without once thanking him from their inmost heart with words like these: 'My Lord and God, how bitter your suffering was, praise and honor be to you for your death' – such words are never heard from their mouth. They then crown him with the crown of derision when they mock his servants and consider it useless to serve him. They give him gall to drink when they rejoice and glory in sin. And not once does the thought arise in their heart of how grave and manifold and dangerous this sin is. They pierce his side when they have the will to continue in sin.

In truth, I tell you - and you can say this to my friends - that such people are more unjust in the sight of my Son than those who judged him, more unkind than those who crucified him, more shameless than those who sold him, and they shall therefore receive a greater torment than the others. Pilate knew very well that my Son had not sinned and did not deserve to die. But he, nonetheless, felt compelled to judge my Son to death because he feared the loss of his worldly power and the revolt of the Jews. But what would these have to fear if they served my Son, or what honor or dignity would they lose if they honored him? They will therefore be judged with a more severe sentence than Pilate's, for they are worse than him in my Son's sight. For Pilate judged him because of the request and will of others and due to fear, but these judge him for their own advantage and without any fear when they dishonor him by committing the sin that they could abstain from if they wanted. But they do not abstain from sin nor are they ashamed of the sins that they have done, for they do not consider that they are unworthy of the good deeds of the One whom they do not serve.

They are also worse than Judas, for when Judas had betrayed his Lord, he knew very well that he was God and that he had sinned heavily against him, but he despaired and hastened his days toward hell, thinking himself to be unworthy to live. But these know their sin very well and yet they continue in it without feeling any remorse about it in their hearts. They want to take the kingdom of Heaven with violence and power when they think they can get it, not through their good deeds but through a vain hope, but it is only given to those who work and suffer something for the sake of God.

They are also worse than those who crucified my Son. For when these saw the good works of my Son, namely, the raising of the dead and the cleansing of leapers, they thought to themselves: 'This man does unheard of and extraordinary miracles. He overcomes anyone he wants with a word, he knows all our thoughts, and he does whatever he wants. If he is successful, we will all have to submit to his power and become his subjects.' Therefore, in order to avoid being subjected to him, they crucified him because of their envy. But if they had known that he was the King of glory, they never would have crucified him.

But these people see his great deeds and miracles everyday, and they take advantage of his good deeds and hear how they should serve him and come to him, but they think to themselves: 'If we must leave all our temporal belongings and follow his will and not our own, it would be heavy and unbearable.' They despise his will so that it should not be placed over their own will, and crucify my Son through their hardened heart when they add sin upon sin against their conscience. They are worse than those who crucified my Son, for the Jews did it for the sake of envy and because they did not know that he was God, but these know him to be God, and yet, in their own malice and presumption and greed, they crucify him spiritually more cruelly than the Jews did physically. For they themselves have been redeemed, but the Jews had not yet been redeemed. Therefore, my bride, obey my Son and fear him, for just as he is merciful, he is also just."

The most pleasant conversation of God the Father with the Son, and about how the Father gave the new bride to the Son, and how the Son received her with pleasure to himself, and about how the bridegroom teaches the bride about patience, obedience and simplicity through an example.

# Chapter 38

The Father spoke to the Son, saying: "I came with love to the Virgin and took your true body from her. You are therefore in me and I in you. Just as fire and heat are never separated, so it is impossible to separate the Divinity from the Manhood." The Son answered: "May all glory and honor be to you Father; may your will be done in me and mine in you." The Father answered him again: "Behold, my Son, I am entrusting this new bride to you like a sheep to be guided and educated. As the owner of the sheep, you will get from her cheese to eat and milk to drink and wool to clothe yourself with. But you, bride, should obey him. You have three things you must do: you have to be patient, obedient and willing to do what is good."

Then the Son said to the Father: "Your will with power, power with humility, humility with wisdom, wisdom with mercy; may your will be done, which is and always will be without beginning or end in me. I take her to myself into my love, into your power and into the guidance of the Holy Ghost, which are not three gods but one God." Then the Son said to his bride: "You have heard how the Father entrusted you to me like a sheep. You must therefore be simpleminded and patient like a sheep and fruitful in producing food and clothing.

Three people are in the world. The first is completely naked, the second is thirsty, and the third is hungry. The first signifies the faith of my Church, and it is naked because everyone is ashamed and afraid to speak of the true faith and of my commandments. And if some people do speak or teach about such things, they are despised and accused of being liars. Therefore, my words which proceed from my mouth, should clothe this faith like wool. For just as wool grows on the body of a sheep by the heat, so too my words proceed from the heat of my Divinity and Manhood to your heart. They will clothe my holy faith with the testimony of truth and wisdom and prove that the faith which is now regarded as vain is true, so that the ones who, up to now, have been lazy in clothing their faith in deeds of love after hearing my words of love, will be converted and enkindled again in order to speak with certitude of faith and act with power.

The second one signifies my friends who have a thirsting desire to make my honor perfect and are saddened at my dishonor. They shall be filled with the sweetness that they heard in my words, and enkindled with a greater love for me, and along with them, others who are now dead in sin, will also be enkindled in my love, when they hear of the mercy I have done with sinners.

The third one signifies those who think thus in their hearts: 'If only we knew the will of God and how we should live, and if anyone taught us about the good way, we would gladly do what we could for the honor of God.' These are hungry to get to know my way and will, but no one feeds them, since no one shows them completely what they should do, and if they are shown or taught what to do, no one lives according to the words with their deeds. And for this reason, the words seem as dead to them. Therefore, I myself shall show and teach them what they should do and I will fill them with my sweetness.

For worldly things, which are seen and desired now almost by everyone, cannot fill mankind but only arouse his desire and greed of the world to win more and more things. But my words and my love will feed men and fill them with an overflowing consolation. Therefore, my bride, who are my sheep, you must take great care to keep your patience and obedience. You are all mine by right and should therefore follow my will. The one who wants to follow the will of another should have three things: First, he should have the same will and opinion as the other; second, have similar deeds; third, he should move away from his enemies. But who are my enemies if not pride and every sin? You should therefore move away from them, if you desire to follow my will."

Christ speaks about how faith, hope and love were found perfectly in him at the moment of his death and are found imperfectly in us wretches.

# Chapter 39

The Son of God said: "I had three things in my death: First, faith, when I bent my knees and prayed to the Father, knowing that he was able to save me from the suffering. Second, hope, when I steadfastly waited and said: 'Not as I will.' Third, love, when I said: 'Thy will be done.' I also had bodily agony from the natural fear of suffering when the sweat of blood went out of my body. Thus, in order that my friends should not fear that they are abandoned when the moment of tribulation comes to them, I showed them in myself that the weak flesh always flees from suffering.

But now you may ask how the sweat of blood went out of my body. Just like the blood of a sick person dries up and is consumed in all his veins, so was my blood consumed by the natural fear of death. My Father wanted to show the way by which Heaven would be opened and the exiled man to be able to enter therein, and therefore he delivered me out of love to my suffering in order that my body would be glorified in honor after the suffering had been fulfilled. For justice did not allow my Manhood to enter into glory without suffering, although I was able to do so by the power of my Divinity.

How then should those deserve to enter into my glory who have little faith, vain hope, and no love? If they believed in the eternal joy of Heaven and in the horrific torments of hell, they would desire nothing but me. If they believed that I see and know all things and have power over all things and that I demand a judgment over all, they would hate the world, and they would fear more to sin before me than before men. If they had a firm and steadfast hope, then their every thought and desire would be directed toward me. If they had a divine love for me, then they would at least think in their soul about what I did for their sake, how much I labored in preaching, how great my pain was in my suffering and how great my love was at my death when I preferred to die rather than to lose and forsake them.

But their faith is sick and wavering, threatening to fall soon, because they believe only when suffering and temptation does not attack them, and they lose their hope as soon as they are met with adversity. Their hope is vain, because they hope that their sin will be forgiven without justice and a right judgment. They hope with self-reliance to receive the kingdom of Heaven for nothing and wish to receive my mercy without the severity of justice. Their love for me is completely cold, for they are never enkindled in seeking or calling me unless they are forced to it by tribulation. How can I be warmed by such people who have neither a right faith nor a firm hope nor a burning love for me?

And therefore, when they cry out to me and say 'O God, have mercy on me', they do not deserve to be heard or to enter into my glory since they did not want to follow their Lord in suffering, and, therefore, they should not follow him to the glory. For no knight can please his Lord and be taken back into his mercy after his fall, unless he first humbles himself in penance for his contempt."

Our Creator asks three questions of his bride. The first is about the servitude of the husband and the dominion of the wife; the second about the work of the husband and the spending of the wife; and the third about the contempt of the Lord and the honoring of the servant.

# Chapter 40

"I am your Creator and Lord. Answer me on the three things I am going to ask you. How is the state of the house where the wife is dressed like a lady and her husband like a slave? Is this right? She answered in her conscience: "No Lord, it is not right." Our Lord said: "I am the Lord of all things and the King of angels. I dressed my servant, namely, my Manhood, with only usefulness and necessity, for I desired nothing from this world except meager food and clothing. But you, who are my bride, want to live like a lady, and wish to have wealth and honor and be held in honor. What is the benefit of all these things? All things are indeed vanity and all things must be left. Mankind was not created for any superfluity but only to have what the necessity of nature requires. This superfluity was invented by pride and it is now held and loved as the law.

Second, tell me if it is right for the man to work from morning to evening and then for the wife to spend everything that has been gathered in a single hour?" She answered: "No, this is not right; the wife is instead obliged to live and act after the will of her man." Our Lord said: "I acted like the man who works from morning to evening, for from my youth up to the time of my suffering, I worked in showing the way to Heaven by preaching and by fulfilling what I preached with deeds. But the wife, that is, the soul, who should be like my wife, wastes all my work when she lives frivolously so that nothing of what I have done and suffered for her sake can benefit her; nor do I find any virtue in her in which I can delight in.

Third, tell me, is it not wrong and abominable for the master of the house to be despised and for the slave to be honored?" She answered: "Yes, it indeed is." Our Lord said: "I am the Lord of all things. My house is the world, and mankind should, by right, be my servant. But I, the Lord, am now despised in the world and the man honored. Therefore shall you, whom I have chosen, take care to do my will, because everything in the world is nothing but sea foam and a false dream."

Our beloved Creator's words in the presence of the heavenly host and the bride, in which he complains about five men signifying the pope and his clergy, the evil laity, the Jews and the heathens; and also about the help he sends to his friends, signifying all mankind, and about the harsh judgment he executes on his enemies.

# Chapter 41

"I am the Creator of all things. I was born of the Father before Lucifer. I am inseparably in the Father and the Father in me and one Spirit in us both. Accordingly, there is one God - Father, Son, and Holy Ghost - and not three gods. I am the one who promised the eternal inheritance to Abraham and led my people out of Egypt through Moses. I am the one who spoke through the prophets. The Father sent me to the womb of the Virgin without separating himself from me but remaining inseparably with me so that mankind, who had abandoned God, would return to God through my love.

But now, in your presence, my heavenly host, although you see and know all things in me, yet for the sake of the knowledge and teaching of my bride standing here, who cannot understand spiritual things except through a corporal parable, I make a complaint before you over these five men who are standing here, for they provoke me to wrath in many ways. Just as I, once, in the Law, with the name of Israel, signified the whole Israelite nation, so now by these five men I signify every man in the world.

The first man signifies the leader of the Church and his priests; the second, the evil laity; the third, the Jews; the fourth, the heathens; and the fifth, my friends. But from you, Jew, I exclude all the Jews who are Christians in secret and who serve me secretly in a pure love, a right faith, and a perfect deed. And from you, heathen, I exclude all those who would gladly walk in the way of my commandments, if they only knew and were taught how they should walk and live, and who with their deeds do as much as they know and are able. These shall by no means be judged with you. I now complain over you, o head of my Church, who sit on my seat which I gave to Peter and his successors to sit on with a threefold dignity and power: First, so that they would have the power of binding and loosing souls from their sins. Second, so that they would open Heaven for the penitent. Third, so that that they would close Heaven to the damned and to those who despise my Law. But you, who should be healing souls and presenting them to me, you are in truth a murderer of souls. I appointed Peter as shepherd and guardian of my sheep. But you, however, scatter and wound them. You are worse than Lucifer. For he was envious of me and desired to kill none but me so that he could rule in my place. But you are so much worse, for you do not only kill me by driving me off from yourself by your bad deeds, but you also kill souls by your bad example. I redeemed the souls with my blood and entrusted them to you as to a faithful friend, but you deliver them back again to the enemy from whom I redeemed them. You are more unrighteous than Pilate. He judged no one else but me to death, but you not only judge me as if I were a powerless lord and worthy of no good thing, no, you also judge and condemn the souls of the innocent and let the guilty go free without any rebuke. You are more cruel than Judas who only sold me, but you not only sell me, but also the souls of my chosen men for your own shameful profit and vain name's sake. You are more despicable than the Jews, for they only crucified my body, but you crucify and torture the souls of my chosen men for whom your malice and your sins are more bitter than from any wound from a sword. And so, since you are like Lucifer and more unrighteous than Pilate and more cruel than Judas and more despicable than the Jews, I complain over you with justice.

To the second man, that is, to the laity, our Lord said: "I created all things for your benefit. You gave your consent to me and I to you. You gave me your faith and promised by oath that you would serve me. But now, you have deserted me like a man who does not know his God. You hold my words for a lie and my deeds as vanity, and you say that my will and my commandments are too heavy. You have violated the faith you promised me. You have broken your oath and abandoned my name. You have separated yourself from the number of my saints and have come to belong to the number of the devils and you have become their friend. You think that no one is worthy of praise and honor but yourself. Everything that belongs to me and that you are bound to do for me appears heavy and bitter for you, but the things that please yourself are very easy for you. Therefore, I complain over you with right, for you have broken the faith you gave me in baptism and later; and for the love I have shown you in word and deed, you mock me and call me a liar, and for my suffering you call me a fool."

To the third man, that is, to the Jews, he said: "I began my deed of love with you and I chose you as my people. I led you out of slavery, I gave you my Law, I brought you into the land I had promised your fathers, and I sent you prophets to console you. Thereafter, I chose a virgin for myself from among you from which I assumed Manhood. But now I complain over you since you do not want not believe in me, but say: 'The Christ has not yet come; he is still to be expected.'"

Our Lord said to the fourth man, that is, to the heathens: "I created and redeemed you like the Christian man, and I created all good things for your sake. But you are like a man out of his senses, because you do not know what you are doing. You are also like a blind man, because you do not see where you are going. You honor and worship the created things instead of the Creator, and the false instead of the true, and you bend your knee before things that have less worth than yourself. That is why I complain about you."

To the fifth man, he said: "My friend, come closer!" And he directly said to the heavenly host: "My beloved friends, I have a friend with which I signify and mean many friends. He is like a man trapped among evil people and harshly shackled in captivity. If he speaks the truth, they beat his mouth with stones. If he does something good, they thrust a spear into his breast. Alas, my friends and saints, how long shall I endure such men, and how long shall I tolerate such contempt?"

Saint John the Baptist answered: "You are like the most pure mirror, for we see and know all things in you as in a mirror without any help of words and speech. You are the sweetness that no one can describe in which we taste all good things. You are like the sharpest of swords for you judge in righteousness."

Our Lord answered him: "Indeed, my friend, you said the truth, for my chosen men see all goodness and righteousness in me, and even the evil spirits see it in their own conscience but not in the light. Just like a man placed in a dark prison, who had earlier learned the letters, knows that which he had learned before even though he is in darkness and currently cannot see, so it is with the devils. Even though they do not see my righteousness in the light of my clarity, they still know and see it in their conscience. I am also like a sword that separates things into two parts. In this way I give each and every person what they deserve."

Then Our Lord said to Saint Peter: "You are the founder and defender of the faith and of my Church. While my host is listening, state the sentence of the five men!" Peter answered: "O Lord, all praise and honor to you, for the love you have shown to your earth. Blessed be you by all your host, for you allow us to see and know all things in you that have been and will be, and that is why we see and know all things in you. It is true justice that the first man who sits upon your seat, while having the deeds of Lucifer, should shamefully lose the seat he dared to sit on and become a partaker in the torment of Lucifer. The right judgment of the second man is that he, who has fallen away from your faith, should fall down to hell with his head down and feet up, for he loved himself and despised you who should have been his head. The right judgment of the third man is that he will not see your face and that he should be tormented for his malice and greed, since unbelievers do not deserve to see your glory and beauty. The right judgment of the fourth is that he should be locked up like a man out of his senses and banished to the city of darkness. The right judgment of the fifth is that help should be sent to him."

Then our Lord answered: "I swear by God the Father, whose voice John the Baptist heard in the Jordan; I swear by the body which John baptized, saw, and touched in the Jordan; I swear by the Holy Ghost who revealed himself in the form of a dove at the Jordan, that I shall do justice with these five men."

Then our Lord said to the first of these five men: "The sword of my severity will go into your body; it shall enter at the top of your head and penetrate you so deeply and violently that it can never be drawn out. Your chair will sink like a heavy stone and never stop before it comes to the lowest of depths. Your fingers, that is, your assistants and advisers, will burn in the inextinguishable sulfurous fire. Your arms, that is, your office-holders, who should have reached out for the help and benefit of souls but instead reached out for worldly honor and profit, will be judged to the torment and suffering of which David speaks: 'His sons shall be fatherless and his wife a widow and others shall take his property.' Who is 'his wife' if not the soul which shall be excluded from the glory of Heaven and be widowed and lose God? 'His sons', that is, the virtues they appeared to have, and my simple and humble men who were under them, shall be separated from them. Their honor and property will be given to others, and they will inherit eternal shame instead of their dignity and glory. Their headgear will sink down into the filth of hell, and they will never be able to get up out of it. Just as they rose above others through their honor and pride, so in hell they will sink so much deeper than others so that it will be impossible for them to ever stand up again. Their limbs, that is, all the priests who followed and helped them in wickedness, will be cut off from them and severed just like the wall that is torn down where not a single stone is left upon another stone and the cement no longer adheres to the stones. No mercy will come to them, for my love will never warm them nor restore or build them up into an eternal house in Heaven, but instead they shall be excluded from all good and endlessly tormented with their headmen and leaders.

But to the second I say: Since you do not want to keep the faith you promised me and have love toward me, I shall send an animal to you that will rise from the surging torrent, and it shall swallow you. Like the torrent always flows downward, so this animal will drag you down to the lowest hell, and just like it is impossible for you to travel upstream against the surging torrent, it will be just as hard for you to ever ascend from hell.

To the third I say: Since you, Jew, do not want to believe that I have come, you will see me when I come on judgment day, but not in my glory but in your conscience, and you will come to know that all the things I said were true. Then there is nothing left for you but to be tormented as you deserve.

To the fourth I say: Since you do not care to believe and do not want to know me, your darkness will become light for you, and your heart will be enlightened so that you may know that my judgments are true, but you will still not come to the light.

To the fifth I say: I shall do three things to you. First, I shall fill you inwardly with my fervor. Second, I shall make your mouth harder and firmer than any stone, so that the stones turn back to the ones throwing them at you. Third, I shall arm you with my weapons so well that no spear will harm you but instead everything will melt before you like wax in the heat of the fire. Be therefore made strong and stand like a man. For just like a knight in battle who hopes for help of his lord and continues fighting as long as he still has some life-force in him, so may you too stand firm and fight like a man; for the Lord, your God, whom none are able to withstand, will give you help. And since your number is small, I will honor you and multiply you greatly. Behold, my friends, you see these things and know them in me, and in this way they stand before me.

The words I have now spoken will be fulfilled. But these other men shall never enter my kingdom, as long as I am King, unless they better themselves. For Heaven will only be given to those who humble themselves and to those who mourn over their sins with penance." Then all the host answered: "Praise be to you, Lord God, who are without beginning and without end."

The Virgin Mary's words of advice to the bride about how she should love her Son above all things, and about how every virtue and gift of grace is contained in the glorious Virgin.

# Chapter 42

The Mother of God spoke: "I had three things by which I pleased my Son: First, humility in such a way that no created creature, whether angel or man, was more humble than I. Second, I had obedience, for I strove to obey my Son in all things. Third, I had a special charity.

For this reason I am honored threefold by my Son: First, I have been made more honorable than angels and men, so that there is no virtue in God that does not shine in me, even though he is the source and beginning of all virtues and the Creator of all things; but I, however, am the creature to whom he has given more grace than all others. Second, for my obedience I received such power that there is no sinner so unclean that he will not receive forgiveness if he turns to me with a will and purpose of amendment and a contrite heart for his sins. Third, for my charity, God is so close to me that the one who sees God sees me, and the one who sees me can see the Divinity and the Manhood in me and me in God as though in a mirror. For the one who sees God, sees three persons in him, and the one who sees me, sees, as it were, three persons. For the Divinity enclosed me in soul and body in himself and filled me with every virtue, so that there is no virtue in God that does not shine and appear in me, although God himself is the Father and giver of all virtues. For as it is with two bodies joined together, that whatever one body receives the other body also receives, so God has done with me.

There is no sweetness that is not found in me. It is like someone who has a sweet nut and gives a part of it to another. My soul and body are clearer than the sun and purer than a mirror, and just as three persons would be seen in the mirror if they stood near it, so the Father and Son and Holy Ghost may also be seen in my purity since I once had my Son in my womb with his Divinity. He is now seen in me with his Divinity and Manhood as in a mirror, for I have been glorified with the honor and glory of the resurrection. Therefore may you, my Son's bride, strive to follow my humility and love nothing but my Son."

The words of the Son to his bride about how people may rise up from a small good deed to the highest good and fall down from a small evil to the greatest punishment and torment.

# Chapter 43

The Son of God said to his bride: "A great reward sometimes arises from a little good. The date-palm has a wonderful smell, and in its fruit there is a stone. If it is planted in rich soil, it feels well, blossoms and makes good fruit and grows into a great tree. But if it is planted in dry soil, it dries out. Very dry and empty of all goodness is the soil that delights in sin, and it does not become better even if the seed of the virtues is sown in there. But rich is the soil of the mind that understands and confesses its sin and cries over their sin which has provoked their Creator to anger. If the date-stone, that is, if the thought of my severe judgment and power is sown in such a mind, it immediately strikes three roots in the mind.

The first one is that he thinks about how he can do nothing without my help, and for this reason he opens his mouth in prayer to me. The second is that he begins to give some small alms to me for the sake of my honor. The third is that he separates himself from worldly affairs in order to better serve me. He then begins to restrain himself from superfluities through daily fasting and abstains from and denies his own will and lust, and this is the trunk of the tree.

After this, the branches of love grow when he leads and draws everyone he can toward the good. Then the fruit grows when he also instructs others in goodness as much as he can and with all piety tries to find ways of increasing my honor. Such a fruit is the best one and most pleasing to me. And so, from a small good, man rises up to perfection. When he first takes root through a little piety, the body grows through abstinence, the branches are multiplied through charity and the fruit is increased through preaching.

In the same way, a man falls down from a small evil to the greatest damnation and torment. Do you know what the heaviest burden is for the things that grow? Surely it is the child who is conceived but cannot be born and dies inside the womb of the mother. And because of this the mother also ruptures and dies, and the father carries her and the child to the grave and buries her with the rotting fetus. This is what the devil does to the soul. The iniquitous soul is indeed like the wife of the devil: she follows his will in everything, and she conceives a child with the devil when sin pleases her and she rejoices in it.

For just as a mother conceives a child and bears fruit through the little seed that is nothing but an unclean rottenness, so too, the soul bears much fruit for the devil when she delights in sin. Thereafter, the strength and limbs of the body get formed as sin gets added to sin and increases daily. When the sins increase, the mother swells up and wants to give birth, but cannot, since her nature is consumed in sin, and her life becomes detestable. She would gladly desire to sin even more, but she cannot, and it is not allowed by God.

Then the fear arrives because she cannot fulfill her will, and her strength and joy are gone. Pain and sorrow are everywhere. While she is now despairing of being able to do any good thing or any good deed, her womb ruptures, and she dies while blaspheming and insulting God's judgment and punishment. Then she is dragged by her father, the devil, down to the grave of hell where she is buried for all eternity with the rot of her sin and the child of her evil lust. Behold how sin increases from a small evil and grows unto damnation."

The Creator's words to his bride about how he is now despised and reproached by men who pay no attention to what he did in love for them, when he admonished them through the prophets and suffered for their sake, and about how they do not care about the anger he exercised against the stubborn by punishing them severely.

# Chapter 44

"I am the Creator and Lord of all things. I created the world and the world despises me. I hear a voice from the world like that of a bumblebee who gathers honey on the earth. For when a bumblebee is flying and begins to land on the ground, it emits a very raspy voice. I now hear this raspy and ignorant voice in the world, saying: 'I do not care what comes after this.' In truth, now everyone is shouting: 'I do not care what comes after this and may I have my own will!'

Indeed, mankind does not care about what I did for the sake of love by preaching and suffering for them and by admonishing them through the prophets, and they do not care about what I did in my anger by executing my vengeance upon the evil and disobedient. They see that they are mortal and that death can strike them unexpectedly, but they do not care. They hear and see my justice which I exercised on Pharaoh and on Sodom for the sake of sin, and how I execute vengeance on other kings and rulers, and how I daily allow it to happen through the sword and other afflictions, but it is as if they were blind to all these things.

And for this reason they fly like bumblebees wherever they desire, and sometimes they fly as if they were jumping and running, for they exalt themselves in their pride, but they come down quickly by returning to their lust and gluttony. They also gather sweetness for themselves from the earth, for man works and gathers for the needs of the body and not for the soul, and for worldly honor but not the eternal. They transform the temporal things into a suffering for themselves, and what is useless, into eternal torment. But, for the sake of the prayers of my Mother, I will send my clear voice to these bumblebees, from which my friends are excluded (for they are in the world only in body), and it shall preach mercy. If they will listen to it, they will be saved.

The answer of the Virgin Mother and the angels, the prophets, the apostles, and the devils to God, in the presence of the bride, testifying about his many virtues and his perfection in creation, incarnation and redemption, and about how evil men nowadays contradict all these things, and about the severe judgment they receive.

# Chapter 45

The Mother of God said: "Bride of my Son, clothe yourself and stand firm, for my Son is approaching you. His flesh was pressed as in a winepress. For since mankind sinned in all limbs, my Son made atonement in all his limbs. His hair was pulled out, his sinews extended, his joints were dislocated, his bones mangled, and his hands and feet were pierced through. His mind was saddened, his heart afflicted by sorrow, his intestines was forced in toward his back, for mankind had sinned in all limbs."

Then the Son spoke, while the heavenly host was present, and he said: "Although you know all things in me, still I speak for the sake of my bride standing here. I ask you, angels: What is it that was without beginning and shall be without end? And what is it that created everything and was created by none? Proclaim it and give your testimony!" All the angels answered as with one voice and said: "Lord, it is you. We give testimony to you about three things: First, that you are our Creator and that you created all things in Heaven and on earth. Second, that you are without beginning and will be without end, and your kingdom and power will stand for all eternity. Without you nothing has been created and without you nothing can be created. Third, we testify that we see all justice in you and all the things that have been and will be, and all things are present to you without beginning or end."

Then he said to the prophets and patriarchs: "I ask you: Who brought you out of slavery into freedom? Who divided the waters for you? Who gave you the Law? Who gave you the prophetic spirit to speak about future things?" They answered him, saying: "You, Lord. You brought us out of slavery. You gave us the Law. You moved our spirit to speak and prophesy about future things."

Then he said to his Mother: "Give true testimony about what you know of me." She answered: "Before the angel, whom you sent, came to me, I was alone in soul and body. But after the angel's words, your body was within me with Divinity and Manhood, and I felt your body in my body. I bore you without pain and suffering. I gave birth to you without anguish and travail. I wrapped you in poor clothes and I fed you with my milk. I was with you from your birth until your death."

Thereafter he said to the apostles: "Say who it was that you saw, heard, and touched?" They answered: "We heard your words and wrote them down. We heard and saw the great works that you did when you gave us the New Law. You commanded the demons with one word to leave humans and they obeyed you and went out, and with your word you raised the dead and healed the sick. We saw you in a human body. We saw your great power and divine glory with your human nature. We saw you handed over to your enemies and we saw you hanging on the cross. We saw you suffer the most bitter pain and we saw you be laid in the grave. We touched you when you were raised from the dead. We touched your hair and your face. We touched the place of your wounds and your limbs. You ate with us and you gave us your eloquence. You are truly the Son of God and the Son of the Virgin. We also observed when you ascended with your Manhood to the right hand of the Father where you now are and will be without end."

Then God said to the unclean demon spirits: "Although you hide the truth in your conscience, still I now command you to say the truth about who it was that reduced your power." They answered him: "Just like thieves do not tell the truth unless their feet are pressed in the hard wood, so we do not speak the truth unless we are forced by your divine and formidable power. You are the one who, with your power, descended into hell. You reduced our power in the world. You took out from hell what was yours by right, namely, your friends."

Then our Lord said: "Behold, all those who have a spirit and are not clothed in a body, bear witness to the truth for me. But those who have a spirit and a body, namely humans, contradict me. Some know the truth of me but do not care about it. Others do not know it and, therefore, they do not care about it but say it is all false." He again said to the angels: "They say that your witness is false, that I am not the Creator of all things and that all things are not known in me. Therefore, they love the created things more than me, who am the Creator." He said to the prophets: "They contradict you and say that the Law is useless, that you can be saved through your own power and wisdom, that the spirit was false and that you spoke according to your own will." He said to his Mother: "Some say that you are not a Virgin and others, that I did not take a body from you. Others know it but do not care about it." He said to the apostles: "They contradict you, for they say that you are liars and that the New Law is irrational and useless. Others believe it to be true but do not care about it. I ask you now: Who will be their judge?"

They all answered him, saying: "You, God, who are without beginning and without end. You, Jesus Christ, who are with the Father, to you is all judgment given by the Father; you are their judge." Our Lord answered: "I who grieved for them am now their judge. But even though I know and can do all things, still, give me your judgment over them."

They answered him: "Just as the whole world perished once at the beginning of the world in Noah's flood, so too now the world deserves to perish by fire, since the wickedness and injustice are much greater now than what it was then."

Then our Lord answered: "Since I am just and merciful, I shall make no judgment without mercy nor mercy without justice, and therefore, I will once more send my mercy to the world for the sake of the prayers of my Mother and my saints. But if they do not want to listen, the most severe and harsh justice will follow and come to them."

The words of praise of the Mother and the Son to each other in the presence of the bride, and about how Christ is now regarded as shameful, dishonest, and despicable by people, and about the horrifying and eternal damnation of these people.

# Chapter 46

The Queen of Heaven spoke to her Son and said: "Blessed be you my God, who are without beginning and without end. You had the most noble and beautiful body. You were the most brave and virtuous man. You are the most worthy creature."

The Son answered: "The words proceeding from your mouth are sweet to me and delight my inmost heart like the sweetest drink. You are more sweet to me than any other creature in existence. For just as different faces can be seen in a mirror by a person but none pleases him more than his own, so too, even though I love my saints, I love you with a special love, because I was born from your blessed flesh. You are like myrrh whose fragrance ascended up to the Divinity and led the Divinity to your body. This same fragrance drew your body and soul up to God, where you now are with soul and body. Blessed be you, for the angels rejoice in your beauty and all are saved by your virtue and power when they call on you with a sincere heart. All the demons tremble in your light and do not dare to stay in your splendor, for they always want to be in darkness.

You gave praise to me for a threefold reason, for you said that I had the most noble body; second, that I was the most brave man; and third, you said that I was the most worthy creature. These three things are only contradicted by those who have a body and soul, that is, human beings. They say that I have a shameful body and that I am the most despicable man and the lowliest of creatures. For what is more shameful than to tempt others to sin? For they claim that my body tempts to sin when they say that sin is not as abominable or displeasing to God as much as is said. They say that nothing exists unless God wants it to be so and that nothing is created but by him. 'Why should we not use the created things to our benefit? Our natural frailty demands it and this is how everyone has lived before us and still do live.' This is how people now speak about me and my Manhood, in which I, the true God, appeared among men. For I advised them to abstain from sinning and showed what a serious and grave matter it is, and this they say was shameful, as if I had advised them to do something useless and shameful. They say that nothing is honorable but sin and that which pleases their will.

They also say that I am the most shameful man. For what is more shameful than someone who, when he speaks the truth, gets his mouth beaten with stones and gets hit in the face and, on top of that, hears people insulting him, saying: 'If he were a man, he would revenge himself over such an injustice.' This is what they do to me. I speak to them through the learned fathers and Holy Scripture, but they say that I lie. They beat my mouth with stones and their fists when they commit adultery, murder, and lying, saying: 'If he were manly, if he were the almighty God, he would revenge himself for such sins and transgressions.' But I endure this with patience, and everyday I hear them saying that the torment is neither eternal nor as severe and bitter as it is said, and my words are judged and said to be lies.

Third, they judge me to be the most ugly and worthless creature. For what is more worthless in the house than a dog or a cat that someone would be glad to exchange for a horse, if he could? But mankind holds me to be of less worth than a dog, for he would not wish to take me if it meant that he would lose the dog, and he would reject and deny me before losing the dog's hide. What is the thing that pleases the mind so little that one does not think of it and desires it more fervently than me? For if they regarded me more worthy than any other created creature, they would love me more than other things. But now they have nothing so small that they do not love it more than me. They grieve over everything but me. They grieve for their own and their friends' losses. They grieve for an injurious word. They grieve over offending or hurting people more highly placed and powerful than they, but they do not grieve about offending or hurting me, who am the Creator of all things. What man is so despicable that he is not listened to if he begs about something and is not given a gift in return if he has given something? But I am utterly vile and despicable in their eyes, for they do not consider me worthy of any good, even though I have given them all good things.

But you, my most dear Mother, have tasted more of my wisdom than others, and never has anything but the truth ever left your mouth, just as nothing but the truth has ever left my own mouth. I will now justify myself in the sight of all the saints. First, against him, who said that I had a shameful body. I shall prove that I indeed have the most noble body without deformity or sin, and he shall fall into eternal shame and reproach which all will see. To the one who said that my words were a lie and that he did not know if I was God or not, I shall prove that I truly am God, and he will flow down like mud to hell. But the third, who regarded me as useless, I shall judge to eternal damnation so that he will never see my glory and my joy."

Thereafter he said to his bride: "Stand firm in my service. You have come to a wall, as it were, in which you are enclosed, so that you cannot flee nor dig through its foundations. Endure this small tribulation willingly, and you will experience eternal rest in my arms. You know the will of the Father, you hear the words of the Son, you feel my Spirit, and you have delight and consolation in the conversation with my Mother and my saints. Therefore, stand firm, or else you will come to feel my justice by which you will be forced to do what I am now kindly urging you to do."

Our Lord's words to his bride about the contempt of the New Law, and about how that same Law is now rejected and despised by the world, and about how bad priests are not God's priests but God's betrayers, and about the punishment and damnation they receive.

# Chapter 47

"I am the God who in ancient days was called the God of Abraham, the God of Isaac and the God of Jacob. I am the God who gave the Law to Moses. This law was like clothing. For as a mother with her child in the womb prepares her infant's clothing, so too I, God, prepared the New Law, for the Old Law was nothing but the clothing and shadow and sign of future things to come. I clothed and wrapped myself in the clothing of this Law. And then when a boy grows up somewhat, his old clothes are laid down and new clothes are taken up. In this way, I fulfilled the Old Law when I put aside the used clothing of the Old Law, and assumed the new clothing, that is, the New Law, and I gave this clothing and myself to everyone who wanted to have it. This clothing is not very tight nor difficult to wear but is well suited everywhere. For my Law does not order people to fast or work too much nor to kill themselves or to do anything beyond the limits of possibility, but it is beneficial for the soul and conducive to the restraining, mortification, and chastisement of the body. For when the body gets too attached to sin, then sin consumes the body.

Two things are found in the New Law: First, a prudent temperance in soul and body and the right use of all things. Second, a readiness for heeding and keeping the Law; for the person who cannot endure to stay in one thing can stand in another. Hereby follows that a person who cannot endure to be a virgin can live in an honorable marriage, and he who falls into sin may get up again and better himself.

But this Law is now rejected and despised by the world. For they say that the Law is narrow, heavy, and ugly. They say it is narrow, for the Law orders one to be satisfied with the necessary and to flee the superfluous. But they want to have all things without reason like senseless cattle and above the necessity of the body, and that is why the Law is too narrow for them. Second, they say it is heavy, because the Law says that one should have enjoyment with reasonable temperance and at established times. But they want to fulfill their lust more than what is good and more than what is established. Third, they say it is unsightly, because the Law bids them to love humility and to accredit every good to God. But they want to be proud and exalt themselves for the good things that God has given them, and that is why the Law seems ugly and vain to them.

See how despised and maltreated my clothes are. I fulfilled everything in the Old Law before I began the New Law. For the Old Law was too difficult, and my intention was that the New Law should remain until I came in judgment. But they shamefully threw away the clothing with which I covered the soul, that is, the right faith. And above this, they add sin to sin, since they also want to betray me. Does not David say in the psalm: 'He who ate my bread thought treason against me'? In these words I want you to note two things. First, he does not say "thinks" but "thought", as if it had already happened. Second, he denotes one man as a betrayer. But I say that it is those who are now present who betray me, not those who have been or who will come, but those who are now alive. I also say that it is not only one man but many.

But now you may ask me: 'Are there not two kinds of bread, one invisible and spiritual, of which angels and saints live, and the other earthly, by which men are fed? But angels and saints do not want anything other than that which is according to your will, and men can do nothing other than that which pleases you. How, then, can they betray you?'

I will answer you in the presence of my heavenly host who knows and sees all things in me, but I say this for your sake so that you may understand: There are indeed two kinds of bread. One is that of the angels who eat my bread in my kingdom so that they may be filled with my indescribable joy. They do not betray me, since they want nothing other than what I want. But those who betray me are the ones who eat my bread at the altar. I truly am that bread. This bread has three characteristics: form, flavor, and roundness. I am indeed the Bread. And, like the bread, I have three things in me: flavor, form, and roundness. I have flavor, for just as all food is tasteless without bread and gives no strength, so without me, everything that exists is tasteless, powerless, and vain. I have also the form of the bread, since I am of the earth. I was born of the Virgin

Mother, and my Mother is of Adam, and Adam is of the earth. I have also roundness wherein there is no end or beginning, since I am without beginning and without end. And no one is able to see or find an end or beginning in my wisdom, power, or charity. I am in all things, over all things, and outside of all things. Even if someone were to fly like the fastest arrow perpetually without end, he would still never find an end or a limit to my power and virtue on account of these three things: namely, flavor, form, and roundness. I am that bread that is seen and touched on the altar and is transformed into my body that was crucified. For just as a dry and easily inflammable piece of wood is quickly consumed if it is placed on the fire, and nothing remains of the wood but all of it is fire, so when these words are said, 'This is my body,' that which before was bread instantly becomes my body, but is not inflamed by fire like wood but by my Divinity.

That is why those who eat my bread betray me. What murder could be more unmanly and abhorrent than when someone kills himself? And what betrayal is worse than when two are joined by an indissoluble bond, and one betrays the other, as is the case of married people? But what does the man do in order to betray his wife? Indeed, he insincerely says to her: 'Let us go to such and such a place so I can fulfill my will with you.' She goes with him in true simplicity, ready for her husband's every wish. But when he finds the proper time and place, he brings against her three means of betrayal: Either something so heavy that it kills her with one blow, or something so sharp that it cuts right through her intestines, or something to smother the spirit of life in her directly. Then, when she is dead, the betrayer thinks to himself: 'Now I have done wrong. If my crime becomes known publicly, I will be judged to death.' Therefore, he goes and lays his dead wife's body in some hidden place, so that his sin may not be revealed.

This is what the priests who are my betrayers do to me. For they and I are joined together by a single bond when they take the bread and pronounce the words that change it into my true body, which I assumed from the Virgin. No angel could do this, for I gave this dignity to priests alone and elected them for the highest office. But now they act towards me like betrayers, for they show me a happy and kind face and lead me to a hidden place to betray me. These priests show me a happy face when they appear to be good and simple, and they treacherously lead me to a hidden place when they approach the altar. There I am ready like a bride or bridegroom to do all of their will, but they betray me.

First they lay something heavy over me when the divine office, which they say for me, is heavy and burdensome to them. They would rather speak a hundred words for the honor of the world than one for my honor. They would rather give a hundred coins of gold for the glory of the world than one penny for my sake. They would rather work a hundred times for their own benefit and that of the world than once for my honor. They press me down with this heavy burden, so that it is as though I am dead in their hearts. Second, they pierce me with a sharp blade that penetrates the intestines whenever the priest goes to the altar with the knowledge that he has sinned and repented, but yet is firmly resolved to sin again when his office is done, thinking thus to himself: 'I truly repent of my sin, but I will not give up the woman with whom I have sinned so that I may not be able to sin any longer with her.' These priests pierce me with the sharpest blade. Third, they smother the spirit when they think inwardly to themselves in this way: 'It is good and delightful to be with the world and good to live in lust and I cannot restrain myself. I will do my will in my youth; when I grow old, I will become restrained and better myself.' And by this wretched thought the spirit of life is smothered.

But now you may ask how their hearts becomes so cold and tepid toward me and everything good so that they can never be warmed or rise again to my love. Just as ice cannot catch fire even if it is laid on the fire, but only melts into water, so too, even if I give them my grace and they hear my words of admonishment, they cannot rise up to the warmth of life, but wither and fade away from everything good.

See how they betray me in that they show themselves to be simple without being so, and are burdened and depressed of my honor, which they instead should delight and rejoice in, and also in that their will is to sin and to continue in sin until the end. They conceal me and place me in a hidden place, when they think to themselves: 'I know I have sinned greatly, but if I refrain from my office, everyone will reproach and condemn me as evil.' And so they shamelessly go up to the altar and place me before them and touch me, who am true God and true man. I am as it were in a hidden place with them, since no one knows or sees how evil and abominable they are. I, true God and man, lie there as in a hidden place, for even if the worst priest said the words "This is my body," he still consecrates my true body, and I, true God and true man, would lie there before him. But when he puts my body to his mouth, then I am no longer present to him through the grace of my Divinity and Manhood; only the form and flavor of bread remain for him, but not because I am not truly present for the evil as with the good due to the office of the sacrament, but because the evil and good do not gain the same benefit or perfection from my body. Behold how these priests are not my priests but true betrayers, since they sell and betray me like Judas. I observe the pagans and the Jews, but I do not see anyone worse than these priests, for they are in the same sin that made Lucifer fall from Heaven.

But now I will also tell you their judgment and whom they are like. Their judgment is damnation. David condemned those who were disobedient to God, and because he was a righteous prophet and king, he did not condemn out of wrath or bad will or impatience, but out of divine justice. So do I too, who am better than David, condemn those who are now priests, not out of wrath or bad will but out of justice.

Accursed be therefore everything of what they take from the earth for their own benefit, for they do not praise their God and Creator who has given them this. Accursed be their food and drink that enters their mouths and nourishes their bodies to become food for worms and destines their souls for hell. Accursed be their bodies that will rise again in hell to suffer and burn for all eternity. Accursed be the years in which they lived uselessly. Accursed be the moment that begins hell for them and that never will end. Accursed be their eyes with which they saw the light of Heaven. Accursed be their ears with which they heard my words and did not care. Accursed be their taste with which they tasted my gifts. Accursed be their touch with which they touched me. Accursed be their smell with which they smelled the delightful things of the world and forgot me, the most delightful of all.

But now you may ask: How will they be accursed spiritually? Well, their sight will be accursed, because they shall not see the vision of God in himself but only the darkness and sufferings of hell. Their ears will be accursed, because they shall not hear my words but only the screams and horrors of hell. Their taste will be accursed, because they shall not taste my eternal goods and joy but only eternal bitterness. Their touch will be accursed, because they shall not touch me but only eternal fire in hell. Their smell will be accursed, because they shall not smell the sweet smell of my kingdom that surpasses all sweet scents, but only have the foul stench of hell which is more bitter than bile and worse than sulfur. They shall be accursed by Heaven and earth and all brute creatures, for these obey God and glorify him, whereas they reject him.

Therefore, I who am the Truth, swear in my truth, that if they die like this and in such a disposition that they are in now, neither my love nor my virtue will ever encompass them, but instead, they will be damned for all eternity, and not only priests, but also everyone who rejects the commandments of God!

About how, in the presence of the heavenly host and of the bride, the Divinity spoke to the Manhood against the Christians, just as God spoke to Moses against the people of Israel, and about how damned priests love the world and despise Christ, and about their condemnation and damnation.

# Chapter 48

A great host was seen in Heaven and God said to it: "My friends, who know and understand and see all things in me, I am speaking in your presence, for the sake of my bride standing here, like someone who speaks to himself, for in this way does my Divinity converse with my Humanity. Moses was with God on the mountain forty days and nights, and when the people saw that he had been gone so long, they took gold and threw it into the fire and shaped a calf out of it, calling it their god.

Then God said to Moses: 'The people have sinned. I will wipe them out, just like something written is erased from a book.' Moses answered: 'No, my Lord, do not. Remember that you led them up from the Red Sea and worked wonders for them. If you erase and destroy them, where is your promise then? I beg you, do not do this, for then your enemies will say: The God of Israel is evil who led the people up from the sea but killed them in the desert.' And God was appeased by these words.

I am this Moses, figuratively speaking. My Divinity speaks to my Manhood just as to Moses, saying: 'Behold what your people have done and see how they have despised me. All the Christians shall be killed and their faith eradicated.' My Humanity answers: 'No, Lord. Remember that I led the people through the sea in my blood when I was bruised from the top of my head to the sole of my foot. I have promised them eternal life; have mercy on them for the sake of my suffering.' After hearing these words the Divinity was appeased and said: 'Thy will be done, for all judgment is given to you.' See what love, my friends!

But now in your presence, my spiritual friends, angels and saints, and in the presence of my bodily friends who are in the world and yet not in the world except with their body, I complain that my people are gathering firewood and lighting a fire, throwing gold into the fire so that a calf emerges for them to adore and worship as a god. It stands like a calf on four feet having a head, a throat, and a tail. When Moses delayed on the mountain a long time without returning, the people said: 'We do not know what may have happened to him after this long time.' And they were displeased that he had led them out of captivity and slavery, and they said: 'Let us find another god to go before us.'

This is what these damned priests are now doing to me. For they say: 'Why should we have a more austere life than others? What is our reward for this? It is better for us to live in peace and as we want. Let us love the world that we are certain about, for we are uncertain about his promise.' Then they gather firewood when they devote all their senses to the love of the world. They light a fire when they have a complete desire for the world. They burn when their lust glows in their mind and proceeds in an act. They throw in gold, which means that all the honor and love they should show to me, they show to get the honor of the world.

Then the calf emerges, which means a complete love of the world. It has four feet of sloth, impatience, superfluous rejoicing, and greediness. For these priests who should be my servants are slothful in honoring me, impatient in suffering anything for my sake, excessive in rejoicing, and never satisfied with the things they have. This calf also has a head and throat, which means a complete will for gluttony that can never be satisfied, not even if the whole sea were to flow into it. The tail of the calf is their malice, for they do not let anyone keep his property if they can take it from him. By their bad example and their contempt, they injure and pervert everyone who serves me. Such is the love for the calf that is in their hearts, and in such they rejoice and lust. They think about me as those others did about Moses, and say: 'He has been gone for a long time. His words appear vain and his deeds burdensome. Let us have our own will, let our power and will be our god.' And they are not even satisfied by these things and forget me entirely, but instead, they have me as their idol.

The heathens used to worship wood and stones and dead men, and among others, an idol called Beelzebub was worshipped whose priests used to offer him incense with devotional genuflections and shouts of praise. And everything in their offering that was useless, they dropped on the ground, and the birds and flies ate it up. But everything that was useful, the priests hid away for themselves. They locked the door on their idol and kept the key for themselves so that nobody could go in.

This is what the priests are doing to me in this time. They offer me incense, that is, they speak and preach beautiful words in order to win praise for themselves and some temporal benefit, but not out of love of me. Just as the scent of the incense cannot be captured but only felt and seen, so their words do not attain any benefit for souls so that it can take root and be kept in their hearts, but they are only heard and seem to please for a short time. They offer me prayers, but not the kind that are pleasing to me. Like those who shouts praise with their mouths and are silent in their hearts, they stand next to me shouting with their mouths while in their hearts and thoughts they wander around in the world. But if they were speaking with a mighty or powerful man, then their hearts would follow their own speech and words so that no one would be able to remark on them.

But in my presence the priests are like men who are mentally deranged, for they say one thing with their mouths and have another in their hearts. No one who hears their words can be certain about their meaning. They bend their knees for me, that is, they promise me humility and obedience, but in truth, their humility is as Lucifer's, and they are obedient to their own desires and not me. They also lock me in constantly and keep the key for themselves. They open up for me and praise me when they say: 'Thy will be done on earth as it is in heaven.' But then they lock me in again by fulfilling their own will, while my will is as an imprisoned and powerless man who can neither be seen nor heard. They keep the key for themselves when they, by their bad example, also lead astray others who want to do my will. And, if they could, they would gladly forbid my will from being fulfilled and accomplished, except when it suits their own will. They also hide anything in the offering that is necessary and useful to them, that is, they demand all their honor and privileges, but the human body, who falls to the ground and dies and for which they should offer the best sacrifice, him they consider as useless and leave the body to the flies, that is, to the worms on the ground. They do not care or bother about their obligation for the salvation of souls.

140

But what was said to Moses? 'Kill those who made this idol!' And some were killed, but not all. In the same way, my words will now come and kill them, some in body and soul by eternal damnation, others unto life so that they should convert and live, others through a fast death, for these priests are altogether abhorrent to me. But what shall I liken them to? They are indeed like the fruit of the thorn-bush, which is beautiful and red on the outside, but inside is full of impurity and stinging thorns. In the same way, these come to me as men who are red with love, and they seem to be pure to men, but inside they are full of all filth. If this fruit is laid in the earth, other thorn-bushes grow up from it. In the same way, these hide their sin and malice in their heart as in the earth, and they become so rooted in evil that they do not even blush to appear in public and boast about their sin. Hence other men not only find a reason to sin but also become deeply wounded in their souls, thinking thus to themselves: 'If priests do this, it is even more permitted for us to do it.' And they are not only like the fruit of the thorn-bush, but also the thorns, for they disdain to be moved by reproach and admonition, and they consider no one to be as wise as them and think that they can do everything they want.

Therefore, I swear by my Divinity and Manhood, in the hearing of all the angels, that I shall break down the door they have closed on my will, and my will shall be fulfilled, and their will shall be annihilated and locked in eternal torment and anguish. For as it was once said: 'I shall begin my judgment with the priests and at my altar.'"

The words of Christ to his bride about how Christ is likened to Moses, in a figurative way, leading the people out of Egypt; and about how the damnable priests, whom he chose in the place of the prophets as his most beloved friends, now cry: "Depart from us!"

# Chapter 49

The Son of God spoke: "Earlier, I likened myself to Moses in a figurative way. When he led the people out, the water stood like a wall to the right and to the left. I am in truth this Moses, figuratively speaking, who led my Christian people out, that is, I opened heaven for them and showed them the way. But now I have chosen other friends for myself more loved and intimate than the prophets, namely, my priests, who not only hear my words and see, when they see me myself, but also touch me with their hands, which none of the prophets or angels could do.

These priests, whom I have chosen in place of the prophets as my friends, cry out to me, but not with such desire and love as the prophets did, no, the priests and the prophets cry out with two opposing voices. For the priests do not cry out as the prophets did: 'Come, Lord, for you are sweet,' but they cry out: 'Depart from us, for your words are bitter and your deeds heavy and they make us ashamed!' Hear what these accursed priests say! I stand before them like the most meek and gentle sheep from which they get wool for their clothing and milk for their food, and yet they despise me for such a great love. I stand before them like a guest saying: 'Friend, give me the necessities of life for my body, for I need it, and you will receive the greatest reward from God in return!'

But even though I appeared with the simplicity of a sheep, they drive me away as a wolf lying in wait for the master's sheep. They do not want to show me any hospitality and refuse to take me into their house, but instead, they affront me like a traitor unworthy of receiving hospitality from them. But what will the guest do when he has been rejected? Should he not bring out arms against the master of the house who drove him away? By no means, for this would not be just since the owner can deny or give his belongings to whomever he wants. But what shall then the guest do? He should indeed say to the one who drove him away: 'My friend, since you do not want to take me into your house, I will go to another who will show mercy to me.' And when he comes to another, he hears him saying: 'You are welcome, my Lord, all that I have is yours. You shall now be the Lord, and I want to be your servant and guest.' Those are the kind of lodgings I am pleased to stay in, where I hear such a voice.

I am indeed like a guest driven away by men. But even though I can enter any place by my power, still, on account of justice I do not, but I only enter to those who receive me with a good will as their true Lord, not as a guest, and entrust all their will into my hands."

The Mother and Son's words of blessing and praise for each other, and about the grace granted by the Son to his Mother for the souls in purgatory and those in this world.

# Chapter 50

The Mother of God spoke to her Son and said: "Blessed be your name, my Son, without end and blessed be your Divinity that is without beginning and without end! In your Divinity there are three wonderful things: namely, power, wisdom, and virtue. Your power is like the most violently burning fire before which everything that is solid and strong is reckoned as dry straw in a fire. Your wisdom is like the ocean that can never be emptied because of its greatness and vastness, and which, when it rises up and flows over, covers valleys and mountains. Neither can your wisdom be comprehended nor fathomed about how wisely you created mankind and placed him over all your creation. How wisely you arranged the birds in the air, the animals on the earth and the fishes in the sea, giving to each one its own time and order. How marvelously you give life to everything and take it away! How wisely you give wisdom to the unwise and take it away from the proud! Your virtue is like the light of the sun which shines in the sky and fills the earth with its light. Likewise, your virtue satisfies high and low and fills all things. Therefore, blessed be you, my Son, for you are my God and my Lord!"

The Son answered: "My most dear Mother, your words are sweet to me, for they come from your soul. You are like the dawn that breaks forth with clarity. You outshine all the heavens and your light and your clarity surpass all the angels. By your clarity, you drew to yourself the true sun, that is, my Divinity, so much so that the sun of my Divinity came to you and settled on you. By his warmth you are warmed in my love over all others and by his splendor you are enlightened in my wisdom more than all others. The darkness of the earth was chased away and all the heavens were enlightened through you. I say in my truth that your purity pleased me more than all the angels, and it drew my Divinity to you so that you were enkindled by the warmth of my Spirit; and through it you enclosed the true God and Man in your womb whereby mankind has been enlightened and the angels made joyful. Therefore, may you be blessed by your blessed Son! And for this reason, no prayer of yours will ever come to me without being heard, and through you, anyone who prays for mercy with the intention of mending their sinful ways will receive grace for your sake. For just as heat comes from the sun, so too all mercy is given through you. You are like a filled and flowing spring from which mercy flows to the help of the wretched."

The Mother answered the Son: "All virtue and glory be yours, my Son! You are my God and my mercy; all good that I have comes from you. You are like the seed that was never sown but still grew and gave fruit a hundredfold and a thousandfold. For all mercy comes from you and since it is innumerable and ineffable, it can indeed be signified by the number one hundred, which signifies perfection, for all perfection comes from you and everyone is perfected in virtue by you."

The Son answered the Mother: "Indeed, my Mother, you likened me rightly to the seed that was never sown but still grew, since I came with my Divinity to you, and my Manhood was not sown by intercourse but still grew in you, and from it mercy flowed out from you to all. Therefore, you have spoken rightly. Since you now draw mercy out of me with the most sweet words of your mouth, ask me what you want, and it shall be given to you."

The Mother answered: "My Son, since I have won mercy from you, I beg for mercy and help for the wretched. For there are namely four places: The first is Heaven, where the angels and the souls of the saints need nothing but you whom they have - for in you they have every good. The second place is hell, and those who stay there are filled with malice and excluded from all mercy. Therefore, nothing good can enter into them any more. The third is the place of those being purged in purgatory, and those who stay there need a threefold mercy since they are tormented in a threefold way. They suffer through their hearing, for they hear nothing but pain, sorrow, and misery. They suffer through their sight, for they see nothing but their own misery. They are tormented through their touch, for they feel the heat of the unbearable fire and of the harsh torment. My Lord and my Son, give them your mercy for the sake of my prayers!"

The Son answered: "I will gladly give them a threefold mercy for your sake. First, their hearing shall be relieved, their sight will be eased, and their torment will be reduced and relieved. And all those who are in the greatest and most severe torment of the fires of purgatory shall from this moment come to the middle torment; those who are in the middle torment shall come to the lightest; and those who are in the lightest torment shall come home to rest."

The Mother answered: "Praise and honor to you, my Lord!" And she immediately said to her Son: "My beloved Son, the fourth place is the world, and its inhabitants are in need of three things: First, repentance for their sins. Second, penance and atonement. Third, the strength to do good deeds."

The Son answered: "Everyone who calls on your name and has hope in you along with a purpose of amendment for his sins shall be given these three things as well as the kingdom of Heaven. Your words are so sweet to me that I cannot deny you anything you plead for, for you want nothing other than what I want. You are indeed like a shining and burning flame by which the extinguished lights are enkindled and the burning lights are strengthened, for by your love which arose in my heart and drew me to you, those who are dead in sin will come to life again and those who are tepid and black like smoke will become strong in my love."

The Mother blesses the Son in the hearing of the bride, and about how the glorious Son makes a wonderful comparison of his most sweet Mother to a flower that grew in a valley but rose up over mountains.

# Chapter 51

The Mother of God spoke to her Son and said: "Blessed be your name, my Son Jesus Christ, and all honor to your Manhood above all that is created! Glory to your Divinity above all good things, which are one God with your Manhood!" The Son answered: "My Mother, you are like a flower that grew in a valley. Around the valley there were five high mountains, and the flower grew out of three roots with a straight stem without any knots. This flower had five leaves that were filled with all sweetness. The valley with its flower grew above these five mountains, and the leaves of the flower spread themselves above every height of heaven and above all the choirs of angels. My beloved Mother, you are this valley for the sake of the great humility you had in comparison with all others. Your humility grew higher than five mountains.

The first mountain was Moses because of his power. For he had power over my people through the Law, as if it were enclosed in his hand. But you enclosed the Lord of all law in your womb and, therefore, you are higher than this mountain. The second mountain was Elijah, who was so holy, that he with soul and body, was assumed into my holy place. But your soul, my most dear Mother, was assumed above all the choirs of angels to the throne of God along with your most pure body. You are therefore higher than Elijah. The third mountain was the strength of Samson that surpassed all other men. Yet the devil defeated him with his treachery. But you defeated the devil with your strength and power. You are therefore stronger than Samson. The fourth mountain was David, who was a man according to my heart and will, but yet fell into sin. But you, my beloved Mother, followed my will in all and never sinned. The fifth mountain was Solomon, who was full of wisdom but nevertheless was fooled. But you, my Mother, were full of all wisdom and were never fooled or deceived. You are therefore higher than Solomon.

The flower grew from three roots, because of the three things you had from your youth: obedience, charity, and divine understanding. Out of these three roots grew the most straight stem without any knots, which means that your will was never bent to anything but my will. This flower also had five leaves that grew above all the choirs of angels. My dear Mother, you are indeed the flower with these five leaves.

The first leaf is your nobleness, which is so great that my angels, who are noble before me, when seeing and considering your nobleness, saw that it was above them and more eminent than their holiness and nobleness. You are therefore higher than the angels. The second leaf is your mercy, which was so great that you, when you saw the misery of all the souls, had compassion over them and suffered the greatest torment at my death. The angels are full of mercy, and yet they never endure sorrow or pain, but you, my loving Mother, were merciful to the wretched when you felt all the sorrow and torment of my death, and you wanted to suffer torment for the sake of mercy rather than being separated from it. Therefore, your mercy surpassed the mercy of all the angels. The third leaf is your loving kindness. The angels are loving and kind and want good for everyone, but you, my dearest Mother, had before your death a will like an angel in your soul and body and did good to everyone. And still you do not refuse anyone who reasonably prays for his own good. Therefore, your kindness is higher and greater than the angels. The fourth leaf is your beauty. The angels behold the beauty of each other and wonder over the beauty of all souls and all bodies, but they see that the beauty of your soul is above all that is created and that the nobleness of your body surpasses all created beings. And so, your beauty surpassed all the angels and everything created. The fifth leaf was your divine joy, for nothing pleased you but God, just as nothing but God delights the angels. Each and every one of them knows and knew his own joy in himself, but when they saw the joy in you to God, they beheld in their conscience how their joy flamed up in them like a light in the love of God. They saw that your joy was like a flaming bonfire, burning with the hottest fire, with flames so high that it came near to my Divinity. And for this reason, my most sweet Mother, your divine joy burned well above all the choirs of angels. Since this flower had these five leaves, namely, nobleness, mercy, loving kindness, beauty, and the highest joy in God, it was full of all sweetness.

But the one who wants to taste of its sweetness should approach the sweetness and assume it into himself. This is also what you did, my most sweet Mother. You were so sweet to my Father that he assumed all of you into his Spirit, and your sweetness delighted him above all other things. The flower also bears a seed by the heat and power of the sun and from it grows a fruit. In this way the blessed sun, my Divinity, assumed Manhood from your virginal womb. For just as the seed makes and grows flowers of the same kind as the seed wherever it is sown, so my limbs were like yours in shape and appearance, even though I was a man and you a woman and a virgin. This valley was uplifted with its flower above all mountains when your body together with your most holy soul was lifted up above all the choirs of angels."

The Mother blesses her Son and prays to him that his words might be spread all over the world and take root in the hearts of his friends. And about how the Virgin is compared to a wonderful flower growing in a garden, and about the words of Christ that were sent through the bride to the pope and to other prelates of the Church.

# Chapter 52

The Holy Virgin spoke to the Son and said: "Blessed be you, my Son and my God, Lord of angels and King of glory! I beg of you that the words that you have spoken may take root in the hearts of your friends and that their minds may cling as firmly to these words as the pitch with which Noah's ark was plastered, which neither storm-waves nor winds could break and dissolve. May they be spread out all over the world like branches and sweet flowers whose fragrance is spread far and wide, in order that they also may bear fruit and become sweet like the date whose sweetness delights the soul exceedingly much."

The Son answered: "Blessed be you, my most beloved Mother! My angel Gabriel said to you: "Blessed art thou, Mary, among women!" And I bear witness to you that you are blessed and most holy above all the choirs of angels. You are like a flower in a garden that is surrounded by other fragrant flowers, but surpasses them all in scent, beauty, and virtue. These flowers are all the chosen men from Adam to the end of the world which were planted in the garden of the world and shone and smelled in manifold virtues. But among all of those who were and who will afterward come, you were the greatest in the fragrance of humility and a good life, in the beauty of the most pleasing virginity, and in the virtue of abstinence. For I bear witness to you that you were more than any martyr at my suffering, more than any confessor in your abstinence, and more than any angel in your mercy and good will. Therefore, for your sake, I will enroot and fasten my words like the strongest pitch in the hearts of my friends. They shall spread out like fragrant flowers and bear fruit like the sweetest and most wonderful date-palm."

Thereafter, our Lord spoke to his bride: "Tell my friend, your father, whose heart is according to my heart, that he carefully present these written words to his own father and also give them to the archbishop and later to the other bishop. And when these have been thoroughly instructed, he may send them to the third bishop. Tell him also on my behalf: "I am your Creator and the Redeemer of souls. I am God whom you love above all things. See and consider how the souls which I redeemed with my blood are like the souls of men who know nothing about God, and they are imprisoned by the devil in such cruelty that he torments them in all their limbs as in a hard press. Therefore, if you savor my wounds in your soul, and if you account anything of the scourging and suffering that I endured as precious, then show by your deeds how much you love me. The words that I have spoken with my own mouth shall be made known publicly and brought to the head of the Church.

I shall namely give you my grace and my Spirit so that, wherever there is a quarrel between two, you may be able to reconcile them in my name through the power given to you, if they believe in my words. And as a further clarification of my words, you shall bring to the pope the testimonies of those who taste and delight in my words. For my words are like fat which melts more quickly when the warmth is greater inside, but if no warmth is found, the fat is thrown up and does not reach the intestines. This is how my words are, since the more a man eats and chews on them with a burning love for me, the more he is fed with the desire for heaven and the sweetness of the divine inner love, and the more he burns in my love and charity. But those who do not delight in my words may be likened to having lard in their mouths which they immediately spit out of their mouths and trample under their feet once they have tasted it. Some people despise my words in this way because they have no taste for the sweetness of spiritual things. But the lord of the land, whom I have chosen as my member and made truly mine, will help you manfully and provide you with the necessary things for your journey out of righteously acquired goods."

The Mother and Son's words of blessing for each other, and about how the Virgin is likened to the ark wherein the staff, the manna, and the tablets of the Law were, and many wonderful things are revealed in this comparison.

# Chapter 53

The Virgin Mary spoke to the Son and said: "Blessed be you, my Son, my God, and Lord of angels! You are the one whose voice the prophets heard, whose body the apostles saw, and the one whom the Jews and your enemies laid their hands on. You are one God with your Divinity and Manhood and Holy Ghost. For the prophets heard the Spirit, the apostles saw the glory of your Divinity, and the Jews crucified your Manhood. Therefore, may you be blessed without beginning and without end."

The Son answered: "Blessed be you, for you are Virgin and Mother. You are the Ark of the Old Law in which there were three things: the staff of Aaron that blossomed, the manna of angels, and the tablets of the Law.

Three things were done with the staff: First, it was transformed into a snake without venom. Second, the ocean was divided by it. Third, it brought forth water out of the rock. I, who lay in your womb and assumed Manhood from you, liken myself with this staff. First, I am as terrifying to my enemies as the snake was to Moses. For they flee from me as from the sight of a snake, and they are terrified of me and abhor me like a venomous snake; and yet I am without the venom of malice and am instead all full of mercy. I allow myself to be held by them, if they want. I return to them if they search for me. I run to them like a mother to her lost and recovered son, if they call on me. I give them my mercy and forgive their sins, if they cry out to me. This is what I do for them, and yet they abhor me like a venomous snake.

Second, the ocean was divided by this staff when the way to heaven, which was closed for the sake of sin, was opened through the shedding of my blood and my pain. The ocean was indeed divided and a way was made, where there before had been no way, when the pain in all my limbs went to my heart, and my heart burst from the violence of the pain. Later, when the people had been led through

152

the ocean, Moses did not lead them to the promised land immediately but to the desert, so that they would be tested and instructed there. This is how it is now, for when the people have accepted my faith and my commandments, they are not led into heaven immediately; for it is necessary that men should be tested in the desert - that is, in the world - as to how much they love God.

However, the people provoked God into anger by three things in the desert: First, because they made an idol and prayed to it. Second, because they longed after the fleshpots that they had in the land of Egypt and third, through their pride, when they, without the will of God, wanted to go and fight against their enemies. People sin against me even now in the world in the same way.

First, they honor and worship an idol: for they love the world and all the things in it more than me, who am their Creator. Therefore, the world is their god, and not I. For I said in my gospel: "Where a man's treasure is, there his heart is also." So, mankind's treasure is the world, since their heart yearns towards it and not to me. Therefore, just as the Jews fell in the desert with a sword in their bodies, so too shall these people fall with the sword of eternal damnation in their soul and they shall live in damnation without end.

Second, they sinned through their longing for fleshpots. I gave mankind everything he needed to use in an honorable and moderate way, but he wants to have all things without moderation and reason. For, if his bodily nature could bear it, he would without end have sex, drink without restraint, desire without measure and limit, and, as long as he could sin, he would never desist from sin. Therefore, the same thing will happen to them that happened to the Jews in the desert, that is, they will die a sudden death in their body. For what is this temporal life other than a single moment compared to eternity? For this reason, they shall die a sudden death in their bodies to be torn away from this short life and live with torment in their souls for all eternity.

Third, they sinned in the desert through their pride, since they wanted to go to battle without God's will. Likewise, people want to go to Heaven through their pride, and they do not trust in me but in themselves, doing their own will and abandoning mine. Therefore, they shall be killed in their souls by devils just as the Jews were killed by their enemies, and their torment shall be everlasting. They thus hate me like a snake, worship an idol instead of me, long for their own desires more than me, and love their own pride instead of my humility. Yet, I am still so merciful that I will turn to them like a loving father and take them to me if they turn to me with a repentant heart.

Third, the rock gave water through this staff. This rock is the hard heart of mankind, for if it is pierced with my fear and love, there immediately flow tears of repentance and penance out of it. No one is so unworthy and no one is so evil that he will not have tears flowing from his eyes and all his limbs awakened to devotion if he turns to me in a heartfelt contemplation of my suffering and bethinks how my power and goodness makes the earth and trees bear fruit.

Second, the manna of angels lay in the ark of Moses. So, too, in you my beloved Mother and Virgin, lay the bread of angels and of holy souls and of righteous men on earth, whom nothing pleases but my sweetness; for all of the world is dead to them, so that they would gladly go even without bodily nourishment if it were my will.

Third, in the ark were the tablets of the Law. So, too, in you lay the Lord of all laws. Therefore, may you be blessed above everything created in Heaven and on earth!"

Then Christ spoke to his bride and said: "Tell my friends three things. When I was bodily in the world, I adjusted my words so that good men were made stronger and more fervent in doing good things, and evil men became better, as was seen in the conversion of Magdalene, Matthew, and many others. I also adjusted my words so that my enemies were not able to refute them. For that reason, may they to whom my words are sent, work with fervor, so that through my words, the good may become more ardent in goodness, the evil repent from wickedness, and that they themselves be on guard against my enemies so that my words are not obstructed. In truth, I do no greater injustice to the devil than to the angels in Heaven. For if I wanted, I could speak my words so that the whole world hears them. I could also open up hell so that everyone may see its torments, but this would not be justice, since all men would then serve me out of fear, when they should serve me out of love. For no other than the one who has love shall enter the kingdom of Heaven. For I would be doing injustice to the devil if I took away from him one who is rightfully his, because of sin, and who is devoid of good deeds. I would also do injustice to the angel in Heaven, if I placed the spirit of an unclean man as an equal to the one who is pure and most fervent in my love.

Therefore, no one shall enter Heaven, but the one who has been purged like gold in the fire of purgatory or who has proved himself over a long duration of time in good deeds on earth so that there is no stain in him left to be purged away. If you do not know to whom my words should be sent, I will tell you: The one who is worthy to have my words is the one who wants to gain merit through good deeds in order to come to the kingdom of Heaven or who already has deserved it with their good deeds in the past. To such as these shall my words be opened up to and enter into them. Those who have a taste for my words and who humbly hope that their names are written in the Book of Life keep my words. But those who have no have taste for my words, consider them first, but then throw up and vomit them out immediately."

The words of an angel to the bride about whether the spirit of her thoughts is good or bad, and about how there are two spirits, one uncreated and one created, and about their characteristics.

# Chapter 54

A holy angel spoke to the bride and said: "There are two spirits, one uncreated and one created. The uncreated Spirit has three characteristics: First, he is hot; second, sweet; and third, pure. First, he gives off warmth, and his warmth does not come from created things but from himself, since he, together with the Father and the Son, is Creator of all things and Almighty. He gives off warmth when the whole soul burns for the love of God. Second, he is sweet, when nothing pleases the soul and nothing delights it but God and the recollection of his deeds. Third, he is so pure that no sin can be found in him, nor any deformity or corruption or mutability. He does not give off warmth like earthly fire, and he does not make things melt like the visible sun, but his warmth is the inner love and desire of the soul that fills the soul and engrosses her in God. He is sweet to the soul, not as a desirable wine or fleshly lust or any other worldly thing, but instead, the sweetness of this Spirit is incomparable to all temporal sweetness and unimaginable to those who have not tasted it. Third, this Spirit is as pure as the rays of the sun in which no blemish can be found.

The second spirit that is created also has three characteristics. He is burning, bitter, and unclean. First, he is burning and consuming like fire, for he completely enkindles the soul he possesses with the fire of lust and evil desire, so that the soul that is filled by him can neither think nor desire anything other than fulfilling this desire; and the consequence of this is that her temporal life is sometimes lost along with all honor and consolation. Second, he is bitter as gall, since he so inflames the soul with his evil lust, that future joys seem like nothing to her and eternal goods but foolishness. And all the things that are of God and which she, the soul, is obligated to do for God, become as bitter and despicable to her as vomit and gall. Third, he is unclean, since he makes the soul so vile and inclined to sin that she does not feel ashamed for any sin, and she would not abstain from any sin, if she did not fear being shamed and judged before men more than before God. This is why this spirit is like a burning fire, because he burns of desire to do evil and enkindles others along with itself. This is why he is bitter, because all good is bitter to him and he wants to make it bitter for others as well as for himself. This is why he is unclean, because he delights in impurity and wants that others shall become like himself.

But now you might ask and say to me: "Are you not also a created spirit like him? Why, then, are you not like that?" I answer you: I am indeed created by the same God as he, for there is only one God, Father, Son and Holy Ghost, and these are not three gods, but one God. Both of us were well made and created for the good, since God has created nothing but good. But I am like a star, for I remained in the goodness and love of God in which I was created. He, however, is like coal, since he left the love of God. Just as a star has brightness and splendor, whereas coal has blackness and filth, so the good angel, who is like a star, has his splendor, that is, the Holy Ghost - since everything he has, he has from God the Father, Son, and Holy Ghost, from whose love he becomes set on fire and from whose splendor he shines - constantly clinging to him and conforming himself after his will without ever wanting anything other than what God wants. And this is why he is burning; this is why he is pure.

The devil however is like ugly coal, and is uglier and more deformed than any other created creature. For just as he once was more beautiful than others, so he had to become uglier than others since he opposed himself against his Creator. Just as the angel of God shines with the light of God and burns incessantly by his love, so the devil is always burning and anguishing in his malice. His malice is insatiable, just as the goodness and grace of the Holy Ghost are inexpressible. For no one in this world is so rooted in the devil that the Holy Ghost does not sometimes visit and touch his heart. Likewise is no one so good that the devil does not gladly try to touch him with temptation. Many good and righteous men are tempted by the devil with God's permission, and this is not because of their wickedness but for their greater glory. Indeed, the Son of God, who is one in Divinity with the Father and the Holy Ghost, was tempted when he had assumed Manhood; and how much more should not his elect be tempted then, so that their reward and glory may become greater!

Again, many good people sometimes fall into sin, and their conscience is darkened by the treachery of the devil, but then they get up again, being stronger and more steadfast than before through the virtue and power of the Holy Ghost. There is no one who does not understand in his conscience whether the suggestion of the devil leads to the ugliness of sin or to the good, if he would only think about and examine his conscience carefully. Therefore may you, bride of my Lord, not doubt whether the spirit of your thoughts is good or bad, for your conscience tells you which things to exclude and which to do.

But what should the one who is full of the devil do, since the good Spirit cannot enter him who is full of evil? He should do three things: First, he should make a pure and complete confession of his sins. Even if he cannot directly feel a complete remorse for his sins due to his hardened heart, still the confession will benefit him so much that the devil ceases with his treachery and yields to the good spirit. Second, he should be humble and wish to amend for all the sins he has committed and do the good deeds he can, and then the devil will begin to leave. Third, he should beseech God with humble prayer in order that he may get the good Spirit back and have contrition for the sins he has committed along with true divine love, since the love for God kills the devil. This devil is so envious and full of malice that he would rather die a hundred times than see someone do God the least little good deed out of love."

Thereafter, the Holy Virgin spoke to the bride, saying: "New bride of my Son, put on your clothes and fasten your brooch, that is, my Son's suffering!" She answered her: "My sweet Lady, put it on me yourself." And the Virgin said: "Yes, I shall do it. I also want to tell you how my Son was disposed and why the holy fathers longed for him so fervently. He stood, as it were, in between two great cities, and a voice from the first city cried out to him saying: "O man, standing in between the cities, you are a wise man, for you know how to beware of coming dangers and injuries. You are also strong in the suffering of overhanging evils, and you are brave as well since you fear nothing. We have longed for and awaited you. Therefore, open our gate, for our enemies are besieging it so that it cannot be opened."

A voice from the second city was heard saying thus: "You, the most kind and strong of men, hear our complaint and lament! We sit in darkness and suffer unbearable hunger and thirst. Consider our misery and our great distress. We are beaten like grass cut by a scythe. All goodness has dried and withered away in us; and all our strength has faded away in us. We beg you to come to us and save us, for you alone are the one we have awaited and hoped for as our liberator! Come and release us from our distress, turn our lamentation into joy, and be our help and salvation! Come, most blessed and worthy body, which proceeded from the pure Virgin!" My Son heard these two voices from the two cities, that is, from Heaven and hell. That is why he had mercy on them and opened up the gates of hell through his most bitter suffering and the shedding of his blood and brought his friends out of there. He opened up Heaven, too, to the joy of the angels, and led the ones into Heaven whom he had rescued from hell. My daughter, think on these things and have them always before your eyes!"

About how Christ is likened to a mighty lord who built a great city and a marvelous castle, signifying the world and the church, and how the judges and defenders and workers in the church of God have been changed into a bad bow.

# Chapter 55

Our Lord Jesus Christ said: "I am like a powerful lord who built a great city and named it after himself. Thereafter, he built a castle in the city in which there were many rooms for storing all kinds of useful necessities. Then, when he had built the castle and arranged all his things, he divided his people into three groups, saying: 'I am going away to a far away country. Stand firm and work manfully for my glory! I have made arrangements for your food and your necessities, and you have judges to judge you and defenders to defend you from your enemies. I have also arranged for working men who shall feed you and give me a tenth part of their work, saving it for my use and my honor.'

But after some time had gone by, the name of the city was forgotten. Then the judges said: 'Our lord has traveled to a far away country. Let us judge righteous judgments and do justice so that, when our lord returns, we may not be punished and be accused but receive honor and blessing.' Then the defenders said: 'Our lord trusts us very much and has left the defense of his house to us. Let us therefore abstain from superfluous food and drink so that we may not become unfit for battle. Let us also abstain from excessive sleep so that we may guard ourselves and not be trapped unawares. May we be well armed and constantly watchful so that we may not be found unprepared when enemies come. The honor of our lord and the salvation of our people depend very much on us.' Then the workers said: 'The glory of our lord is great and his reward is glorious and grand. Let us therefore work mightily and give him not only a tenth of our work but also offer him everything above our living expenses! Our reward shall become more glorious the greater the love he sees in us.'

Thereafter, some time went by, and the name of the city and the lord of the castle became forgotten. Then the judges said to themselves: 'The delay of our lord is long, and we do not know if he will return or not. Let us therefore judge according to our own will and do what we please.' The defenders said: 'We are fools, because we work and know not what reward we shall receive. Let us enter into a covenant with our enemies instead and sleep and drink with them, for we do not care about whose enemies they have been.' Thereafter, the workers said: 'Why do we save our gold for others, when we do not know who will get it after us? It is better that we use it ourselves and dispose of it after our own will. Let us therefore give the tenth to the judges and placate them so that we then can do what we want.'

In truth, I am like this mighty lord, for I built myself a city, that is, the world, and placed a castle there, that is, the church. The name of the world was divine wisdom, for the world had this name from the beginning, since it was created in divine wisdom. This name was venerated by all, and God was praised in his wisdom and wondrously proclaimed by his creatures. But now the name of the city has been dishonored and changed, and a new name has been taken, that is, human wisdom.

For the judges, who before had made judgments in righteousness and the fear of the Lord, have now turned to pride and are trying to deceive simple men. They desire to be eloquent so that they may win human praise, and they speak and preach that which pleases men so that they may obtain favors. They tolerate calmly all words so that they may be called good and patient, and they accept bribes to overturn righteous judgments. They are wise for the sake of their own temporal benefit and their own will, but dumb when it comes to my praise. They trample and press down simple men under their feet and force them into silence. They extend their greed to all and make right into wrong. This is the kind of wisdom that is loved now, while my wisdom is forgotten.

The defenders of the church, who are the noblemen and knights, see my enemies and the attackers of my Church but do not care about it. They hear their words of blasphemy and mockery but do not care about it. They perceive and understand the deeds of those who attack my commandments and still bear them patiently. They behold them daily committing all kinds of mortal sins, as if they were allowed, and feel no compunction about it, but sleep and associate with them, binding themselves by oath to their company.

The workers, that is, the entire people, reject my commandments and withhold my gifts and my tenth. They offer gifts to their judges and show them honor and reverence in order to win their favor and goodwill. In truth, I can boldly say that the sword of fear for me and for my Church is thrown away in the world, and that a sack of money has been put in its place."

The words in which God explains the nearest preceding Chapter, and about the judgment that he makes against such people, and about how God for a while endures the evil for the sake of the good.

# Chapter 56

"I told you before that the sword of my Church is thrown away and that a sack of money has been put in its place, which is open at one end. The other end is so deep, that whatever one puts into it never reaches the bottom, and so the sack never gets filled. This sack is greed, which exceeds all measures and now has become so powerful that the Lord is scorned and nothing is desired but money and the selfish will of man. But I am like a lord who is both father and judge. When he shall go forth and judge, the bystanders say to him: 'Lord, proceed quickly and make your judgment!' The Lord answers them: 'Wait a little until tomorrow, because perhaps my son will still amend himself in the meantime.'

When he comes back the next day, the people say to him: 'Proceed, Lord, and make your judgment! Why are you postponing the judgment for so long and do not judge the guilty?' The Lord answers them: 'Wait a little while longer, to see if my son betters himself, and if he then does not repent, I shall make a just judgment over him.' In this way I patiently endure mankind even until the last moment, since I am both father and judge. But my justice is unchangeable, and even though it sometimes is postponed a long time, I will still either punish sinners who do not better themselves or show them mercy if they amend themselves.

I also told you before that I divided the people into three groups: namely, judges, defenders, and workers. What do these judges signify if not the priests who have turned the divine wisdom into an evil and useless wisdom? Like clerks who take many words and assemble them into a few words, which say the same thing as the many did, so too have these present-day clerics taken my ten commandments and assembled them into a single one. And what is this single word if not: 'Reach out your hand and give us money!' This is their wisdom, to speak beautifully, to act badly and to pretend to be my servants while yet acting maliciously against me. For the sake of gifts, they gladly put up with sinners in their sins and bring about the downfall of simpleminded people through their bad example. Furthermore, they hate those who walk on my way. Second, the defenders of the Church, that is, the knights, are unfaithful, since they have broken their promise and their oath and gladly endure those who sin against the faith and law of my Holy Church. Third, the workers, that is, the whole people, are like untamed bulls which have three things: First, they dig the earth with their feet; second, they fill themselves to satiety; third, they fulfill their own lusts according to their own desire. Likewise does now the whole people crave after temporal goods with all of their desire, filling itself with immoderate gluttony and worldly vanity and practicing its carnal lust and delight without reason.

But even though my enemies are many, I still have many friends among them, although hidden. As it was said to Elijah, who thought none of my friends were left in the world but himself: "I have seven thousand men who have not bowed their knees to Baal." So, even though my enemies are many, I still have some friends hidden among them who cry daily because my enemies are superior and because my name is despised. Therefore, for the sake of their prayers, I shall do like a charitable and good king who knows the evil deeds of the city but patiently endures its residents and sends letters to his friends to forewarn them of their danger. In this way I send my words to my friends; and they are not so obscure as the words in the Apocalypse which I revealed to John in an obscure way in order that they would be interpreted by my Spirit at the time that pleased me. Nor are they so hidden that they cannot be proclaimed - as when Paul saw many of my hidden secrets that he was not allowed to speak about - but they are so plain, that all, both small and big, can understand them, and so easy, that all who want to, can grasp and understand them.

Therefore, let my friends see to it that my words reach my enemies, so that they, perhaps, convert themselves and feel sorrow and remorse for their sins, when their peril and my judgment are made known to them. Otherwise, the city will be judged so severely that, just as a wall is torn down without leaving stone upon stone, so that not even two stones join to each other in the foundation, so shall it be with the city, that is, with the world.

The judges shall burn in the hottest fire. There is no fire hotter than the one that is fed with some fat. These judges were fat, since they had more opportunities of fulfilling their lust and will than others; they surpassed others in honor and temporal abundance, and abounded more in malice and unrighteousness. Therefore, they will burn in the hottest pan, that is, in the torments of hell!

The defenders shall be hanged on the highest gallows. A gallows consists of two vertical timber beams with a third placed above the others horizontally. This gallows with two wooden beams signifies their cruel and severe torment, which is, so to speak, made from two pieces of wood. The first beam signifies that they did not hope for my eternal reward nor worked for it with their good deeds. The second beam signifies that they did not trust in my power and goodness, when they thought I was not able to do all things or did not want to provide for them sufficiently. The wooden crossbeam signifies their evil conscience, for they understood very well what they should do but, instead, did evil and felt no shame about acting against their conscience. The rope of the gallows signifies the everlasting fire which can neither be extinguished by water nor cut by scissors nor be destroyed and broken by old age. On this gallows of the most cruel torment and inextinguishable fire, they will hang and feel shame and distress like unhappy traitors, since they were disloyal. They will hear insults, since my words displeased them. A woe shall be in their mouths, since their own honor and praise delighted them. They shall be mangled on this gallows by living crows, that is, by devils who can never get their fill, and even though they be wounded, they shall never be consumed, but they shall live in torment without end and their torturers shall also live without end. There shall be a woe that will never end and a misery that will never be mitigated. Woe unto them, that they were ever born! Woe unto them, that their life was so long!

And lastly concerning the workers, their just sentence will be the same as for bulls. For the bulls have very hard flesh and skin. Therefore, their judgment shall be the sharpest steel. This most sharp steel is the death of hell that will torment those who scorned me and loved their own will instead of my commandments.

165

The letter, that is, my words, are now written. May my friends work wisely and reasonably so that it comes to my enemies, for perhaps they will want to hear them and repent from their wickedness. But if some, after having heard my words, should say: "Let us wait a little moment, the judgment is not yet coming, it is not yet his time," then I swear by my Divinity which cast out Adam from paradise and sent ten plagues over Pharaoh, that I will come to them faster than they think.

I swear by my Manhood, which I assumed without sin from the Virgin for the salvation of mankind, and in which I endured sorrow in my heart and suffered bodily torment and death for the eternal life of men, and in which I rose again from the dead and ascended into heaven and am seated at the right hand of the Father, true God and true Man in one person, that I shall fulfill my words.

I swear by my Spirit, which descended over the apostles on the day of Pentecost and inflamed them so that they spoke in the language of all peoples, that unless they better themselves and return to me like weak servants, I shall execute vengeance over them in my wrath. Then there shall be a woe in soul and body! Woe unto them that they came alive into the world and lived in the world! Woe unto them, for their lust was small and vain but their torment shall be everlasting! Then they shall perceive what they now scorn to believe, namely, that my words were words of love. Then they shall understand that I admonished them like a father, even though they did not want to hear me. In truth, if they do not want to believe in my words of goodwill, they will have to believe in the deeds when they come.

The words of our Lord to the bride about how he is loathsome and despicable food for the souls of Christians, and how the world, instead, is loved and found to be delightful by them, and about the terrifying judgment that is executed over such people.

# Chapter 57

The Son of God spoke to his bride: "Christians are now acting towards me as the Jews acted towards me. The Jews drove me out of the temple and had a complete will to kill me, but since my hour had not yet come, I escaped from their hands. Christians act towards me in the same way now. They drive me out of their temple (that is, out of their soul, which should be my temple) and they would gladly want to kill me if they could. I am like rotten and stinking flesh in their mouths. I seem, to them, to be like a man who utters lies, and they do not care about me at all. They turn their backs to me, but I will turn my neck to them, since there is nothing but craving in their mouths and irrational beastly lust in their flesh. Only pride is delightful in their ears, only the lust of the world delights their eyes. My suffering and my love are detestable to them and my life heavy and burdensome. Therefore, I shall do as the animal which had many dens: when hunters pursued and drove it from one den, it escaped into another. This is what I will do, because Christians are chasing me away with their bad deeds and driving me out of the den of their hearts.

Therefore, I want to go to the heathens in whose mouths I am now bitter and distasteful, but I will become sweeter than honey in their mouths. Nevertheless, I am still so merciful that I will happily receive each and everyone who begs for my forgiveness and says: 'Lord, I know that I have sinned severely and I gladly want to better myself through your grace. Have mercy on me for the sake of your bitter suffering.' But to those who harden themselves in their evil, I shall come like a warrior that has three characteristics: namely, dreadfulness, strength, and severity. I shall come and be so terrifying to the Christians that they will not dare to move the least finger against me. I shall also come to them with such strength that they will be like mosquitoes before me. Third, I shall come to them with such severity that they will feel a woe in this world and a woe without end."

The words of the Mother to the bride about how sweet the Mother and the Son are to each other. How Christ is bitter, bitterer, and most bitter for the evil, and how he is sweet, sweeter, and most sweet for the good.

# Chapter 58

The Mother of God said to the bride: "Consider, new bride of my Son, the suffering of my Son, which surpassed in bitterness the suffering of all the saints. Just as a mother would feel the most bitter sorrow and anguish if she saw her son being cut to pieces alive, so, too, was I grieving at the torments of my Son when I saw his bitter sufferings." Then she spoke to her Son, saying: "Blessed be you, my Son, for you are holy, as it is sung: 'Holy, holy, holy, Lord God Sabaoth.' Blessed be you, for you are sweet, sweeter, and most sweet! You were holy before you assumed Manhood, holy in my womb, and holy after you assumed Manhood. You were sweet before the creation of the world, sweeter to the angels, and most sweet to me when you assumed Manhood from me."

The Son answered: "Blessed be you, my beloved Mother, above all the angels. Just as I, in a threefold way, was most sweet for you, as you were saying now, so I am bitter, bitterer, and most bitter for the wicked. I am bitter for those who say I have created many things without a reason and who scornfully say I have created mankind for death and not for life. What a miserable and foolish thought! Did I, who am the most righteous and virtuous, create the angels without a reason? Would I have enriched mankind with so many good things if I had created him for damnation? By no means! I created all things well and gave every good to mankind out of my love. But he, however, turned all good things into evil for himself. It is not because I created anything evil, but mankind moves his will in another way than he should, and not according to God's law, and this is evil.

But I am bitterer for those who say that I have given them a free will to sin and not to do good, who say I am unjust since I condemn some and justify others, and who blame me for their own wickedness because I withhold my grace from them. I am most bitter for those who say that my law and commandments are exceedingly harsh and difficult and that no one is able to keep them, who say my suffering is worth nothing for them, and who therefore count it for nothing.

Therefore, I swear by my life, as once I swore through the prophets, that I shall justify myself before the angels and all my saints. Those for whom I am bitter shall understand that I created all things reasonably and well for the use and education of mankind, and that not the smallest worm exists without a reason. Those for whom I am bitterer shall understand that I wisely gave men a free will for their own good. They will also know that I am just, giving the eternal kingdom to good men, but everlasting torment to the wicked. For it would not be proper for the devil, who was created good by me but who fell through his own malice, to have fellowship with the good. The wicked will also understand that it is not my fault that they are evil, but their own fault. For if it were possible, I would gladly take upon myself the same torment for each and every man that I once suffered on the cross for all, if thereby they could return to their promised inheritance. But the will of mankind is always opposed to mine. I gave him liberty to serve me, if he would, and to gain the eternal reward; but if he does not want to, he should be tormented together with the devil and his followers, for whose malice, hell was justly created.

But because I am full of charity, I do not want mankind to serve me out of fear or be forced to do so like an irrational animal but out of love for God, for no one who serves me unwillingly or out of fear of torment can see my face. But those for whom I am most bitter will understand in their consciences that my law was most easy and my yoke most sweet. They will feel inconsolable sadness that they despised my law and instead loved the world, whose yoke is heavier and much more difficult than my yoke."

Then the Mother of God answered: "Blessed be you, my Son, my God, and my Lord! Since you were most sweet for me, I beg of you that others may be made partakers of my sweetness!" The Son answered: "Blessed be you, my most dear Mother! Your words are sweet and full of love. Therefore shall each and everyone who takes your sweetness into his mouth and keeps it perfectly be benefited thereby. But the one who takes it and spits it out again will be tormented all the more bitterly." Then the Virgin answered: "Blessed be you, my Son, for all your mercy and love!"

The words of Christ, in the presence of the bride, about how Christ is likened to a peasant, good priests to a good shepherd, bad priests to a bad shepherd, and good Christians to a wife. Many useful things are also explained in this parable.

# Chapter 59

"I am the one who never said anything false. The world considers me to be a peasant whose name seems contemptible. My words are counted as foolish and my house is considered a despicable shed. This peasant had a wife who wanted nothing other than what he wanted, who owned everything with him and had him as her master, obeying him in all things as her master. This peasant also had many sheep, and he hired a shepherd to watch over them for five gold coins and for the necessities of his bodily needs. Since this was a good shepherd, he used the gold to his benefit and the food for his sustenance. After some time had gone by, this shepherd moved and another shepherd came who was worse, who bought himself a wife with the gold and brought her his food, constantly taking his rest with her without caring about the sheep that were being lamentably scattered by cruel beasts.

When the peasant saw how his sheep were being scattered, he cried out saying: 'My shepherd is unfaithful to me! My sheep are scattered by the most cruel beasts. Some of them are completely devoured by the beasts with body and fleece, while others are dead but their bodies left uneaten.' Then the wife said to her husband the peasant: 'My Lord, it is certain that we will not get back the bodies that are devoured, but the bodies who have remained unharmed, even though they are without life, should be brought home and made use of by us. For it would be unbearable for us if we lost everything.' The husband answered her: 'But what shall we do? Since the animals had venomous teeth, the flesh of the sheep has also become poisoned with deadly venom, the hide is ruined, and the wool is all tangled.' The wife answered: 'If everything is infected and ruined and everything taken from us, what shall we then live on?'

The husband answered her: 'I see that there are sheep still alive in three places. Some are like the dead sheep and do not dare to breathe out of fear. Other sheep are lying deep in filth and cannot raise themselves up. Still others lie in hiding places and dare not come forth. Come therefore, my wife, and let us lift up the sheep that are trying to raise themselves up but cannot do so without help, and let us make use of them to our own benefit.'

Behold, I the Lord am this peasant, for men consider me to be a donkey raised in its stall according to its ways and habits. My name is the foundation of the Holy Church, but she is now considered to be contemptible, since the sacraments of the Church, namely baptism, confirmation, anointing, penance, and matrimony, are taken, as it were, with derision and given to others for the sake of greed. My words and deeds are considered and judged to be foolish and vain, for the words that I spoke in parables with my own mouth, have now been converted from a spiritual understanding to temporal entertainment. My house is looked on as contemptible, for the things of the earth are loved instead of the things of Heaven.

With this first shepherd I had, I symbolize my friends the priests, which I used to have in the Holy Church; for by a single word, I mean and signify many. I entrusted them with my sheep, that is, to consecrate my most venerable body and to rule and defend the souls of my chosen ones. I also gave them five good things more precious than all gold: First, an insight and understanding about all abstruse things so that they will be able to distinguish between good and evil, and between truth and falsehood. Second, I gave them understanding and wisdom in spiritual things; this has now been forgotten and human wisdom is loved instead. Third, I gave them chastity; fourth, temperance in all things and abstinence for the restraining and guidance of their body; fifth, steadfastness in good habits, words, and deeds.

After this first shepherd, that is, after these friends of mine, who used to be in my Church in days of old, other unrighteous shepherds came that bought a wife for themselves with the gold, that is, they took to themselves the body of a woman and intemperance instead of chastity and these five good things, and that is why my Spirit departed from them. For when they have a complete will to sin and to satisfy their wife, that is, to satisfy their lust, then my Spirit is absent from them, since they do not care about the perdition of the sheep so long as they can fulfill their evil lust. But the sheep that are completely devoured are those whose souls are in hell and whose bodies are buried in the grave awaiting the resurrection of the eternal damnation. The sheep whose flesh remains but whose spirit is taken away, are those who neither love me nor fear me nor feel any devotion or care toward me. My Spirit is far away from them, since their flesh is poisoned by the venomous teeth of the beasts, that is, their soul and their thoughts, which are symbolized by the sheep's flesh and intestines, are in every way as disgusting to me and as repulsive to taste as is poisoned meat. From their hide, that is, from their body, has all goodness and charity dried out and it is unfit for any service in my kingdom and shall be delivered to the everlasting fire of hell after the judgment. Their wool, that is, their deeds, are so altogether useless that there is nothing in them that would make them worthy to receive my love and grace.

But what shall we do then, my wife, that is, good Christians, whom the wife symbolizes, what should we do? I see that sheep are alive in three places. Some of them look like the dead sheep and do not dare to breathe out of fear. These are the gentiles who would gladly have the right faith, if only they knew how, but who do not dare to breathe, that is, they do not dare to leave the faith that they have and take the right faith. The second sheep are those lying in hiding places who do not dare to come forth, and these are the Jews who live, so to speak, under a veil, and who would gladly come forth if they knew for certain that I was born. They namely hide themselves under a veil, since their hope for salvation is in the figures and signs that used to symbolize me in the Old Law but which in truth have been fulfilled in me, and because of this vain hope they are afraid to come forth to the right faith. The third sheep that lie in the filth are Christians in the state of mortal sin. They would gladly raise themselves up because of their fear of the torment, but they cannot due to their heavy sins and because they have no divine love. Therefore, my wife, that is, good Christians, help me! For just as a wife and a man should be one flesh and one limb, so the Christian is my limb and I am his, since I am in him and he is in me.

Therefore, o wife of mine, that is, good Christians, run with me to the sheep that still have a breath of life and let us lift them up and refresh them! Have compassion on me, for I bought them at a very high price! Let us lift them up, you with me and me with you, you at the back and I at the head! I gladly carry them with my hands. Once I carried them all on my back when it was all lacerated and fastened to the cross. O my friends, I love these sheep so dearly that, if it were possible for me to suffer such a death for each sheep as I once suffered on the cross for all of them, I would rather redeem them than want to lose them. That is why I cry out to my friends with all my heart that they should not spare goods or work for my sake; for if I was not spared from reproaching and insulting words while I was in the world, they should not spare themselves in speaking the truth about me. I was not ashamed to suffer a contemptible death for their sake, but stood there naked, just as I was born, before the eyes of my enemies. I was struck in the teeth with their fists. I was dragged by the hair with their fingers and scourged by their scourges. I was fastened to the cross with their tools, and I hung on the cross between thieves and robbers. Therefore, my friends, do not spare yourself in working for me since I endured such things out of love for you. Work manfully and bring help to all my sheep in distress.

I swear by my Manhood, which is in the Father as the Father is in me, and by my Divinity, which is in my Spirit as the Spirit is in the Divinity and the same Spirit is in me and I in him, and these are one God in three persons, that I shall run out to meet those halfway who work in carrying my sheep with me and help them, and I shall give them the most precious reward, namely, myself unto their everlasting joy."

The words of the Son to the bride about the three kinds of Christians that are symbolized by the Jews living in Egypt, and about how the things which have been revealed to the bride should be transmitted, published and preached to ignorant persons by the friends of God.

# Chapter 60

The Son of God spoke to the bride and said: "I am the God of Israel and the one who spoke with Moses. When Moses was sent to my people, he begged for a sign, saying: 'The people will not believe me otherwise.' But if the people to whom Moses was sent were the Lord's people, why did they not believe? You should know that this people consisted of three kinds of men: Some believed in God and Moses. Others believed in God but distrusted Moses, in that they thought that he, perhaps of his own invention and presumption, had presumed to say and do these things. The third were those who neither believed in God nor in Moses.

In the same way, there are now three kinds of men among Christians who are symbolized by the Hebrew people: There are some who rightly believe in God and in my words. There are others who believe in God but distrust my words, because they cannot distinguish between the good and the evil spirit. The third are those who neither believe in me nor in you to whom I have spoken my words. But, as I said, even though some of the Hebrews distrusted Moses, nevertheless they all went through the Red Sea with him and into the desert where those who had not believed worshipped idols and provoked God into wrath, which is why they also died in the most miserable of deaths. But only those who had an evil faith did so.

Therefore, my friend shall carry my words to those who believe him, since the human soul is slow to believe. And these shall afterwards spread them to others who do not know how to distinguish between the good and the evil spirit. But if the hearers beg them for a sign, let them show those men the staff, just as Moses did, that is, let them explain my words to them. For just as the staff of Moses was straight and terrifying (for it was transformed into a snake), so are my words straight so that no falsehood can be found in them. They are terrifying, since they proclaim the righteous judgment. Let them also explain and testify that, by a word and sound of a single mouth, the devil yielded from the creature of God - he who could move mountains, if he were not restrained by my power. What kind of power belonged to him when, with God's permission, he was driven away by the sound of a single word?

Therefore, just as those Hebrews, who neither believed in God nor in Moses, yet went out of Egypt for the promised land when they, as it were, were forced along together with the others, so too, many Christians go out unwillingly together with my chosen men since they do not trust in my power to heal them. They do not believe in my words and they have a false hope in my power. Nevertheless, my words shall be fulfilled without their will and shall be, as it were, forced along to fulfillment until they get to the place that pleases me."

# Book 2

The Son's instruction to the bride about the devil; the Son's answer to the bride about why he does not remove evildoers before they fall into sin; and about how the kingdom of heaven is given to baptized persons who die before reaching the age of discretion.

## Chapter 1

The Son spoke to the bride, saying: "When the devil tempts you, tell him these three things: 'The words of God cannot be anything but true.' Second: 'Nothing is impossible for God, because he can do all things.' Third: 'You, devil, could not give me so great a fervor of love as that which God gives me.' " Again the Lord spoke to the bride, saying: "I look at people in three ways: first, their outer body and what condition it is in; second, their inner conscience, what it tends toward and in what way; third, their heart and what it desires. Like a bird that sees a fish in the sea and assesses the depth of the water and also takes note of storm winds, I, too, know and assess the ways of each person and take note of what is due to each, for I am keener of sight and can assess the human situation better than a person knows his own self.

Therefore, because I see and know all things, you might ask me why I do not take evildoers away before they fall into the depths of sin. I myself asked the question and I myself will answer it for you: I am the Creator of all things, and all things are foreknown to me. I know and see all that has been and all that will be. But, although I know and can do all things, still, for reasons of justice, I no more interfere with the natural constitution of the body than I do with the inclination of the soul. Each human being continues in existence according to the natural constitution of the body such as it is and was from all eternity in my foreknowledge. The fact that one person has a longer life and another a shorter has to do with natural strength or weakness and is related to a person's physical constitution. It is not due to my foreknowledge that one person loses his sight or another becomes lame or something like that, since my foreknowledge of all things is such that no one is the worse for it, nor is it harmful to anyone.

Moreover, these things do not occur because of the course and position of the heavenly elements, but due to some hidden principle of justice in the constitution and conservation of nature. For sin and natural disorder bring about the deformity of the body in many ways. This does not happen because I will it directly, but because I permit it to happen for the sake of justice. Even though I can do all things, still I do not obstruct justice. Accordingly, the length or brevity of a person's life is related to the weakness or strength of his physical constitution such as it was in my foreknowledge that no one can contravene.

You can understand this by way of a simile. Imagine that there were two roads with one road leading up to them. There were a great many graves in both roads, crossing and overlapping one another. The end of one of the two roads dropped directly downward; the end of the other tended upward. At the crossroads was written: 'Whoever travels this road begins it in physical pleasure and delight and ends it in great wretchedness and shame. Whoever takes the other road begins it in moderate and endurable exertion but reaches the end in great joy and consolation.' A person walking along on the single road was completely blind. However, when he reached the crossroads, his eyes were opened, and he saw what was written about how the two roads ended.

While he was studying the sign and thinking it over to himself, there suddenly appeared next to him two men who were entrusted with guarding the two roads. As they observed the wayfarer at the crossroads, they said to each other: 'Let us carefully observe which road he chooses to take and then he will belong to that one of us whose road he selects.' The wayfarer, however, was considering to himself the ends and advantages of each road. He made the prudent decision of selecting the road whose beginning involved some pain but had joy at the end, rather than the road that began in joy but ended in pain. He decided that it was more sensible and endurable to get tired from a little exertion at the start but rest in safety at the end.

Do you understand what all this means? I shall tell you. These two roads are the good and the evil within human reach. It lies within a person's power and free will to choose whatever he or she likes upon reaching the age of discretion. A single road leads up to the two roads of the choice between good and evil; in other words, the time of childhood leads up to the age of discretion. The man walking on this first road is like a blind man because he is, as it were, blind from his childhood up until he reaches the age of discretion, not knowing how to distinguish between good and evil, between sin and virtue, between what is commanded and what is forbidden.

The man walking on this first road, that is, in the age of boyhood, is like a blind man. However, when he reaches the crossroads, that is, the age of discretion, the eyes of his understanding are opened. He then knows how to decide whether it is better to experience a little pain but eternal joy or a little joy and eternal pain. Whichever road he chooses, he will not lack those who carefully count his steps. There are many graves on these roads, one after the other, one over against the other, because, both in youth and in old age, one person may die earlier, another later, one in youth, another in old age. The end of this life is fittingly symbolized by graves: it will come to everyone, one in this way, another in that, according to each one's natural constitution and exactly as I have foreknown it.

If I took anyone away against the body's natural constitution, the devil would have grounds of accusation against me. Accordingly, in order that the devil might not find anything in me that goes against justice in the least, I no more interfere with the natural constitution of the body than I do with the constitution of the soul. But consider my goodness and mercy! For, as the teacher says, I give virtue to those who do not have any virtue. By reason of my great love I give the kingdom of heaven to all of the baptized who die before reaching the age of discretion. As it is written: It has pleased my Father to give the kingdom of heaven to such as these. By reason of my tender love, I even show mercy to the infants of pagans.

If any of them die before reaching the age of discretion, given that they cannot come to know me face to face, they go instead to a place that it is not permitted for you to know but where they will live without suffering. Those who have advanced from the one road reach those two roads, that is, the age of discretion between good and evil. It is then in their power to choose what pleases them most. Their reward will follow the inclination of their will, since by that time they know how to read the sign written at the crossroads telling them that it is better to experience a little pain at the start and joy ready and waiting for them than experience joy at the start and pain at the end. Sometimes it does happen that people are taken away earlier than their natural physical constitution would normally allow, for example, through homicide, drunkenness, and things of that kind.

This is because the devil's wickedness is such that the sinner in this case would receive an extremely long-lasting punishment if he were to continue in the world for any great length of time. Therefore, some people are taken away earlier than their natural physical condition would allow due to the demands of justice and because of their sins. Their removal has been foreknown to me from all eternity, and it is impossible for anyone to contravene my foreknowledge. Sometimes good people are also taken away earlier than their natural physical constitution would allow. Because of the great love I have toward them, and because of their burning love and their efforts to discipline the body for my sake, justice sometimes requires that they be taken away, as foreknown to me from all eternity. Thus, I no more interfere with the natural constitution of the body than I do with the constitution of the soul."

The Son's indictment of a certain soul who was to be condemned in the presence of the bride, and Christ's answer to the devil about why he permitted this soul and permits other evildoers to touch and take or receive his own true body.

# Chapter 2

God appeared angry and said: "This work of my hands, whom I destined for great glory, holds me in much contempt. This soul, to whom I offered all my loving care, did three things to me: He averted his eyes from me and turned them toward the enemy. He fixed his will on the world. He put his confidence in himself, because he was free to sin against me. For this reason, because he did not bother to have any regard for me, I brought my sudden justice upon him. Because he had fixed his will against me and put false confidence in himself, I took away from him the object of his desire." Then a devil cried out, saying: "Judge, this soul is mine." The Judge answered: "What grounds do you bring against him?" He answered: "My accusation is the statement in your own indictment that he despised you, his Creator, and because of that his soul has become my handmaid.

Besides, since he was suddenly taken away, how could he suddenly begin to please you? For, when he was of sound body and living in the world, he did not serve you with a sincere heart, since he loved created things more fervently, nor did he bear illness patiently or reflect on your works as he ought to have. In the end he was not burning with the fire of charity. He is mine because you have taken him away suddenly."

The Judge answered: "A sudden end does not condemn a soul, unless there is inconsistency in her actions. A person's will is not condemned forever without careful deliberation." Then the Mother of God came and said: "My Son, if a lazy servant has a friend who is on intimate terms with his master, should not his intimate friend come to his aid? Should he not be saved, if he asks for it, for the sake of the other?" The Judge answered: "Every act of justice should be accompanied by mercy and wisdom - mercy with respect to remitting severity, wisdom to ensure that equity is maintained. But if the transgression is of such a kind as not to deserve remission, the sentence can still be mitigated for the sake of friendship with out infringing justice. Then his Mother said: "My blessed Son, this soul had me constantly in mind and showed me reverence and was often moved to celebrate the great solemnity for my sake, even though he was cold toward you. So, have mercy on him!"

The Son answered: "Blessed Mother, you know and see all things in me. Even though this soul kept you in mind, he did so more for the sake of his temporary than his spiritual welfare. He did not treat my most pure body as he should have. His foul mouth kept him from enjoying my charity. Worldly love and dissolution hid my suffering from him. His taking my pardon too much for granted and not thinking about his end accelerated his death. Although he received me continuously, it did not improve him much, because he did not prepare himself properly. A person who wishes to receive his noble Lord and guest should not only get the guest room ready but also all the utensils. This man did not do so, since, although he cleaned the house, he did not sweep it reverently with care. He did not strew the floor with the flowers of his virtues or fill the utensils of his limbs with abstinence. Therefore, you see well enough that what must be done to him is what he deserves.

Although I may be invulnerable and beyond comprehension and am everywhere by reason of my divinity, my delight is in the pure, even if I enter the good and the damned alike. The good receive my body, which was crucified and ascended into heaven, which was prefigured by the manna and by the widow's flour. The wicked do so likewise, but, whereas for the good it leads to greater strength and consolation, for the wicked it leads to an even more just condemnation, inasmuch as they, in their unworthiness, are not afraid to approach so worthy a sacrament." The devil answered: "If he approached you unworthily and his sentence was made stricter because of this, why did you permit him to approach you and touch you despite his unworthiness?"

The Judge answered: "You are not asking this out of love, since you have none, but my power compels you to ask it for the sake of this bride of mine who is listening. In the same way in which both the good and bad handled me in my human nature in order to prove the reality of my human nature as well as my patient humility, so too good and wicked alike eat me at the altar - the good unto their greater perfection, the bad in order that they may not believe themselves to be already damned and so that, having received my body, they might be converted, provided they decide to reform their intention. What greater love can I show them than that I, the most pure, will enter even the impurest of vessels (although like the material sun I cannot be defiled by anything)? You and your comrades despise this love, for you have hardened yourselves against love."

Then the Mother spoke again: "My good Son, whenever he approached you, he was still reverent toward you, though not as he should have been. He also repents of having offended you, though not perfectly. My Son, for my sake, consider this to his advantage." The Son answered: "As the prophet said, I am the true sun, although I am far better than the material sun. The material sun does not penetrate mountains or minds, but I can do both.

A mountain can stand in the way of the material sun with the result that the sunlight does not reach the land nearby, but what can stand in my way except the sinfulness that prevents this soul from being affected by my love? Even if a part of the mountain were removed, the neighboring land would still not receive the warmth of the sun. And if I were to enter into one part of a pure mind, what consolation would it be to me if I could smell a stench from another part? Therefore, one should get rid of everything that is dirty, and then sweet enjoyment will follow upon beautiful cleanliness." His Mother answered: "May your will be done with all mercy!"

## Explanation

This was a priest who had often received warnings regarding his incontinent behavior and who did not want to listen to reason. One day when he went out to the meadow to groom his horse, there came thunder and lightning that struck and killed him. His whole body was left unscathed except for his private parts, which could be seen to be completely burned. Then the Spirit of God said: "Daughter, those who get themselves entangled in such wretched pleasures deserve to suffer in their souls what this man suffered in his body."

Words of amazement from the Mother of God to the bride, and about five houses in the world whose inhabitants represent five states of people, namely unfaithful Christians, obstinate Jews and pagans separately, Jews and Pagans together, and the friends of God. This Chapter contains many useful remarks.

# Chapter 3

Mary said: "It is a terrible thing that the Lord of all things and the King of glory is despised. He was like a pilgrim on earth, wandering from place to place, knocking on many doors, like a wayfarer seeking welcome. The world was like an estate that had five houses. When my Son came dressed as a pilgrim to the first house, he knocked on the door and said: 'Friend, open up and let me enter to rest and stay with you, so that the wild animals do not harm me, so that storm-showers and rain may not fall upon me! Give me some of your clothes to warm me from the cold, to cover me in my nakedness! Give me some of your food to refresh me in my hunger and something to drink to revive me. You will receive a reward from your God!'

The person inside answered: 'You are far too impatient, so you are unable to live with us peaceably. You are far too tall. For that reason we are unable to clothe you. You are far too greedy and gluttonous, so we are unable to satisfy you, for there is no end to your greedy appetite.' Christ the pilgrim responded from outside: 'Friend, let me in cheerfully and voluntarily. I do not need much room. Give me some of your clothes, since there are no clothes in your house so small that they will not be able to offer me at least some warmth! Give me some of your food, since even a tiny morsel can satisfy me and a mere drop of water will refresh and strengthen me.' The person inside replied: 'We know you well enough.

You are humble in speech but importunate in your requests. You seem easily contented but are in fact insatiable when it comes to having your fill. You are far too cold and hard to clothe. Go away, I will not take you in!' Then he came to the second house and said: 'Friend, open up and look at me! I will give you what you need. I will defend you from your enemies.' The person inside answered: 'My eyes are weak. It would hurt them to look at you. I have plenty of everything and I have no need of anything of yours. I am strong and powerful. Who can harm me?' Coming, then, to the third house, he said: 'Friend, lend me your ears and hear me! Stretch forth your hands and take hold of me! Open your mouth and taste me!'

The inhabitant of the house answered: 'Shout louder so I can hear you better! If you are nice, I will draw you to myself. If you are pleasant, I will you let in.' Then he went to the fourth house whose door was about half-open. He said: 'Friend, if you were to consider that your time has been uselessly spent, you would take me in. If you were to understand and to listen to what I have done for you, you would have compassion on me. If you paid heed to how much you have offended me, you would sigh and beg for forgiveness.' The man answered: 'We are nearly dead from waiting and longing for you. Have compassion on our wretchedness and we will be most ready to give ourselves to you. Behold our misery and look on the anguish of our body, and we will be ready for your every wish.' Then he came to the fifth house, which was completely open. He said: 'Friend, I would gladly enter here, but know that I seek a softer resting-place than that provided by a feather-bed, a greater warmth than can be had from wool, a fresher food than fresh animal meat can offer.'

Those who were inside answered: 'We have hammers lying here at our feet. We will gladly use them to shatter our feet and legs, and we will give you the marrow flowing from them to be your resting-place. We will gladly open up our inmost parts and entrails for you. Come right in! There is nothing softer than our marrow for you to rest upon, and nothing better than our inmost parts to warm you. Our heart is fresher than the fresh meat of animals. We shall be happy to cut it up for your food. Just come in! For you are sweet to taste and wonderful to enjoy!' The inhabitants of these five houses represent five different states of people in the world. The first are the unfaithful Christians who call my Son's sentences unjust, his promises false, and his commandments unbearable.

These are the ones who in their thoughts and in their minds and in their blasphemy say to my Son's preachers: 'Almighty he may well be, but he is far away and cannot be reached. He is high and wide and cannot be clothed. He is insatiable and cannot be fed. He is most impatient and there is no getting along with him.' They say he is far away because they are weak in good deeds and charity and do not try to rise up to his goodness. They say he is wide, because their own greediness knows no limit: they are always pretending they lack or need something and are always imagining problems before they come. They also charge him with being insatiable, because heaven and earth are not enough for him, but he demands even greater gifts from mankind.

They think it foolish to give up everything for the sake of their soul in accordance with the precept, and harmful to give the body less. They say he is impatient, because he hates vice and sends them things against their will. They think nothing is fine and useful except that which the pleasure of the body suggests to them. Of course, my Son is indeed almighty in heaven and on earth, the Creator of all things and created by none, existing prior to everything, after whom no one is to come. He is indeed farthest away and widest and highest, within and without and above all things.

Yet although he is so powerful, still in his love he wants to be clothed with human help - he who has no need of clothing, who clothes all things and is himself clothed eternally and unchangeably in perpetual honor and glory. He, who is the bread of angels and of men, who feeds all things and himself needs nothing, wants to be fed with human love. He who is the restorer and author of peace asks for peace from men. Therefore, whoever wants to welcome him in a cheerful mind can satisfy him with even a morsel of bread, so long as his intention is good. He can clothe him with a single thread, so long as his love is burning. A single drop can still his thirst, provided a person has the right dispositions.

So long as a person's devotion is fervent and steadfast, he is capable of welcoming my Son into his heart and speaking with him. God is spirit and, for that reason, he has willed to transform creatures of flesh into spiritual beings and ephemeral beings into eternal ones. He thinks that whatever happens to the members of his body also happens to himself. He takes into account not only a person's work or abilities, but also the fervor of his will and the intention with which a work is carried out. In truth, the more my Son cries out to these people through hidden inspirations, and the more he admonishes them through his preachers, the more they harden their will against him.

They do not listen or open the door of their will to him or let him in by means of charitable acts. Therefore, when their time comes, the falsehood they rely on will be annihilated, truth will be exalted, and the glory of God made manifest. The second ones are obstinate Jews. These people seem to themselves to be reasonable in every way and they regard wisdom as being legal justice. They assert their own deeds and hold them to be more honorable than the works of others. If they hear of the things my Son has done, they hold them in contempt. If they hear his words and commandments, they react with scorn.

Worse still, they would regard themselves as sinful and unclean if they were but to hear and reflect on anything having to do with my Son and as even more wretched and miserable if they were to imitate his works. But while the winds of worldly fortune still blow upon them, they think themselves most lucky. So long as their physical forces are sound, they believe themselves to be most strong. For that reason, their hopes will come to nothing and their honor will turn into shame.

The third ones are the pagans. Some of them cry out in mockery each day: 'Who is this Christ? If he is gracious in giving present goods, we shall gladly receive him. If he is gentle in condoning sins, we shall even more gladly honor him.' But these people have closed the eyes of their mind so as not to perceive the justice and mercy of God. They stop up their ears and do not hear what my Son has done for them and for everyone. They shut their mouths and do not inquire what their future will be like or what is to their advantage. They fold their arms and refuse to make an effort to search out the way in which they might escape lies and find the truth. Therefore, since they do not want to understand or take precautions, although they can and have the time to do so, they and their house will fall and be enveloped by the tempest.

The fourth ones are those Jews and pagans who would like to be Christians, if they only knew how and in what way to please my Son and if only they had a helper. They hear from people in neighboring regions everyday, and also know from the appeals of love within themselves, as well as from other signs, how much my Son has done and suffered for everyone. This is why they cry out to him in their conscience and say:

'O Lord, we have heard that you promised to give yourself to us. So we are waiting for you. Come and fulfill your promise! We see and understand that there is no divine power in those who are worshipped as gods, no love of souls, no appreciation of chastity. We only find in them carnal motives, a love for the honors of the present world. We know about the Law and hear about the great works you have performed in mercy and justice, We hear from the sayings of your prophets that they were awaiting you whom they had foretold. So come, kind Lord! We would like to give ourselves to you, because we understand that in you there is love for souls, the right use of all things, perfect purity, and life everlasting. Come without delay and enlighten us, for we are nearly dead from waiting for you!' That is how they cry out to my Son. This explains why their door is half-open, because their intention is complete with respect to the good, but they have not yet attained its fulfillment. These are people who deserve to have the grace and consolation of my Son.

In the fifth house are the friends of my Son and me. The door of their mind is completely open for my Son. They are glad to hear him calling. They not only open when he knocks but joyfully run to meet him as he comes in. With the hammers of the divine precepts they shatter anything they find distorted in themselves. They prepare a resting-place for my Son, not out of the feathers of birds but out of the harmony of the virtues and the curbing of evil affections, which is the very marrow of all the virtues. They offer my Son a kind of warmth that does not come from wool but from a love so fervent that they not only give their belongings to him but their very selves as well. They also prepare food for him that is fresher than any meat: it is their perfect heart that does not desire or love anything but its God.

The Lord of Heaven dwells in their hearts, and God who nourishes all things is sweetly nourished by their charity. They keep their eyes continually on the door lest the enemy enter, they keep their ears turned toward the Lord, and their hands ready for doing battle against the enemy. Imitate them, my daughter, as far as you are able, because their foundation is built on solid rock The other houses have their foundations in mud, which is why they will be shaken when the wind comes."

*The words of the Mother of God to her Son on behalf of his bride, and about how Christ is compared to Solomon, and about the severe sentence against false Christians.*

# Chapter 4

The Mother of God spoke to her Son, saying: "My Son, look how your bride is crying because you have few friends and many enemies." The Son answered: "It is written that the sons of the kingdom will be cast out and will not inherit the kingdom. It is likewise written that a certain queen came from far away to see the riches of Salomon and to hear his wisdom. When she saw it all, she was breathless from sheer amazement. The people of his kingdom, however, paid no attention to his wisdom nor admired his riches. I am prefigured by Solomon, although I am far richer and wiser than Solomon was, inasmuch as all wisdom comes from me and anyone who is wise gets his wisdom from me. My riches are eternal life and indescribable glory. I promised and offered these goods to Christians as to my own children, in order that they might possess them forever, if they imitated me and believed in my words. But they pay no attention to my wisdom.

They hold my deeds and my promises in scorn and regard my riches as worthless. What shall I do with them then? Surely, if the sons do not want their inheritance, then strangers, that is, pagans will receive it. Like that foreign queen, whom I take to represent faithful souls, they will come and admire the wealth of my glory and charity, so much so that they will fall away from their spirit of infidelity and be filled with my Spirit. What, then, shall I do with the sons of the kingdom? I will deal with them in the manner of a skillful potter who, when he observes that the first object he has made out of clay is neither beautiful nor useable, throws it to the earth and crushes it. I will deal with Christians in the same way. Although they ought to be mine, since I formed them in my image and redeemed them with my blood, they have turned out to be pitiably deformed. Therefore, they will be trampled down like earth and thrown into hell."

The Lord's words in the presence of the bride concerning his own majesty, and a wonderful parable comparing Christ to David, while Jews, bad Christians, and pagans are compared to David's three sons, and about how the church subsists in the seven sacraments.

# Chapter 5

"I am God, not made of stone or wood nor created by another but the Creator of the universe, abiding without beginning or end. I am he who came into the Virgin and was with the Virgin without losing my divinity. Through my human nature I was in the Virgin while still retaining my divine nature, and I am that same person who, through my divine nature, continued to rule over heaven and earth together with the Father and the Holy Ghost. Through my Spirit I set the Virgin on fire - not in the sense that the Spirit that set her on fire was something separate from me, but the Spirit that set her on fire was the same one who was in the Father and in me, the Son, just as the Father and the Son were in him, these three being one God, not three gods.

I am like King David who had three sons. One of them was called Absalom, and he sought the life of his father. The second, Adonijah, sought his father's kingdom. The third son, Solomon, obtained the kingdom. The first son denotes the Jews. They are the people who sought my life and death and scorned my counsel. Consequently, now that their requital is known, I can say what David said upon the death of his son: 'My son, Absalom!" that is: O my Jewish children, where is your longing and expectation now? O my children, what will be your end now? I felt compassion for you because you longed for me to come - for me whom you learned from many signs had come - and because you longed for quickly fading glory, all of which now has faded. But I feel greater compassion for you now, like David repeating those first words over and over, because I see that you will end in a wretched death.

Therefore, again like David, I say with all my love: 'My son, who will let me die in your stead?' David knew well that he could not bring back his dead son by dying himself, but, in order to show his deep fatherly affection and the eager yearning of his will, even though he knew it was impossible, he was prepared to die in the place of his son. In the same way, I now say: O my Jewish children, although you had ill-will toward me and did as much as you could against me, if it were possible and if my Father allowed it, I would willingly die once again for you, for I take pity on the misery you have brought upon yourselves as required by justice. I told you what was to be done by my words and showed you by my example. I went ahead of you like a hen protecting you with wings of love, but you spurned it all. Therefore, all the things that you longed for have fled away. Your end is misery and all your labor wasted.

Bad Christians are denoted by David's second son who sinned against his father in his old age. He reasoned with himself in this way: 'My father is an old man and failing in strength. If I say anything wrong to him, he does not respond. If I do anything against him, he does not avenge himself. If I assail him, he endures it patiently. Therefore, I will do what I want.' With some of his father David's servants, he went up to a grove of few trees in order to play the king. But when the wisdom and intention of his father became evident, he changed his plan and those who were with him fell into discredit.

This is what Christians are doing to me now. They think to themselves: 'God's signs and decisions are not as manifest now as they were before. We can say what we like, since he is merciful and pays no attention. Let us do as we please, since he gives way easily.' They have no faith in my power, as if I were weaker now in accomplishing my will than I was before.

They imagine my love to be less, as if I am no longer as willing to have mercy on them as on their fathers. They also think that my judgment is a thing to be laughed at and that my justice is meaningless. Therefore, they, too, go up to a grove with some of David's servants in order to play the king with presumption. What does this grove of few trees denote, if not the Holy Church subsisting through the seven sacraments as through just a few trees? They enter into this church along with some of David's servants, that is, with a few good works, in order to gain God's kingdom with presumption.

They do a modest number of good works, confident that thereby, no matter what state of sin they are in or whatever sins they have committed, they can still gain the kingdom of heaven as if by hereditary right. David's son wanted to obtain the kingdom against

David's will but was driven away in disgrace, inasmuch as both he and his ambition were unjust, and the kingdom was given to a better and wiser man. In the same way, these people will also be driven away from my kingdom.

It will be given to those who do the will of David, since only a person who has charity can obtain my kingdom. Only a person who is pure and is led by my heart can approach me who am the most pure of all.

Solomon was the third son of David. He represents the pagans. When Bathsheba heard that someone other than Solomon - whom David had promised would be king after him - had been elected by certain persons, she went to David and said: 'My lord, you swore to me that Solomon would be king after you. Now, however, someone else has been elected.

If this is the case and it goes on in this way, I will end up being sentenced to the fire as an adulteress and my son will be regarded as illegitimate.' When David heard this, he stood up and said: 'I swear to God that Solomon will sit on my throne and be king after me.' He then ordered his servants to set Solomon on the throne and proclaim as king the man of David's choice. They carried out the orders of their lord and raised up Solomon to great power, and all those who had given their vote to his brother were scattered and reduced to servitude. This Bathsheba, who would have been accounted an adulteress had another king been elected, stands for nothing other than the faith of the pagans.

No kind of adultery is worse than selling oneself into prostitution away from God and from the true faith and believing in a god other than the Creator of universe. Just as Bathsheba did, some of the Gentiles come to me with humble and contrite hearts, saying: 'Lord, you promised that in the future we would be Christians. Carry out your promise! If another king, if another faith other than yours should gain the ascendancy over us, if you remove yourself from us, we will burn in misery and die like an adulteress who has taken an adulterer instead of a lawful husband. Besides, although you live forever, nevertheless, you will die to us and we to you in the sense that you will remove your grace from our hearts and we will set ourselves up against you due to our lack of faith. Therefore, fulfill your promise and strengthen our weakness and enlighten our darkness! If you delay, if you remove yourself from us, we will perish.' Having heard this, I will stand up like David through my grace and mercy.

I swear by my divine nature, which is joined to my humanity, and by my human nature, which is in my Spirit, and by my Spirit, which is in my divine and human natures, these three being not three gods but one God, that I will fulfill my promise. I will send my friends to bring my son Solomon, that is, the pagans, into the grove, that is, into the church, which subsists through the seven sacraments as through seven trees (namely baptism, penance, the anointment of confirmation, the sacrament of the altar and of the priesthood, matrimony, and extreme unction). They will take their rest upon my throne, that is, in the true faith of the Holy Church.

Moreover, the bad Christians will become their servants. The former will find their joy in an everlasting heritage and in the sweet nourishment that I will prepare for them. The latter, however, will groan in the misery that will begin for them in the present and last forever. And so, since it is still the time for vigilance, may my friends not fall asleep, may they not grow weary, for a glorious reward awaits their toil!"

The Son's words in the presence of the bride concerning a king standing on a battlefield with friends to his right and enemies to his left, and about how the king represents Christ who has Christians to the right and pagans to the left, and about how the Christians are rejected and he sends his preachers to the pagans.

# Chapter 6

The Son said: "I am like a king standing in a battlefield with friends standing to his right and enemies to his left. The voice of someone shouting came to those who stood on the right where everyone was well armed. Their helmets were fastened and their faces were turned to their lord. The voice shouted to them: 'Turn to me and trust me! I have gold to give you.' When they heard this, they turned toward him. The voice spoke a second time to those who had turned around: 'If you want to see the gold, unfasten your helmets, and if you want to keep it, I will fasten your helmets on again as I wish.' When they assented, he fastened their helmets on back to front. The result was that the front part with the apertures to see through was at the back of their heads while the helmets' back part covered their eyes so that they were unable to see. Shouting like this, he led them after him like blind men.

When this had been done, some of the king's friends reported to their lord that his enemies had tricked his men. He said to his friends: 'Go out among them and cry out: Unfasten your helmets and see how you have been deceived! Turn back to me and I will welcome you in peace!' They did not want to listen, but regarded it as mockery. The servants heard this and reported it to their lord. He said: 'Well then, since they have scorned me, go quickly toward the left-hand side and tell those who stand on the left these three things: The way that leads you to life has been prepared for you. The gate is open. And the lord himself wants to come to meet you with peace. Believe therefore firmly that the way has been prepared! Have a steadfast hope that the gate is open and his words are true! Go to meet the lord with love, and he will welcome you with love and peace and lead you to everlasting peace!' When they heard the messengers' words, they believed in them and were welcomed in peace.

I am that king. I had Christians to my right, since I had prepared an eternal reward for them. Their helmets were fastened and their faces were turned toward me so long as they wholly intended to do my will, to obey my commandments, and so long as all their desire aimed at heaven. By and by the devil's voice, that is, pride, sounded in the world and showed them worldly riches and carnal pleasure. They turned toward it by yielding their assent and desires to pride. Because of pride, they took off their helmets by putting their desires into effect and preferring temporal to spiritual goods. Now that they have put aside the helmets of God's will and the weapons of virtue, pride has got such a hold of them and so bound them to itself that they are only too happy to go on sinning right to the end and would be glad to live forever, provided they could sin forever.

Pride has so blinded them that the apertures of the helmets through which they should be able to see are at the back of their heads and in front of them is darkness. What do these apertures in the helmets represent if not the consideration of the future and the provident circumspection of present realities? Through the first aperture, they should see the delight of future rewards and the horrors of future punishments as well as the awful sentence of God. Through the second aperture, they should see God's commandments and prohibitions, also how much they may have transgressed God's commandments and how they should improve. But these apertures are at the back of the head where nothing can be seen, which means that the consideration of heavenly realities has fallen into disregard.

Their love for God has grown cold, while their love for the world is considered with delight and embraced in such away that it leads them like a well-oiled wheel whither it will. However, seeing me dishonored and souls falling away and the devil gaining control, my friends cry out daily to me in their prayers for them. Their prayers have reached heaven and come to my hearing. Moved by their prayers, I have daily sent my preachers to these people and shown them signs and increased my graces to them. But, in their scorn for it all, they have piled sin upon sin.

Therefore, I shall now say to my servants and I shall put my words most assuredly into effect: My servants, go to the left-hand side, that is, to the pagans, and say: 'The Lord of heaven and the

Creator of the universe would have the following said to you: The way of heaven is open for you. Have the will to enter it with a firm faith! The gate of heaven stands open for you. Hope firmly and you will enter through it! The King of heaven and the Lord of angels will personally come out to meet you and give you everlasting peace and blessing. Go out to meet him and receive him with the faith he has revealed to you and that has made ready the way to heaven! Receive him with the hope by which you hope, for he himself has the intention of giving you the kingdom.

Love him with your whole heart and put your love into practice and you will enter through the gates of God from which those Christians were thrust away who did not want to enter them and who made themselves unworthy by their own deeds.' By my truth I declare to you that I will put my words into practice and will not forget them. I will receive you as my children and I will be your father, I, whom Christians have held in scornful scorn.

You then, my friends, who are in the world, go forth without fear and shout out loud, announce my will to them and help them to carry it out. I will be in your hearts and in your words. I will be your guide in life and your savior in death. I will not abandon you. Go forth boldly - the more the toil, the greater the glory!

I can do all things in a single instant and with a single word, but I want your reward to grow through your own efforts and my glory to grow through your bravery. Do not be surprised at what I say. If the wisest man in the world could count up how many souls fall into hell each day, they would outnumber the sands of the sea or the pebbles on the shore. This is a matter of justice, because these souls have separated themselves from their Lord and God. I am saying this so that the devil's numbers may decrease, and the danger become known, and my army be filled up. If only they would listen and come to their senses!"

Jesus Christ speaks to the bride and compares his divine nature to a crown and uses Peter and Paul to symbolize the clerical and the lay state, and about the ways of dealing with enemies, and about the qualities that knights in the world should have.

# Chapter 7

The Son spoke to the bride, saying: "I am King of the crown. Do you know why I said 'King of the crown'? Because my divine nature was and will be and is without beginning or end. My divine nature is aptly likened to a crown, because a crown has neither starting-point nor end. Just as a crown is reserved for the future king in a kingdom, so too my divine nature was reserved for my human nature to be its crown.

I had two servants. One was a priest, the other a layman. The first was Peter who had a priestly office, while Paul was, as it were, a layman. Peter was bound in marriage, but when he saw that his marriage was not consistent with his priestly office, and considering that his upright intention might be endangered by a lack of continence, he separated himself from the otherwise licit marriage, in which he divorced himself from his wife's bed, and he devoted himself to me wholeheartedly.

Paul, however, did observe celibacy and kept himself unstained by the marriage-bed. See what great love I had for these two! I gave the keys of heaven to Peter so that whatever he bound or loosed on earth might be bound or loosed in heaven. I allowed Paul to become like Peter in glory and honor. As they were equals together on earth, so now they are united in everlasting glory in heaven and glorified together. However, although I mentioned these two expressly by name, by and through them I mean to denote other friends of mine as well. In similar fashion, under the earlier Covenant, I used to speak to Israel as if I were addressing just one person, although I meant to designate the entire people of Israel by that one name. In the same way now, using these two men, I mean to denote the multitude of those whom I have filled with my glory and love.

With the passage of time, evils began to multiply and the flesh began to grow weaker and to be more than usually prone to evil.

Therefore, I set up norms for each of the two, that is, for the clergy and laity, represented here by Peter and Paul. In my mercy I decided to allow the clergy to own a moderate amount of church property for their bodily needs in order that they might grow more fervent and constant in serving me. I also allowed the laity to join in marriage according to the rites of the church. Among the priests there was a certain good man who thought to himself: 'The flesh drags me toward base pleasure, the world drags me toward harmful sights, while the devil sets various traps to get me to sin. Therefore, in order not to be ensnared by carnal pleasure, I will observe moderation in all my actions. I will be moderate in my rest and recreation.

I will dedicate the proper time to work and prayer and restrain my carnal appetites through fasting. Second, in order that the world may not drag me away from the love of God, I will give up all worldly things, for they are all perishable. It is safer to follow Christ in poverty. Third, in order not to be deceived by the devil who is always showing us falsehoods instead of the truth, I will submit myself to the rule and obedience of another; and I will reject all selfishness and show that I am ready to undertake whatever is commanded me by the other person.' This man was the first to establish a monastic rule. He persevered in it in praiseworthy fashion and left his life as an example to be imitated by others.

For a time the class of the laity was well organized. Some of them tilled the soil and bravely persevered in working the land. Others sailed on ships and carried merchandise to other regions so that the resources of one region supplied the needs of another. Others were diligent craftsmen and artisans. Among these were the defenders of my church who are now called knights.

They took up arms as avengers of the Holy Church in order to do battle against her enemies. There appeared among them a good man and friend of mine who thought to himself: 'I do not till the soil as a farmer. I do not toil on the seas as a merchant. I do not work with my hands as a skilled craftsman.

What, then, can I do or with what works can I please my God? I am not energetic enough in the service of the church. My body is too soft and weak to bear physical injuries, my hands lack the force to strike down enemies, and my mind grows uneasy in pondering the things of heaven. What can I do then?

I know what I can do. I will go and bind myself by a stable oath to a secular prince, swearing to defend the faith of the Holy Church with my strength and with my blood.' That friend of mine went to the prince and said: 'My lord, I am one of the defenders of the church. My body is all too weak to bear physical injuries, my hands lack the force to strike down others; my mind is unstable when it comes to thinking about and carrying out what is good; my self-will is what pleases me; and my need for rest does not let me take a strong stance for the house of God. I bind myself therefore with a public oath of obedience to the Holy Church and to you, o Prince, swearing to defend her all the days of my life in order that, although my mind and will may be lukewarm with respect to the struggle, I can be held and compelled to toil because of my oath.' The prince answered him: 'I will go with you to the house of the Lord and be a witness to your oath and your promise.' Both of them came up to my altar, and my friend genuflected and said: 'I am too weak of body to bear physical injuries, my self-will is all too pleasing to me, my hands are too lukewarm when it comes to striking blows.

Therefore, I now pledge obedience to God and to you, my chief, binding myself by an oath to defend the Holy Church against her enemies, to comfort the friends of God, to do good to widows, orphans, and God's faithful, and never to do anything contrary to God's church or the faith. Moreover, I will submit myself to your correction, if I should happen to err, in order that, bound by obedience, I might fear sin and selfishness all the more and apply myself more fervently and readily to carrying out God's will and your own will, knowing myself to be only the more worthy of condemnation and contempt if I should presume to violate obedience and transgress your commands.' After this profession had been made at my altar, the prince wisely decided that the man should dress differently than other laymen as a sign of his self-renouncement and as a reminder to him that he had a superior to whom he had to submit.

The prince also placed a sword in his hand, saying: 'This sword is for you to use to threaten and slay the enemies of God.' He placed a shield on his arm, saying: 'Defend yourself with this shield against the missiles of the enemy and patiently endure whatever is thrown against it. May you sooner see it shattered than run away from battle!' In the presence of my priest who was listening, my friend made the firm promise to observe all of this. When he had made his promise, the priest gave him my body to provide him strength and fortitude so that, once united with me through my body, my friend might never be separated from me. Such was my friend George as well as many others. Such, too, should the knights be. They should get to hold their title as a result of merit and to wear their knightly attire as a result of their actions in defense of the Holy Faith.

Hear how my enemies are now going against the earlier deeds of my friends. My friends used to enter the monastery out of their wise reverence and love for God. But those who are in monasteries nowadays go out into the world because of pride and greed, following self-will, fulfilling the pleasure of their bodies. Justice demands that people who die in such a disposition should not experience the joy of heaven but rather obtain the endless punishment of hell. Know, too, that the cloistered monks who are forced against their will to become prelates out of love for God are not to be counted among their number. The knights who used to bear my arms were ready to lay down their lives for justice and shed their blood for the sake of the holy faith, bringing justice to the needy, putting down and humbling the doers of evil.

But hear how they have now been corrupted! Now they would rather die in battle for the sake of pride, greed, and envy at the promptings of the devil instead of living after my commandments and obtaining eternal joy. Just wages will therefore be dealt out at the judgment to all the people who die in such a disposition, and their souls will be yoked to the devil forever. But the knights who serve me will receive their due wages in the heavenly host forever. I, Jesus Christ, true God and man, one with the Father and the Holy Ghost, one God forever and ever, have said this."

Christ's words to the bride about a certain knight's desertion from the true army, that is, from humility, obedience, patience, faith, etc., to the false one, that is, to the opposing vices, pride, etc., and the description of his condemnation, and about how one can meet with condemnation because of an evil will just as much as because of evil deeds.

# Chapter 8

"I am the true Lord. There is no other lord greater than I. There was no lord before me nor will there be any after me. All lordship comes from me and through me. This is why I am the true Lord and why no one but I alone can truly be called Lord, for all power comes from me.

I was telling you earlier that I had two servants, one of whom manfully took up a praiseworthy way of life and kept at it manfully to the end. Countless others followed him in that same way of knightly service. I will now tell you about the first man to desert the profession of knighthood as instituted by my friend. I will not tell you his name, because you do not know him by name, but I will disclose his purpose and desire.

A man who wanted to become a knight came to my sanctuary. When he went in, he heard a voice: 'Three things are necessary if you want to be a knight: First, you must believe that the bread you see on the altar is true God and true man, the Creator of heaven and earth. Second, once you take up your knightly service, you must exercise more self-restraint than you were accustomed to doing before. Third, you should not care about worldly honor. Rather I will give you divine joy and everlasting honor.

Hearing this and pondering these three things to himself, he heard an evil voice in his mind making three proposals contrary to the first three. It said: 'If you serve me, I will make you three other proposals. I will let you take what you see, hear what you like, and obtain what you desire.' When he heard this, he thought to himself: 'The first lord bade me to have faith in something I do not see and promised me things unknown to me. He bade me abstain from the delights that I can see, and that I desire, and to hope for things of which I am uncertain. The other lord promised me the worldly honor that I can see and the pleasure that I desire without forbidding me to hear or see the things I like.

Surely, it is better for me to follow him and to have what I see and to enjoy the things that are sure rather than to hope for things of which I am uncertain.' With thoughts such as these, this man was the first to commence the desertion from the service of a true knight. He rejected the true profession and broke his promise. He threw down the shield of patience at my feet and let the sword for the defense of the faith drop from his hands and left the sanctuary. The evil voice told him: 'If, as I said, you would be mine, then you should walk proudly in the fields and streets. That other Lord commands his men to be constantly humble. Therefore, be sure not to avoid any sign of pride and ostentation! While that other Lord made his entrance in obedience and subjected himself to obedience in every way, you should let no one be your superior. Bend not your neck in humility to another. Take up your sword to shed the blood of your neighbor and brother in order to acquire his property!

Strap the shield to your arm and risk your life for the sake of winning renown! Instead of the faith that he holds out, give your love to the temple of your own body without abstaining from any of the pleasures that delight you.' While the man was making up his mind and strengthening his resolve with such thoughts, his prince laid his hand on the man's neck in the appointed place. No place whatsoever can harm anyone who has a good will or help anyone whose intention is wicked. After the confirmation of his knighthood, the wretch betrayed his knightly service, exercising it only with a view to worldly pride, making light of the fact that he was now under a greater obligation to live an austere life than before. Countless armies of knights imitated and still imitate this knight in his pride, and he has sunk all the deeper into the abyss due to his knightly vows.

But, given that there are many people who want to rise in the world and achieve renown but do not manage to do so, you might ask: Are these people to be punished for the wickedness of their intentions as much as those who achieve their desired success? To this I answer you: I assure you that anyone who fully intends to rise in the world and does all he can to do so in order to gain an empty title of worldly honor, although his intention never achieves its effect due to some secret decision of mine, such a man will be punished for the wickedness of his intention just as much as the one who does manage to achieve it, that is, unless he rectifies his intention through penance.

Look, I will put to you the example of two persons known well enough to many people. One of them prospered according to his wishes and obtained almost everything he desired. The other had the same intention, but not the same possibilities. The first one obtained worldly renown; he loved the temple of his body in its every lust; he had the power he wanted; everything he put his hand to prospered. The other was identical to him in intention but received less renown. He would willingly have shed his neighbor's blood a hundred times over in order to be able to realize his plans of greed.

He did what he could and carried out his will in accordance with his desire. These two were alike in their horrible punishment. Although they did not die at exactly the same time, I can still speak of one soul rather than two, since their condemnation was one and the same. Both had the same thing to say when body and soul were separated and the soul departed. Once having left the body, the soul said to it: 'Tell me, where now are the sights to delight my eyes that you promised me, where is the pleasure you showed me, where are the pleasant words that you bade me use?' The devil was there and answered:

'The promised sights are no more than dust, the words are but air, the pleasure is but mud and rot. Those things are of no value to you now.' The soul exclaimed then: 'Alas, alas, I have been wretchedly deceived! I see three things.

I see him who was promised to me under the semblance of bread. He is the very King of kings and Lord of lords. I see what he promised, and it is indescribable and inconceivable. I hear now that the abstinence he recommended was really most useful.' Then, in an even louder voice, the soul cried out 'woe' three times: 'Woe is me that ever I was born! Woe is me that my life on the earth was so long! Woe is me that I shall live in a perpetual and neverending death!'

Behold what wretchedness the wretched will have in return for their contempt of God and their fleeting joy! You should therefore thank me, my bride, for having called you away from such wretchedness! Be obedient to my Spirit and to my chosen ones!"

Christ's words to the bride giving an Explanation of the immediately preceding Chapter, and about the devil's attack on the aforementioned knight, and about his terrible and just condemnation.

# Chapter 9

"The entire span of this life is but as a single hour for me. Therefore, what I am telling you now has always been in my foreknowledge. I told you before about a man who began the true knighthood, and about another who deserted it like a scoundrel. The man who deserted from the ranks of true knights threw down his shield at my feet and his sword at my side by breaking his sacred promises and vows. The shield he threw down symbolizes nothing other than the upright faith by which he was to defend himself against the enemies of the faith and of his soul.

The feet, on which I walk toward humanity, symbolize nothing other than the divine delight by which I attract a person to myself and the patience by which I patiently bear with him. He threw this shield down when he entered my sanctuary, thinking to himself: I want to obey the lord who counseled me not to practice abstinence, the one who gives me what I desire and lets me hear things pleasant to my ears. This was how he threw down the shield of my faith by wanting to follow his own selfish desire rather than me, by loving the creature more than the Creator.

If he had had an upright faith, if he had believed me to be almighty and a just judge and the giver of eternal glory, he would not have wished for anything but me, he would not have feared anything but me. But he threw down my faith at my feet, despising it and counting it for nothing, because he did not seek to please me and had no regard for my patience. Then he threw down his sword at my side. The sword denotes nothing other than the fear of God, which God's true knight should continuously have in his hands, that is, in his acts. My side symbolizes nothing other than the care and protection with which I shelter and defend my children, like a mother hen sheltering her chicks, so that the devil does not harm them and no unendurable trials come upon them.

But that man threw away the sword of my fear by not bothering to think about my power and by not having any regard for my love and patience.

He threw it down at my side as if to say: 'I neither fear nor care about your defense. I got what I have by my own doing and my noble birth.' He broke the promise he made to me. What is the true promise that a man is bound to vow to God? Surely, it is deeds of love: that whatever a person does, he should do out of love for God. But this he set aside by twisting his love for God toward self-love; he preferred his selfishness to future and eternal delight.

In this way he separated himself from me and left the sanctuary of my humility. The body of any Christian ruled by humility is my sanctuary. Those ruled by pride are not my sanctuary but the sanctuary of the devil who steers them toward worldly desire after his own purposes. Having gone out of the temple of my humility, and having rejected the shield of holy faith and the sword of fear, he walked out proudly to the fields, cultivating every selfish lust and desire, scorning to fear me and growing in sin and lust.

When he reached the final end of his life and his soul had left the body, the demons charged out to meet him. Three voices from hell could be heard speaking against him. The first said: 'Is not this the man who deserted from humility and followed us in pride? If his two feet could take him up even higher in pride so as to surpass us and hold the primacy in pride, he would be quick to do so.' The soul answered him: 'I am the one.' Justice answered him: 'This is the reward of your pride: you will descend handed by one demon down to the next until you reach the lowest part of hell. And given that there was no demon who did not know his own particular punishment and the torment to be inflicted for every useless thought and deed, neither will you escape punishment at the hands of any one of them but share in the malice and evil of them all.' The second voice cried out saying: 'Is not this the man who separated himself from his professed service to God and joined our ranks instead?'

The soul answered: 'I am the one.' And Justice said: 'This is your allotted reward: that everyone who imitates your conduct as a knight will add to your punishment and sorrow by his own corruption and pain and will strike you at his coming as though with a deadly wound. You will be like a man afflicted by a severe wound, indeed like one afflicted by wound upon wound until his whole body is full of wounds, who endures intolerable suffering and bewails his fate constantly. Even so, you will experience misery upon misery. At the height of your pain, your pain will be renewed, and your punishment will never end and your woes will never decrease.' The third voice cried out: 'Is not this the man who exchanged his Creator for creatures, the love of his Creator for his own selfishness?' Justice answered: 'It certainly is.

Therefore, two holes will be opened in him. Through the first the re will enter into him every punishment earned for his least sin up to his greatest, inasmuch as he exchanged his Creator for his own lust. Through the second there will enter into him every kind of pain and shame, and no divine consolation or charity will ever come to him, inasmuch as he loved himself rather than his Creator. His life will last forever and his punishment will last forever, for all the saints have turned away from him.' My bride, see how miserable those people will be who despise me and how great will be the pain they purchase at the price of so little pleasure!"

As God spoke to Moses from the burning bush, Christ speaks to the bride about how the devil is symbolized by Pharaoh, present-day knights by the people of Israel, and the Virgin's body by the bush, and about how present-day knights and bishops are, at present, preparing a home for the devil.

# Chapter 10

"It is written in the law of Moses that Moses was watching over the flocks in the desert when he saw a bush that was on fire without being burned up, and he became afraid and covered his face. A voice spoke to him from the bush: 'I have heard of my people's suffering and feel pity for them, for they are oppressed in harsh slavery.' I who am now speaking with you am that voice heard from the bush. I have heard the misery of my people. Who were my people if not Israel? Using this same name I now designate the knights in the world who have taken the vows of my knighthood and who should be mine but are being attacked by the devil.

What did Pharaoh do to my people Israel in Egypt? Three things. First, when they were building his walls, they were not to be helped by those gatherers of straw who earlier had helped them in making bricks. Instead, they had to go themselves and gather the straw wherever they could throughout the entire country. Second, the builders did not get any thanks for their labor, despite their producing the number of bricks set them as a goal. Third, the foremen beat them harshly whenever they fell short of their normal production. In the midst of their great affliction, this people of mine built two cities for pharaoh.

This pharaoh is none another than the devil who attacks my people, that is, the knights, who ought be my people. Truly I tell you that if the knights had kept the arrangement and rule established by my first friend, they would have been among my dearest friends. Just as Abraham, who was the first to be given the commandment of circumcision and was obedient to me, became my dearest friend, and anyone who imitated Abraham's faith and works shared in his love and glory, so too the knights were especially pleasing to me among all the orders, since they promised to shed for me that which they held most dear, their own blood. By this vow they made themselves most pleasing to me, just as Abraham did in the matter of circumcision, and they purified themselves daily by living up to their profession and by taking up the practice of holy charity.

These knights are now so oppressed by their wretched slavery under the devil that the devil is wounding them with a lethal wound and throwing them into pain and suffering. The bishops of the church are building two cities for him just like the children of Israel. The first city stands for physical toil and meaningless anxiety over the acquisition of worldly goods. The second city stands for spiritual unrest and distress, inasmuch as they are never allowed to rest from worldly desire. There is toil on the outside and restlessness and anxiety on the inside, rendering spiritual things a burden.

Just as Pharaoh did not supply my people with the things necessary for making bricks or give them fields full of grain, or wine and other useful things, but the people had to go and find them for themselves in sorrow and tribulation of heart, so the devil deals likewise with them now. Although they toil for and covet the world with their inmost heart, they are still unable to fulfill their desire and sate the thirst of their greed. They are consumed on the inside with sorrow and on the outside with toil. For that reason, I pity them their sufferings, because my knights, my people, are building homes for the devil and toiling ceaselessly, because they cannot get what they desire, and because they worry themselves over meaningless goods, although the fruit of their anxiety is not a blessing but rather the reward of shame.

When Moses was sent to the people, God gave him a miraculous sign for three reasons. First, it was because each person in Egypt worshipped his own individual god, and because there were innumerable beings who were said to be gods. Therefore it was fitting that there should be a miraculous sign so that, through it and by the power of God, people would believe that there was one God and one Creator of all things because of the signs, and so that all the idols would be proved worthless. Second, a sign was also given to Moses as a symbol prefiguring my future body. What did the burning bush that was not consumed symbolize if not the Virgin who conceived by the Holy Ghost and gave birth without corruption? From this bush I came forth, assuming a human nature from the virginal body of Mary. Similarly, the serpent given as a sign to Moses symbolized my body. In the third place, a sign was given to Moses in order to confirm the truth of coming events and to prefigure the miraculous signs to be done in the future, proving the truth of God to be so much the truer and more certain the more clearly those things signified by the signs were in time fulfilled.

I am now sending my words to the children of Israel, that is, to the knights. They need no miraculous signs for three reasons. This is, first of all, because the one God and Creator of all things is already worshipped and known through Holy Scripture as well as through many signs. Second, they are not now waiting for me to be born, because they know that I was truly born and became incarnate without corruption, inasmuch as scripture has been completely fulfilled. And there is no better or more certain faith to be held and believed than the one that has already been preached by me and by my holy preachers. Nevertheless, I have done three things through you by which it may be believed. First, these are my true words and do not differ from the true faith.

Second, a demon went out of a possessed man at my word. Third, I gave a certain man the power to unite mistrustful hearts in mutual charity. Therefore, do not have any doubts about those who will believe in me. Those who believe in me believe also in my words. Those who savor me savor also my words. It is written that Moses covered his face after speaking with God.

You, however, do not need to cover your face. I opened your spiritual eyes so that you might see spiritual things. I opened your ears so that you might hear the things that are of the Spirit. I will show you a likeness of my body as it was during and before my passion, and such as it was after the resurrection, as Magdalene and Peter and others saw it. You will also hear my voice as it spoke to Moses from within the bush. This same voice is now speaking within your soul."

Christ's delightful words to the bride about the glory and honor of the good and true knight, and about how the angels come out to meet him, and about how the glorious Trinity welcomes him affectionately and takes him to a place of indescribable rest as a reward for but a little struggle.

# Chapter 11

"I told you before about the end and punishment of that knight who was the first to desert from the knightly service he had promised me. I will now describe for you by way of metaphors (for otherwise you are unable to understand spiritual things) the glory and honor of him who first manfully took up the true knightly service and manfully kept at it to the end. When this friend of mine came to the end of his life and his soul left his body, five legions of angels were sent to greet him. Along with them there also came a multitude of demons in order to find out if they could lay any claim to him, for they are full of malice and never rest from malice.

A bright clear voice was then heard in heaven, saying: 'My Lord and Father, is not this the man who bound himself to your will and carried it out to perfection?' The man himself then answered in his own conscience: 'Indeed I am.' Three voices were then heard. The first was that of the divine nature, which said: 'Did I not create you and give you a body and soul? You are my son and you have done your Father's will. Come to me, your almighty Creator and dear Father! An eternal inheritance is owed to you, for you are a son. Your Father's inheritance is owed to you, for you have been obedient to him.

So, dear son, come to me then! I will welcome you with joy and honor.' The second voice was that of the human nature, which said: 'Brother, come to your brother! I offered myself for you in battle and shed my blood for you. You, who obeyed my will, come to me! You, who paid blood for blood and were prepared to offer death for death and life for life, come to me! You, who imitated me in your life, enter now into my life and into my neverending joy! I recognize you as my true brother.' The third voice was that of the Spirit (but the three are one God, not three gods) that said: 'Come, my knight, you whose interior life was so attractive that I longed to dwell with you!

In your exterior conduct you were so manly that you deserved my protection. Enter, then, into rest in return for all your physical troubles! In return for your mental suffering, enter into a consolation beyond description! In return for your charity and your manly struggles, come into me and I will dwell in you and you in me! Come to me, then, my excellent knight, who never yearned for anything but me! Come and you will be filled with holy pleasure!' Afterward five voices were heard from each of the five legions of angels.

The first one spoke, saying: 'Let us march ahead of this excellent knight and carry his weapons ahead of him, that is, let us present to our God the faith he preserved unshaken and defended from the enemies of justice.' The second voice said: 'Let us carry his shield ahead of him, that is, let us show our God that patience of his which, although it is already known to God, will be even more glorious because of our testimony. By his patience he not only bore adversities patiently but also thanked God for those same adversities.'

The third voice said: 'Let us march ahead of him and present his sword to God, that is, let us show him the obedience by which he remained obedient in both difficult and easy times in accordance with his pledge.' The fourth voice said: 'Come and let us show our God his horse, that is, let us offer the testimony of his humility. As a horse carries the body of a man, so his humility both preceded and followed him, carrying him forth to the performance of every good work. Pride found nothing of its own in him, which is why he rode in safety.' The fifth voice said: 'Come and let us present his helmet to our God, that is, let us bear witness to the divine yearning he felt for God!

He meditated on him in his heart at all times. He had him on his lips, in his works, and yearned for him above all things. Out of his love and veneration he caused himself to die to the world. So, let us present these things to our God, for, in return for a little struggle, this man has deserved eternal rest and joy with his God for whom he yearned so much and so often!' Accompanied by the sounds of these voices and a wonderful choir of angels, my friend was carried to eternal rest.

His soul saw it all and said to itself in exultation: 'Happy am I to have been created! Happy am I to have served my God whom I now behold! Happy am I, for I have joy and glory that will never end!' In such a way did my friend come to me and receive such a reward. Although not everyone sheds his blood for the sake of my name, nevertheless, everyone will receive the same reward, provided they have the intention of giving their lives for me if the occasion presents itself and the needs of the faith demand it. See how important a good intention is!"

Christ's words to the bride about the unchanging nature and eternal duration of his justice, and about how, after taking a human nature, he revealed his justice through his love in a new light, and about how he tenderly exercises mercy toward the damned and gently teaches his knights mercy.

# Chapter 12

"I am the true King. No one deserves to be called king except me, because all honor and power come from me. I am he who rendered judgment upon the first angel to fall through pride, greed, and envy. I am he who rendered judgment upon Adam and Cain as well as upon the whole world by sending it the flood due to the sins of the human race. I am the same one who allowed the people of Israel to come into captivity and miraculously led it out with miraculous signs. All justice is to be found in me. Justice always was and is in me without beginning or end. It does not at any time grow less in me but remains in me true and unchangeable. Although at the present time my justice seems to be somewhat gentler and God seems to be a more patient judge now, this represents no change in my justice, which never changes, but only shows my love the more. I now judge the world by that same justice and that same true judgment as when I permitted my people to become slaves in Egypt and made them suffer in the desert.

My love was hidden prior to my incarnation. I kept it hidden in my justice like light obscured by a cloud. Once I had taken a human nature, although the law that had been given was changed, justice itself was not changed but was all the more clearly visible and was shown in a more abundant light in love through God's Son. This happened in three ways. First, the law was mitigated, since it had been severe because of disobedient and hardened sinners and it was difficult in order to tame the proud. Second, the Son of God suffered and died. Third, my judgment now appears to be farther away and both seems to be postponed out of mercy and to be gentler toward sinners than before. Indeed, the acts of justice concerning the first parents or the flood or those who died in the desert seem rigid and strict. But that same justice is still with me and ever has been. However, mercy and love are now more apparent. Earlier, for wise reasons, love was hidden in justice and displayed with mercy, albeit in a more hidden manner, because I never carried out and never do carry out justice without mercy or kindness without justice. Now, however, you might ask: if I show mercy in all my justice, in what way am I merciful toward the damned? I will answer you by way of a parable.

It is as if a judge were seated in judgment and his brother came along to be sentenced. The judge says to him: 'You are my brother and I am your judge and, although I sincerely love you, I cannot nor is it right for me to counteract justice. In your conscience you see what is just with respect to what you deserve. It is necessary to sentence you accordingly. If it were possible to go against justice, I would willingly take your sentence upon myself.' I am like that judge. This person is my brother because of my human nature. When he comes to be judged by me, his conscience informs him of his guilt and he understands what his sentence should be. Since I am just, I reply to the soul - figuratively speaking - and tell it: 'You see all that is just for you in your conscience. Tell me what you deserve.' The soul answers me then: 'My conscience informs me of my sentence. It is the punishment due to me, because I did not obey you.' I answer: 'I, your judge, took on myself all your punishment and made your danger known to you as well as the way to escape punishment. It was simple justice that you could not enter heaven before atoning for your guilt. I took on your atonement, because you were incapable of bearing it your self.

Through the prophets I showed you what would happen to me, and I did not omit a single detail of what the prophets foretold. I showed you all the love I could in order to make you turn to me. However, since you have turned away from me, you deserve to be sentenced, because you scorned mercy. However, I am still so merciful that, if it were possible for me to die again, for your sake I would again endure the same torment I once endured on the cross rather than see you sentenced to such a sentence. Justice, however, says that it is impossible for me to die again, even if mercy tells me to want to die for your sake again, if it were possible. This is how I am merciful and loving even toward the damned. I loved mankind from the start, even when I seemed to be angry, but nobody cared about or paid any attention to my love.

Because I am just and merciful, I warn the so-called knights that they should seek my mercy, lest my justice find them. My justice is as immovable as a mountain, it burns like fire, it is as frightening as thunder, and as sudden as a bow fitted with an arrow. My warning is threefold. First, I warn them as a father does his children, in order to make them turn back to me, because I am their Father and Creator. Let them return, and I will give them the patrimony due to them by right. Let them return, because, although I have been spurned, I will still welcome them with joy and go out to meet them with love. Second, I ask them like a brother to recall my wounds and my deeds. Let them return, and I will receive them like a brother, Third, as their Lord I ask them to return to the Lord to whom they pledged their faith, to whom they owe their allegiance and to whom they have sworn themselves by oath.

Wherefore, o knights, turn back to me, your father, who brought you up with love. Think on me, your brother, who became as one of you for your sakes. Turn back to me, your kind Lord. It is highly dishonest to pledge your faith and allegiance to another lord. You pledged me that you would defend my church and help the needy. See now how you pledge allegiance to my enemy, and throw away my banner and hoist the banner of my enemy!

Wherefore, O knights, come back to me in true humility, since you deserted me through pride. If anything seems hard to suffer for me, consider what I did for you! For your sakes, I went to the cross with my feet bleeding; my hands and feet were pierced for you; I spared not a single limb of mine for you. And yet you ignore all this by running away from me. Come back, and I will give you three kinds of help. First, fortitude, so as to be able to withstand your physical and spiritual enemies. Second, a brave generosity, so that you may fear nothing but me and may deem it a joy to exert yourselves for my sake. Third, I shall give you wisdom to make you understand the true faith and the will of God. Therefore, come back and take your stand like men! For I, who am giving you this warning, am the same one whom the angels serve, the one who freed those forefathers of yours who were obedient but sentenced the disobedient and humbled the proud. I was first in war, first in suffering. Follow me, then, so that you will not be melted like wax by fire. Why are you breaking your promise? Why do you scorn your oath? Am I of less value or more unworthy than some worldly friend of yours to whom, once you pledge your faith, you keep it? To me, however, the giver of life and honor, the preserver of health, you do not render what you have promised.

For this reason, good knights, fulfill your promise and, if you are too weak to do so in deeds, at least have the will to do so! I feel pity due to the slavery the devil has imposed on you and so I will accept your intention as a deed. If you come back to me in love, then exert yourselves in the faith of my church, and I will come out to meet you like a kind father together with all my army. I will give you five good things as a reward. First, neverending praise will always sound in your ears. Second, the face and glory of God will always be before your eyes. Third, the praise of God will never leave your lips. Fourth, you will have everything your soul can desire, and you will desire nothing more than you have. Fifth, you will never be separated from your God, but your joy will endure without end and you will live your life in joy without end.

Such will be your reward, my knights, if you defend my faith and exert yourselves more for the sake of my honor than for your own. If you have any sense, remember that I have been patient with you and that you have insulted me in a way you yourselves would never tolerate. However, although I can do all things by reason of my omnipotence, and although my justice cries out to be revenged upon you, still my mercy, which is in my wisdom and goodness, spares you. Therefore, ask for mercy! In my love I grant that which a person asks me for in humility."

Christ's strong words to the bride against present-day knights, and about the proper way of creating knights, and about how God gives and bestows strength and help to them in their actions.

# Chapter 13

"I am one God together with the Father and the Holy Ghost in a trinity of persons. None of the three can be separated or divided from the others, but the Father is in both the Son and the Spirit, and the Son is in both the Father and the Spirit, and the Spirit is in both. The Divinity sent its Word to the Virgin Mary through the angel Gabriel. Yet the same God, both sending and being sent by himself, was with the angel, and he was in Gabriel, and he was in the Virgin prior to Gabriel. After the angel had delivered his message, the word was made flesh in the Virgin. I, who speak with you, am that Word.

The Father sent me through himself together with the Holy Ghost into the womb of the Virgin, although not in such away that the angels would be left without the vision and presence of God. Rather, I, the Son, who was with the Father and the Holy Ghost in the virginal womb, remained the same God in the sight of the angels in heaven together with the Father and the Spirit, ruling and sustaining all things. However, the human nature assumed by the only Son lay in the womb of Mary. I, who am one God in my divine and human natures, do not disdain to speak with you and thus manifest my love and strengthen the holy faith.

Although my human form seems to be here before you and to be speaking with you, nonetheless it is truer to say that your soul and your conscience are with me and in me. Nothing in heaven or on earth is impossible or difficult for me. I am like a powerful king who comes to a city with his troops and takes up the whole place, occupying all of it. In like manner, my grace fills all of your limbs and strengthens them all. I am within you and with out you. Although I may be speaking with you, I remain the same in my glory. What could possibly be difficult for me who sustains all things with my power and arranges all things in my wisdom, surpassing everything in excellence? I, who am one God together with the Father and the Holy Ghost, without beginning or end, who assumed a human nature for the sake of the salvation of humankind, the divine nature remaining intact, who suffered, rose again, and ascended into heaven, I am now truly speaking with you.

I told you earlier about the knights who were once most pleasing to me because they were bound to me by the bond of charity. They bound themselves by their oath to offer up their body for my body, their blood for my blood. This is why I gave them my consent, why I joined them to myself in a single bond and a single company. Now, however, my grievance is that these knights, who ought to be mine, have turned away from me. I am their Creator and redeemer as well as their helper. I made a body with all its limbs for them. I made everything in the world for their use. I redeemed them with my blood. I bought an eternal inheritance for them with my passion. I protect them in every danger.

Now, however, they have turned away from me. They hold my passion for naught, they neglect my words that should delight and nourish their soul. They despise me, preferring with all their heart and soul to offer up their body and let it be wounded in return for human praise, to shed their blood for the sake of satisfying their greed, happy to die on account of worldly, devilish, empty speech. But still, although they have turned away, my mercy and justice is upon them. I mercifully watch over them so that they may not be handed over to the devil. In justice I bear with them patiently and, if they would turn back again, I would welcome them joyfully and gladly run out to meet them.

Tell that man who wants to put his knighthood at my service that he can please me once again through the following ceremony. Anyone who wants to be made a knight should proceed with his horse and armor to the churchyard and leave his horse there, since it was not made for human pride but in order to be useful in life and in defense and in fighting the enemies of God. Then let him put on his cloak, placing its clasp to his forehead, similar to what a deacon does when he puts on his stole as a sign of obedience and holy patience. In like manner, he should put on his cloak and place the clasp to his forehead as a sign both of his military vows and of the obedience undertaken for the defense of Christ's cross.

A banner of the secular government should be carried before him, reminding him that he should obey his worldly government in all the things that are not against God. Once he has entered the churchyard, the priests should go out to meet him with the banner of the church. On it the passion and wounds of Christ should be depicted as a sign that he is obliged to defend the church of God and comply with her prelates. When he enters the church, the banner of the temporal government should remain outside the church while the banner of God should go before him into the church as a sign that divine authority precedes secular authority and that one should care more about spiritual things than temporal things.

When Mass has been said up to the Agnus Dei, the presiding officer, that is, the king or someone else, should go up to the knight at the altar and say: 'Do you want to be made a knight?' When the candidate answers, I do,' the other should add the words: 'Promise to God and to me that you will defend the faith of the Holy Church and obey its leaders in all the things pertaining to God!'

When the candidate answers 'I do,' the other should place a sword in his hands, saying: 'Behold, I place a sword in your hands so that you may not spare even your own life for the sake of God's church, so that you may crush the enemies of God and protect the friends of God.' Then he should give him the shield and say: 'Behold, I give you a shield so that you may defend yourself against the enemies of God, so that you may offer assistance to widows and orphans, so that you may add to the glory of God in every way.' Then he should place his hand on the other's neck, saying: 'Behold, you are now subject to obedience and to authority. Know, then, that you must carry out in practice what you have bound yourself to by your pledges!' After this, the cloak and its clasps should be fitted on him in order to remind him daily both of his vows to God and that, by his profession before the church, he has bound himself to do more than others to defend the church of God.

Once these things are done and the Agnus Dei has been said, the priest celebrating the Mass should give him my body in order that he may defend the faith of the Holy Church. I will be in him and he in me. I will furnish him with help and strength, and I will make him burn with the fire of my love so as to desire nothing but me and to fear nothing but me, his God. If he should happen to be on a campaign when he undertakes this service for my glory and the defense of my faith, it will still benefit him, provided his intention is upright.

I am everywhere by virtue of my power, and all people can please me by an upright intention and a good will. I am love, and no one can come to me but a person who has love. Therefore I do not order anyone to do this, since in that case they would be serving me out of fear. But those who want to undertake this form of knightly service can be pleasing to me. It would be fitting for them to show through humility that they want to return to the true exercise of knighthood, inasmuch as desertion from the profession of true knighthood occurs through pride."

## Explanation

This knight was believed to have been Sir Karl, the son of St. Bridget.

About Christ as symbolized by a goldsmith and the words of God as gold, and about how these words should be transmitted to people with the love of God, an upright conscience, and their five senses under control, and about how the preachers of God should be diligent rather than lazy in selling the gold, that is, in transmitting the word of God.

# Chapter 14

"I am like a skilled goldsmith who sends his servant to sell his gold throughout the land, telling him: 'You must do three things. First of all, you must not entrust my gold to anyone except those who have calm and clear eyes. Second, do not entrust it to people who have no conscience. Third, put my gold on sale for ten talents weighed twice over! A person who refuses to weigh my gold twice will not get it. You must beware of three weapons my enemy uses against you. First of all, he wants to make you slow to put my gold on display. Second, he wishes to mix inferior metal into my gold so that those who see and test it think my gold is just rotten clay.

Third, he instructs his friends to contradict you and to claim constantly that my gold is no good.' I am like that goldsmith. I forged everything in heaven and on earth, not with hammers and tools but by my power and strength. All that is and was and will be is foreknown to me. Not the least little worm or the smallest grain can exist or continue in existence without me. Not the least little thing escapes my foreknowledge, since everything comes from me and is foreknown to me. Among all the things I have made, however, the words I have spoken with my own lips are of the greatest value, just as gold is more valuable than other metals.

This is why my servants, whom I dispatch with my gold throughout the world, must do three things. First of all, they are not to entrust my gold to people who do not have calm and clear eyes. You may ask: 'What does it mean to have clear eyesight?' Well, a clear-sighted person is one who has divine wisdom along with divine charity. But how are you to know this? It is obvious. That person is clear-sighted and can be entrusted with my gold who lives according to reason, who removes himself from worldly vanity and curiosity, who seeks nothing so much as his God. But that person is blind who has knowledge but does not put the divine charity he understands into practice. He seems to have his eyes on God but he does not, for his eyes are on the world and he has turned his back to God.

Second, my gold is not to be entrusted to someone with no conscience. Who has a conscience if not the person who manages his temporal, perishable goods with a view to eternity, who has his soul in heaven and his body on earth, who ponders daily how he is going to depart from earth and answer to God for his deeds? My gold should be entrusted to such a person. Third, he should put my gold on sale for ten talents weighed two times over. What do the scales with which the gold is weighed symbolize if not conscience? What do the hands that weigh the gold symbolize if not a good will and desire? What are the counterweights to be used if not spiritual and corporal works?

A person who wants to buy and keep my gold, that is, my words, should examine himself uprightly on the scales of his conscience and consider how he is to pay for it with ten talents carefully weighed out in accordance with my wishes. The first talent is the person's disciplined eyesight. This makes him consider the difference between corporal and spiritual vision, what use there is in physical beauty and appearance, how much excellence there is in the beauty and glory of the angels and of the heavenly powers that surpass all the stars of the sky in splendor, and what joyful delight a soul possesses in God's commandments and in his glory.

This talent, I mean, physical vision and spiritual vision, which is found in God's commandments and in chastity, are not to be measured on the same scale. Spiritual vision counts for more than the corporal kind and weighs more, inasmuch as a person's eyes must be open to what is beneficial for the soul and necessary for the body, but closed to foolishness and indecency.

The second talent is good hearing. A person should consider the worth of indecent, silly, and derisive language. Surely, it is worth nothing more than an empty puff of air. This is why a person should hear God's praises and hymns. He should listen to the deeds and sayings of my saints. He should hear what he needs in order to foster his soul and body in virtue. This kind of hearing weighs more on the scales than the hearing of indecency. This good kind of hearing, when it is weighed on the scales against the other kind, will sink the scales all the way down, while the other, empty kind of hearing will get lifted up and weigh nothing at all.

The third talent is that of the tongue. A person should weigh the excellence and usefulness of edifying and measured speech on the scales of his conscience. He should also take note of the harmfulness and uselessness of vain and idle speech. He should then put away vain speech and love the good kind.

The fourth talent is taste. What is the taste of the world if not misery? Toil at the start of an enterprise, sorrow as it continues, bitterness at the end. Accordingly, a person should carefully weigh spiritual taste against the worldly kind, and the spiritual will outweigh worldly taste. The spiritual taste is never lost, never becomes wearisome, never diminishes. This kind of taste begins in the present through the restraint of lust and through a life of moderation and lasts forever in heaven through the enjoyment and sweet delight of God.

The fifth talent is that of the sense of touch. A person should weigh how much care and misery he feels because of the body, all the worldly cares, all the many problems with his neighbor. Then he experiences misery everywhere. Let him also weigh how great the peace of soul and of a well-disciplined mind is, how much good there is in not being worried about vain and superfluous possessions. Then he will experience consolation everywhere. Whoever wants to measure it well should put the spiritual and physical senses of touch on the scales, and the result will be that the spiritual outweighs the corporal. This spiritual sense of touch begins and develops through the patient endurance of setbacks and through perseverance in the commandments of God, and it lasts forever in joy and peaceful rest. A person who gives more weight to physical rest and to worldly feelings and joy than to those of eternity is not worthy to touch my gold or to enjoy my happiness.

The sixth talent is human work. A person should carefully weigh in his conscience both spiritual and material work. The former leads to heaven, the latter to the world; the former to an eternal life without suffering, the latter to tremendous pain and suffering. Whoever desires my gold should give more weight to spiritual work, which is done in my love and for my glory, than to material work, since spiritual things endure, while material things will pass away.

The seventh talent is the orderly use of time. A person is given certain times to devote to spiritual things alone, other times for bodily functions, without which life is impossible (if these are used reasonably, they are counted as a spiritual use of time), and other times for physically useful activity. Since a person must render an account of his time as well as of his deeds, he should therefore give priority to the spiritual use of time before turning to material labor, and manage his time in such away that spiritual things are given more priority than temporal things so that no time is allowed to pass without the examination and right balance required by justice.

The eighth talent is the just administration of the temporal goods given to one, meaning that a rich person, as far as his means allow, should give to the poor with divine charity. But you might ask: 'What should a poor person who owns nothing give?' He should have the right intention and think the following thoughts: 'If I had anything, I would gladly give it generously.' Such an intention is counted for him as a deed. If the poor man's intention is such that he would like to have temporal possessions like others but only intends to give a small sum and mere trifles to the poor, this intention is reckoned for him as a small deed. Therefore a rich person with possessions should practice charity. A needy person should have the intention of giving, and it will gain him merit. Whoever gives more weight to the temporal than to the spiritual, whoever gives me one shilling and the world a hundred and himself a thousand does not use a fair measuring standard. A person who uses a measuring standard like that does not deserve to have my gold. I, the giver of all things, who can also take all things away, deserve the worthier share. Temporal goods were created for human use and necessity, not for superfluity.

The ninth talent is the careful examination of times gone and past. A person should examine his deeds, what sort of deeds they were, their number, how he has corrected them and with what merit. He should also consider whether his good works were fewer than his bad. If he should find his bad works to be more numerous than his good, then he should have a perfect purpose of amendment and be truly contrite for his misdeeds. This intention, if it be true and firm, will weigh more in God's sight than all his sins.

The tenth talent is the consideration of and planning for future time. If a person has the intention of not wanting to love anything but the things of God, of not desiring anything but what he knows to be pleasing to God, of willingly and patiently embracing difficulties, even the pains of hell, were that to give God any consolation and were it to be God's will, then this talent excels all the rest. Through this talent all dangers are easily avoided. Whoever pays these ten talents will get my gold.

However, as I said, the enemy wants to impede the people delivering my gold in three ways. First he wants to make them slow and lazy. There is both a physical and a spiritual laziness. The physical kind is when the body tires of working, getting up, and so forth. Spiritual laziness is when a spiritually minded person, knowing the sweet delight and grace of my Spirit, prefers to rest in that delight rather than to go out and help others to partake of it with him. Did not Peter and Paul experience the overflowingly sweet delight of my Spirit? If it had been my will, they would rather have lain hidden in the lowest part of the earth with the interior delight they had than to go out into the world.

However, in order that others might be made participants in their sweet delight and in order to instruct others along with themselves, they preferred to go out for other people's sake as well as for their own greater glory and not to remain by themselves without strengthening others with the grace given them. In like manner my friends, although they would like to be alone and to enjoy that sweet delight they have already, should now go forth so that others might also become participants in their joy. Just as someone with abundant possessions does not use them for himself alone but entrusts them to others, so too my words and my grace should not be kept hidden but should be broadcast to others so that they, too, may be edified.

My friends can give aid to three kinds of people. First, to the damned; second, to sinners, that is, to those who fall into sins and get up again; third, to the good who stand firm. But you may ask: 'How can a person give aid to the damned, seeing that they are unworthy of grace and it is impossible for them to return to grace?' Let me answer you by way of a simile. It is as though there were countless holes at the bottom of a certain precipice and anyone falling into them would necessarily sink to the depths. However, if someone were to block up one of the holes, the person falling would not sink down as deeply as if no hole had been blocked up. This is what happens to the damned. Although by reason of my justice and their own hardened malice they have to be condemned at a definite and foreknown time, still their punishment will be lighter if they are held back by others from doing certain evils and instead urged to do something good. That is how I am merciful even toward the damned. Although mercy pleads for leniency, justice and their own wickedness countermand it.

In the second place, they can give aid to those who fall down but get back up again by teaching them how to get up, by making them take care not to fall, and by instructing them how to improve and to resist their passions.

In the third place, they can be of benefit to the righteous and perfect. Do not they themselves fall as well? Of course they do, but it is for their greater glory and the devil's shame. Just as a soldier lightly wounded in battle gets all the more stirred up because of his wound and becomes that much keener for battle, so too the diabolical temptation of adversity stirs up my chosen ones all the more for the spiritual struggle and for humility, and they make all the more fervent progress toward winning the crown of glory. Therefore my words should not be kept hidden from my friends, for, having heard of my grace, they will get all the more stirred up as to devotion toward me.

My enemy's second method is to use deception in order to make my gold look like clay. For this reason, when any of my words are being transcribed, the transcriber should bring two trusty witnesses or one man of proven conscience to certify that he has examined the document. Only then may it be transmitted to whomever he wants, in order not to come uncertified into the hands of enemies who could add something false, which could lead to the words of truth being denigrated among simple folk.

My enemy's third method is to make his own friends preach resistance to my gold. My friends should then say to those who contradict them: 'The gold of these words contains, as it were, only three teachings. They teach you to fear rightly, to love piously, to desire heaven intelligently. Test the words and see for yourselves, and, if you find anything else there, contradict it!' "

Christ's words to the bride about how the way to paradise was opened by his coming, and about the ardent love he showed us in bearing so many sufferings for us from his birth to his death, and about how the way to hell has now been made wide and the way to paradise narrow.

# Chapter 15

"You are wondering why I am telling you such things and why I am revealing such marvels to you. Is it for your sake alone? Of course not, it is for the edification and salvation of others. You see, the world was like a kind of wilderness in which there was one road leading down to the great abyss. In the abyss were two chambers. One was so deep that it had no bottom and the people who went down into it never came up again. The second was not so deep or frightening as the first. Those who went down into it had some hope of help; they experienced longing and delay but not misery, darkness but not torment. The people who lived in this second chamber kept sending their cries daily to a magnificent city nearby that was filled with every good thing and every delight.

They cried out hardily, for they knew the way to the city. However, the wild forest was so thick and dense that they were unable to cross it or make any advance because of its density, and they had not the strength to forge a path through it. What was their cry? Their cry was this: 'O God, come and give us help, show us the way and enlighten us, we are waiting for you! We cannot be saved by anyone but you.' This cry came to my hearing in heaven and moved me to mercy. Appeased by their crying, I came to the wilderness like a pilgrim.

But before I began to work and make my way, a voice spoke out ahead of me, saying: 'The ax has been laid to the tree.' This voice was none other than John the Baptist. He was sent before me and cried out in the desert: 'The ax has been laid to the tree,' which is to say: 'Let the human race be ready, for the ax is now ready, and he has come to prepare a way to the city and is uprooting every obstacle.' When I came, I worked from sunrise to sunset, that is, I devoted myself to the salvation of humankind from the time of my incarnation until my death on the cross. At the start of my undertaking, I took flight into the wilderness away from my enemies, more precisely, from Herod who was pursuing me; I was put to the test by the devil and suffered persecution from men. Later, while enduring much toil, I ate and drank and sinlessly complied with other natural needs in order to build up the faith and to show that I had truly taken a human nature.

While I prepared the way to the city, that is, to heaven, and uprooted all the obstacles that had sprung up, brambles and thorns scratched my side and harsh nails wounded my hands and feet. My teeth and my cheeks were badly mishandled. I bore it with patience and did not turn back but went ahead all the more zealously, like an animal driven by starvation that, when it sees a man holding a spear against it, charges into the spear in its desire to get at the man. And the more the man thrusts the spear into the entrails of the animal, the more the animal thrusts itself against the spear in its desire to get at the man, until at last its entrails and entire body are pierced through and through. In like manner, I burned with such love for the soul, that, when I beheld and experienced all these harsh torments, the more eager men were to kill me, the more ardent I became to suffer for the salvation of souls.

Thus I made my way in the wilderness of this world and prepared a road through my blood and sweat. The world might well be called a wilderness, since it was lacking in every virtue and remained a wilderness of vice. It had only one road on which everyone was descending into hell, the damned toward damnation, the good towards darkness. I heard mercifully their longstanding desire for future salvation and came like a pilgrim in order to work. Unknown to them in my divinity and power, I prepared the road that leads to heaven. My friends saw this way and observed the difficulties of my work and my eagerness of heart, and many of them followed me in joy for a long time.

But now there has been a change in the voice that used to cry out: 'Be ready!' My road has been altered, and thickets and thorn bushes have grown up, and those who were advancing on it have halted. The way to hell has been opened up. It is broad, and many people travel by it. However, in order not to let my road become altogether forgotten and neglected, my few friends still travel it in their longing for their heavenly homeland, like birds moving from bush to bush, hidden, as it were, and serving me out of fear, since everyone nowadays thinks that to travel by the way of the world leads to happiness and joy.

For this reason, because my road has become narrow while the road of the world has been widened, I am now shouting out to my friends in the wilderness, that is, in the world, that they should remove the thorn bushes and brambles from the road leading to heaven and recommend my road to those who are making their way.

As it is written: 'Blessed are those who have not seen me and have believed'. Likewise, happy are they who now believe in my words and put them into practice. As you see, I am like a mother who runs out to meet her roving son. She holds out a light for him on the way so that he can see the road. In her love, she goes to meet him on the way and shortens his journey. She goes up to him and embraces and greets him. With love like that I shall run out to meet my friends and all the people returning to me, and I shall give their hearts and souls the light of divine wisdom. I will embrace them with glory and surround them with the heavenly court where there is neither heaven above nor earth below but only the vision of God; where there is neither food nor drink, but only the enjoyment of God.

The road to hell is open for the wicked. Once they enter into it, they will never come up again. They will be without glory or bliss and will be filled with misery and everlasting reproach. This is why I speak these words and reveal this love of mine, so that those who have turned away may turn back to me and recognize me, their Creator, whom they have forgotten."

Christ's words to the bride about why he speaks with her rather than with others better than she, and about three things commanded, three forbidden, three permitted, and three recommended to the bride by Christ; a most excellent lesson.

# Chapter 16

"Many people wonder why I speak with you and not with others who live a better life and have served me for a longer time. I answer them by way of a parable: A certain lord owns several vineyards in several different regions. The wine of each vineyard has the particular taste of the region where it comes from. Once the wine has been pressed, the owner of the vineyards sometimes drinks the mediocre and weaker wine and not the better kind. If any of those present sees him and asks their lord why he does so, he will answer that this particular wine tasted good and sweet to him at the time. This does not meant that the lord gets rid of the better wines or holds them in disdain, but that he reserves them for his use and privilege on an appropriate occasion, each of them for the occasion for which it is suited. This is the way I deal with you.

I have many friends whose life is sweeter to me than honey, more delicious than any wine, brighter in my sight than the sun. However, it pleased me to choose you in my Spirit, not because you are better than they are or equal to them or better qualified, but because I wanted to - I who can make sages out of fools and saints out of sinners. I did not grant you so great a grace because I hold the others in disdain. Rather, I am reserving them for another use and privilege as justice demands. Humble yourself then in every way, and do not let anything trouble you but your sins. Love everyone, even those who seem to hate and slander you, for they are only providing you with a greater opportunity to win your crown! Three things I command you to do. Three things I command you not to do. Three things I permit you to do. Three things I recommend you to do.

I command you to do three things, then. First, to desire nothing but your God; second, to cast off all pride and arrogance; third, always to hate the lust of the flesh. Three things I order you not to do. First, neither to love vain, indecent speech nor, second, excessive eating and superfluity in other things, and, third, to flee from worldly merriment and frivolity. I permit you to do three things. First, to sleep moderately for the sake of good health; second, to carry out temperate vigils to train the body; third, to eat moderately for the strength and sustenance of your body.

I recommend three things to you. First, to take pains to fast and carry out good works that earn the promise of the kingdom of heaven; second, to dispose of your possessions for the glory of God; third, I counsel you to think on two things continually in your heart. First, think on all that I have done for you by suffering and dying for you. Such a thought stirs up love for God. Second, consider my justice and the coming judgment. This instills fear in your mind. Finally, there is a fourth thing which I both order and command and recommend and permit. This is to obey as you ought. I order this, inasmuch as I am your God. I command you not to act otherwise, inasmuch as I am your Lord. I permit this to you, inasmuch as I am your bridegroom. I also recommend it, inasmuch as I am your friend."

Christ's words to the bride about how God's divinity can truly be named virtue, and about the manifold downfall of humankind instigated by the devil, and about the manifold remedy to aid humankind that was given and provided for through Christ.

# Chapter 17

The Son of God spoke to the bride saying: "Do you firmly believe that what the priest holds in his hands is the body of God?" She answered: "I firmly believe that, just as the word sent to Mary was made flesh and blood in her womb, so too that which I now see in the hands of the priest I believe to be true God and man." The Lord answered her: "I am the same who am speaking to you, remaining eternally in the divine nature, having become human in the womb of the Virgin but without losing my divinity. My divinity can rightly be named virtue, since there are two things in it: power most powerful, the source of all power, and wisdom most wise, the source and seat of all wisdom. In this divine nature all things that exist are ordered wisely and rationally.

There is not one little tittle in heaven that is not in it and that has not been established and foreseen by it. Not a single atom on earth, not one spark in hell is outside its rule and can hide itself from its foreknowledge. Do you wonder why I said 'not one little tittle in heaven'? Well, a tittle is the final stroke on a glossed word. Indeed God's word is the final stroke on all things and was ordained for the glorification of all things. Why did I say 'not a single atom on earth,' if not because all earthly things are transitory? Not even atoms, however small they are, are outside of God's plan and providence. Why did I say 'not one spark in hell,' if not because there is nothing in hell except envy? Just as a spark comes from fire, so all kinds of evil and envy come from the unclean spirits, with the result that they and their followers always have envy but never love of any kind.

Therefore, perfect knowledge and power are in God, which is why each thing is so arranged that nothing is greater than God's power, nor can anything be caused to be made contrary to reason, but all things have been made rationally, suitable to the nature of each thing. The divine nature, then, inasmuch as it can rightly be named virtue, showed its greatest virtue in the creation of the angels. It created them for its own glory and for their delight, so that they might have charity and obedience: charity, by which they love none but God; obedience, by which they obey God in all things. Some of the angels went wickedly astray and wickedly set their will against these two things. They turned their will directly against God, so much so that virtue became odious to them and, therefore, that which was opposed to God became dear to them. Because of this disordered direction of their will, they deserved to fall. It was not that God caused their fall, but they themselves brought it about through the abuse of their own knowledge.

When God saw the reduction in the numbers of the heavenly host that had been caused through their sin, he again showed the power of his divinity. For he created human beings in body and soul. He gave them two goods, namely the freedom to do good and the freedom to avoid evil, because, given that no more angels were to be created, it was fitting that human beings should have the freedom of rising, if they wished, to angelic rank. God also gave the human soul two goods, namely a rational mind to order to distinguish opposite from opposite and better from best; and fortitude in order to persevere in the good. When the devil saw this love of God for mankind, he considered thus in his envy: 'So then, God has made a new thing that can rise up to our place and by its own efforts gain that which we lost through neglect!

If we can deceive him and cause his downfall, he will cease his efforts, and then he will not rise up to such a rank.' Then, having thought out a plan of deception, they deceived the first man and prevailed over him with my just permission. But how and when was the man defeated? To be sure, when he left off virtue and did what was forbidden, when the serpent's promise pleased him more than obedience to me. Due to this disobedience he could not live in heaven, since he had despised God, and not in hell either, since his soul, using reason, carefully examined what he had done and had contrition for his crime.

For that reason, the God of virtue, considering human wretchedness, arranged a kind of imprisonment or place of captivity, where people might come to recognize their weakness and atone for their disobedience until they should deserve to rise to the rank they had lost. The devil, meanwhile, taking this into consideration, wanted to kill the human soul by means of ingratitude. Injecting his filth into the soul, he so darkened her intellect that she had neither the love nor the fear of God. God's justice was forgotten and his judgment scorned. For that reason, God's goodness and gifts were no longer appreciated but fell into oblivion.

Thus God was not loved, and the human conscience was so darkened that humanity was in a wretched state and fell into even greater wretchedness. Although humanity was in such a state, still God's virtue was not lacking; rather, he revealed his mercy and justice. He revealed his mercy when he revealed to Adam and other good people that they would obtain help at a predetermined time. This stirred up their fervor and love for God. He also revealed his justice through the flood in Noah's day, which filled human hearts with the fear of God. Even after that the devil still did not leave off further molesting humankind, but attacked it by means of two other evils. First, he inspired faithlessness in people; second, hopelessness. He inspired faithlessness in order that people might not believe in the word of God but would attribute his wonders to fate. He inspired hopelessness lest they hope to be saved and obtain the glory they had lost.

The God of virtue supplied two remedies to fight these two evils. Against hopelessness he offered hope, giving Abram a new name and promising him that from his seed there would be born the one who would lead him and the imitators of his faith back to the lost inheritance. He also appointed prophets to whom he revealed the manner of redemption and the times and places of his suffering. With respect to the second evil of faithlessness, God spoke to Moses and revealed his will and the law to him and backed his words up with portents and deeds. Although all this was done, still the devil did not desist from his evil. Constantly urging humankind on to worse sins, he inspired two other attitudes in the human heart: first, that of regarding the law as unbearable and losing peace of mind over trying to live up to it; second, he inspired the thought that God's decision to die and suffer out of charity was too incredible and far too difficult to believe.

Again God provided two further remedies for these two evils. First, he sent his own Son into the womb of the Virgin so that nobody would lose peace of mind over how hard the Law was to fulfill, since, having assumed a human nature, his Son fulfilled the requirements of the Law and then made it less strict. With respect to the second evil, God displayed the very height of virtue. The Creator died for creation, the righteous one for sinners. Innocent, he suffered to the last drop, as had been foretold by the prophets. Even then the wickedness of the devil did not cease, but again he rose up against humanity, inspiring two further evils. First, he inspired the human heart to hold my words in contempt and, second, to let my deeds fall into oblivion.

God's virtue has again begun to indicate two new remedies against these two evils. The first is to return my words to honor and to undertake to imitate my deeds. This is why God has led you in his Spirit. He has also revealed his will on earth to his friends through you, for two reasons in particular. The first is in order to reveal God's mercy, so that people might learn to recall the memory of God's love and suffering. The second is to remind them of God's justice and to make them fear the severity of my judgment.

Therefore, tell this man that, given that my mercy has already come, he should bring it out into the light so that people might learn to seek mercy and to beware of the judgment on themselves. Moreover, tell him that, although my words have been written down, still they must first be preached and put into practice. You can understand this by way of a metaphor. When Moses was about to receive the Law, a staff was made and two stone tablets were hewn. Nevertheless, he did not work miracles with the staff until there was a need for it and the occasion demanded it. When the acceptable time came, then there was a show of miracles and my words were proved by deeds.

Likewise, when the New Law arrived, first my body grew and developed until a suitable time and from then on my words were heard. However, although my words were heard, still they did not have force and strength in themselves until accompanied by my deeds. And they were not fulfilled until I fulfilled all the things that had been foretold about me through my passion. It is the same now. Although my loving words have been written down and should be conveyed to the world, still they cannot have any force until they have been completely brought out into the light."

About three wonderful things that Christ has done for the bride, and about how the sight of angels is too beautiful and that of devils too ugly for human nature to bear, and about why Christ has condescended to come as a guest to a widow like her.

# Chapter 18

"I have done three wonderful things for you. You see with spiritual eyes. You hear with spiritual ears. With the physical touch of your hand you feel my spirit in your living breast. You do not see the sight you see as it is in fact. For if you saw the spiritual beauty of the angels and of holy souls, your body could not bear to see it but would break like a vessel, broken and decayed due to the soul's joy at the sight. If you saw the demons as they are, you would either go on living in great sorrow or you would die a sudden death at the terrible sight of them. This is why spiritual beings appear to you as if they had bodies.

The angels and souls appear to you in the likeness of human beings who have soul and life, because angels live by their spirit. The demons appear to you in a form that is mortal and belongs to mortality, such as in the form of animals or other creatures. Such creatures have a mortal spirit, since when their body dies, their spirit dies too. However, devils do not die in spirit but are forever dying and live forever. Spiritual words are spoken to you by means of analogies, since you cannot grasp them otherwise. The most wonderful thing of all is that you feel my spirit move in your heart."

Then she replied: "O my Lord, Son of the Virgin, why have you condescended to come as a guest to so base a widow, who is poor in every good work and so weak in understanding and discernment and ridden with sin for so long?" He answered her: "I can do three things. First, I can make a poor person rich and a foolish person of little intelligence capable and intelligent. I am also able to restore an aged person to youth. It is like the phoenix that brings together dried twigs. Among them is the twig of a certain tree that is dry by nature on the outside and warm on the inside. The warmth of the sunbeams comes to it first and kindles it, and then all the twigs are set on fire from it. In the same way you should gather together the virtues by which you can be restored from your sins.

Among them you should have a piece of wood that is warm on the inside and dry on the outside; I mean your heart, which should be dry and pure from all worldly sensuality on the outside and so full of love on the inside that you want nothing and yearn for nothing but me. Then the fire of my love will come into the heart first and in that way you will be enkindled with all the virtues. Thoroughly burned by them and purged from sins, you will arise like the rejuvenated bird, having put off the skin of sensuality."

Christ's words to the bride about how God speaks to his friends through his preachers and through sufferings, and about Christ as symbolized by an owner of bees and the church by a beehive and Christians by bees, and about why bad Christians are allowed to live among good ones.

# Chapter 19

"I am your God. My Spirit has led you to hear and see and feel: to hear my words, to see visions, to feel my Spirit with the joy and devotion of your soul. All mercy is found in me together with justice, and there is mercy in my justice. I am like a man who sees his friends fall away from him, down on to a road where there is a horrible yawning gap out of which it is impossible to climb. I speak to these friends through those people who have an understanding of scripture. I speak with a lash, I warn them of their danger. But they just act contrariwise. They head for the impasse and do not care about what I say.

I have only one thing to say: 'Sinner, turn back to me! You are headed for danger; there are traps along the way of a kind that are hidden from you due to the darkness of your heart.' They scorn what I say. They ignore my mercy. However, though my mercy is such that I warn sinners, my justice is such that, even if all the angels were to drag them back, they could not be converted unless they themselves direct their own will toward the good. If they turned their will to me and gave me their heart's consent, not all the demons together could hold them back.

There is an insect called the bee that is kept by its lord and master. The bees show respect in three ways to their ruler, the queen bee, and derive benefit from her in three ways. First, the bees carry all the nectar they find to their queen. Second, they stay or go at her beck and call, and wherever they fly and wherever they appear, their love and charity is always for the queen. Third, they follow and serve her, sticking steadily close by her side. In return for these three things, the bees receive a threefold benefit from their queen.

First, her signal gives them a set time to go out and work. Second, she gives them direction and mutual love. Because of her presence and rule and because of the love she has toward them and they toward her, all the bees are united with one another in love, and each one rejoices over the others and at their advancement. Third, they are made fruitful through their mutual love and the joy of their leader. Just as fish discharge their eggs while playing together in the sea, and their eggs fall into the sea and bear fruit, so bees are also made fruitful through their mutual love and their leader's affection and joy. By my wondrous power, a seemingly lifeless seed comes forth from their love and will receive life through my goodness.

The master, that is, the owner of the bees, speaks to his servant in his concern for them: 'My servant,' he says, 'it seems to me that my bees are ill and do not fly at all.' The servant answers: 'I do not understand this illness, but if it is so, I ask you how I can learn about it.' The master answers: 'You can infer their illness or problem by three signs. The first sign is that they are weak and sluggish in flight, which means that they have lost the queen from whom they receive strength and consolation. The second sign is that they go out at random and unplanned hours, which means that they are not getting the signal of their leader's call.

The third sign is that they show no love for the beehive, and therefore return home carrying nothing back, sating themselves but not bringing any nectar to live on in the future. Healthy and fit bees are steady and strong in their flight. They keep regular hours for going out and returning, bringing back wax to build their dwellings and honey for their nourishment.' The servant answers the master: 'If they are useless and infirm, why do you allow them to go on anymore and do not do away with them?' The master answers: 'I permit them to live for three reasons, inasmuch as they provide three benefits, although not by their own power.

First, because they occupy the dwellings prepared for them, horseflies do not come and occupy the empty dwellings and disturb the good bees that remain. Second, other bees become more fruitful and diligent at their work due to the badness of the bad bees. The fruitful bees see the bad and unfruitful bees working only to satisfy their own desires, and they become the more diligent in their work of gathering for their queen the more eager the bad bees are seen to be in gathering for their own desires. In the third place, the bad bees are useful to the good bees when it comes to their mutual defense.

For there is a flying insect accustomed to eating bees. When the bees perceive this insect coming, all of them hate it in common.

Although the bad bees fight and hate it out of envy and self-defense, while the good ones do so out of love and justice, both the good and bad bees work together to attack these insects. If all the bad bees were taken away and only the good ones were left, this insect would quickly prevail over them, since then they would be fewer. That is why,' the master said, 'I put up with the useless bees. However, when autumn comes, I shall provide for the good bees and shall separate them from the bad ones that, if they are left outside the beehive, will die from the cold.

But if they remain inside and do not gather, they will be in danger of starvation, inasmuch as they have neglected to gather food when they could.' I am God, the Creator of all things; I am the owner and the lord of the bees. Out of my ardent love and by my blood I founded my beehive, that is, the Holy Church, in which Christians should be gathered and dwell in unity of faith and mutual love. Their dwelling-places are their hearts, and the honey of good thoughts and affections should inhabit it. This honey ought to be brought there through considering my love in creation and my toils in redemption and my patient support and mercy in calling back and restoring.

In this beehive, that is, in the Holy Church, there are two kinds of people, just as there were two kinds of bees. The first ones are those bad Christians who do not gather nectar for me but for themselves. They return carrying nothing back and do not recognize their leader. They have a sting instead of honey and lust instead of love. The good bees represent good Christians. They show me respect in three ways. First, they hold me as their leader and lord, offering me sweet honey, that is, works of charity, which are pleasing to me and useful to themselves. Second, they wait upon my will. Their will accords with my will, all their thought is on my passion, all their actions are for my glory. Third, they follow me, that is, they obey me in everything.

Wherever they are, whether outside or inside, whether in sorrow or in joy, their heart is always joined to my heart. This is why they derive benefit from me in three ways. First, through the call of virtue and my inspiration, they have fixed and certain times, night at nighttime and daylight at daytime. Indeed, they change night into day, that is, worldly happiness into eternal happiness, and perishable happiness into everlasting stability. They are sensible in every respect, inasmuch as they make use of their present goods for their necessities; they are steadfast in adversity, wary in success, moderate in the care of the body, careful and circumspect in their actions. Second, like the good bees, they have mutual love, in such away that they are all of one heart toward me, loving their neighbor as themselves but me above all else, even above themselves.

Third, they are made fruitful through me. What is it to be fruitful if not to have my Holy Ghost and be filled with him? Whoever does not have him and lacks his honey is unfruitful and useless; he falls down and perishes. However, the Holy Ghost sets the person in whom he dwells on fire with divine love; he opens the senses of his mind; he uproots pride and incontinence; he spurs the soul on to the glory of God and the contempt of the world.

The unfruitful bees do not know this Spirit and therefore scorn discipline, fleeing the unity and fellowship of love. They are empty of good works; they change daylight into darkness, consolation into mourning, happiness into sorrow. Nevertheless, I let them live for three reasons. First, so that horseflies, that is, the infidels, do not get into the dwelling-places that have been prepared. If the wicked were removed all at once, there would be too few good Christians left, and, because of their small numbers, the infidels, being greater in number, would come and live side by side with them, causing them much disturbance. Second, they are tolerated in order to test the good Christians, for, as you know, the perseverance of good people is put to the test by the wickedness of the wicked.

Adversity reveals how patient a person is, while prosperity makes plain how persevering and temperate he is. Since vices insinuate themselves into good characters from time to time and virtues can often make people proud, the wicked are allowed to live alongside the good in order that good people may not become enervated from too much happiness or fall asleep out of sloth, and also in order that they may frequently fix their gaze on God. Where there is little struggle, there is also little reward. In the third place, they are tolerated for their assistance so that neither the gentiles nor other hostile infidels might harm those seeming to be good

Christians , but that they might rather fear them because there are more of them. The good offer resistance to the wicked out of justice and love of God, while the wicked do so only for the sake of self-defense and to avoid God's wrath. In this way, then, the good and wicked help each other, with the result that the wicked are tolerated for the sake of the good and the good receive a higher crown on account of the wickedness of the wicked.

The beekeepers are the prelates of the church and the princes of the land, whether good or bad. I speak to the good keepers and I, their God and keeper, admonish them to keep my bees safe. Have them consider the comings and goings of the bees! Let them take note of whether they are sick or healthy! If they happen not to know how to discern this, here are three signs I give them to recognize it. Those bees are useless that are sluggish in flight, erratic in their hours, and contribute nothing to bringing in honey. The ones that are sluggish in flight are those who show greater concern for temporal goods than for eternal ones, who fear the death of the body more than that of the soul, who say this to themselves: 'Why should I be full of disquiet, when I can have quiet and peace? Why should I die to myself when I can live?'

These wretches do not reflect on how I, the powerful King of glory, chose to be powerless. I know the greatest quiet and peace and, indeed, I am peace itself, and yet I chose to give up peace and quiet for their sake and freed them through my own death. They are erratic in their hours in that their affections tend toward worldliness, their conversation toward indecency, their labor toward selfishness, and they arrange their time according to the cravings of their bodies. The ones who have no love for the beehive and do not gather nectar are those who do some good works for my sake but only out of fear of punishment. Even though they do perform some works of piety, still they do not give up their selfishness and sin. They want to have God but without giving up the world or enduring any wants or hardship.

These bees are the kind that hurry home with empty feet, but their hurry is unwise, since they do not fly with the right sort of love. Accordingly, when autumn comes, that is, when the time of separation comes, the useless bees will be separated from the good ones and they will suffer eternal hunger in return for their selfish love and desires. In return for scorning God and for their disgust at virtue they will be destroyed by excessive cold but with out being consumed.

However, my friends should be on their guard against three evils from the bad bees. First, against letting their rottenness enter the ears of my friends, since the bad bees are poisonous. Once their honey is gone, there is nothing sweet left in them; instead they are full of poisoned bitterness. Second, they should guard the pupils of their eyes against the wings of the bad bees that are as sharp as needles. Third, they should be careful not to expose their bodies to the tails of the bees, for they have barbs that sting sharply. The learned who study their habits and temperament can explain the meaning of these things. Those who are unable to understand it should be wary of the risks and avoid their company and example.

Otherwise, they will learn by experience what they did not know how to learn by listening." Then his Mother said: "Blessed are you, my Son, you who are and were and always will be! Your mercy is sweet and your justice great. You seem to remind me, my Son - to speak figuratively - of a cloud rising up to heaven preceded by a light breeze. A dark spot appeared in the cloud, and a person who was out of doors, feeling the light breeze, raised his eyes and saw the dark cloud and thought to himself: 'This dark cloud seems to me to indicate rain.' And he prudently hurried into a shelter and hid himself from the rain.

Others, however, who were blind or who perhaps did not care, made little of the light breeze and were unafraid of the dark cloud, but they learned by experience what the cloud meant. The cloud, taking over the whole sky, came with violent commotion and so furious and mighty a fire that living things were expiring at the very commotion. The fire was consuming all the inner and outer parts of man so that nothing remained.

My Son, this cloud is your words, which seem dark and incredible to many people since they have not been heard much and since they have been given to ignorant people and have not been confirmed by portents. These words were preceded by my prayer and by the mercy with which you have mercy on everyone and, like a mother, draw everyone to yourself.

This mercy is as light as a light breeze because of your patience and sufferance. It is warm with the love with which you teach mercy to those who provoke you to anger and offer kindness to those who scorn you. Therefore, may all those who hear these words raise their eyes and see and know their source. They should consider whether these words signify mercy and humility. They should reflect on whether the words signify present or future things, truth or falsehood. If they find that the words are true, let them hurry to a shelter, that is, to true humility and love of God. For, when justice comes, the soul will then be separated from the body and engulfed by fire and burn both outwardly and inwardly. It will burn, to be sure, but it will not be consumed. For this reason, I, the Queen of mercy, cry out to the inhabitants of the world: may they raise their eyes and behold mercy! I admonish and beseech like a mother, I counsel like a sovereign lady.

When justice comes, it will be impossible to withstand it. Therefore, have a firm faith and be thoughtful, test the truth in your conscience, change your will, and then the one who has shown you words of love will also show the deeds and proof of love!" Then the Son spoke to me, saying: "Above, regarding the bees, I showed you that they receive three benefits from their queen. I tell you now that those crusaders whom I have placed at the borders of Christian lands should be bees like that. But now they are fighting against me, for they do not care about souls and have no compassion on the bodies of those who have been converted from error to the Catholic faith and to me.

They oppress them with hardships and deprive them of their liberties. They do not instruct them in the faith, but deprive them of the sacraments and send them to hell with a greater punishment than if they had stayed in their traditional paganism.

Furthermore, they fight only in order to increase their own pride and augment their greed. Therefore, the time is coming for them when their teeth will be ground, their right hand mutilated, their right foot severed, in order that they may live and know themselves."

God's grievance concerning three men now going around in the world, and about how from the start God established three estates, namely those of the clergy, the defenders, and the laborers; and about the punishment prepared for the thankless and about the glory given to the thankful.

# Chapter 20

The great host of heaven was seen, and God spoke to it, saying: "Although you know and see all things in me, however, because it is my wish, I will state my complaint before you concerning three things. The first is that those lovely beehives, which were built in heaven from all eternity and from which those worthless bees went out, are empty. The second is that the bottomless pit, against which neither rocks nor trees are of any help, stands ever open. Souls descend into it like snow falling from the sky down to earth. Just as the sun dissolves snow into water, so too souls are dissolved of every good by that terrible torment and are renewed unto every punishment. My third complaint is that few people notice the fall of souls or the empty dwellings from which the bad angels have strayed. I am therefore right to complain.

I chose three men from the beginning. By this I am figuratively speaking of the three estates in the world. First, I chose a cleric to proclaim my will in his words and to demonstrate it in his actions. Second, I chose a defender to defend my friends with his own life and to be ready for any undertaking for my sake. Third, I chose a laborer to labor with his hands in order to provide bodily food through his work.

The first man, that is, the clergy, has now become leprous and mute. Anyone who looks to see a fine and virtuous character in him shrinks back at the sight and shudders to approach him because of the leprosy of his pride and greed. When he wants to listen to him, the priest is mute about praising me but a chatterbox in praising himself.

So, how is the path to be opened that leads the way to great joy, if the one who should be leading the way is so weak? And if the one who should be proclaiming it is mute, how will that heavenly joy be heard of? The second man, the defender, trembles at heart and his hands are idle. He trembles at causing scandal in the world and losing his reputation. His hands are idle in that he does not perform any holy works. Instead, everything he does, he does for the world. Who, then, will defend my people if the one who should be their leader is afraid?

The third man is like an ass that lowers its head to the ground and stands with its four feet joined together. Sure, indeed, the people are like an ass that longs for nothing but things of the earth, which neglects the things of heaven and goes in search of perishable goods. They have four feet, since they have little faith and their hope is idle; third, they have no good works and, fourth, they are entirely intent upon sinning. This is why their mouth is always open for gluttony and greed. My friends, how can that endless yawning pit be reduced or the honeycomb be filled by people such as these?"

God's Mother replied: "May you be blessed, my Son! Your grievance is justified. Your friends and I have only one word of excuse for you to save the human race. It is this: 'Have mercy, Jesus Christ, Son of the living God!' This is my cry and the cry of your friends." The Son replied: "Your words are sweet to my ears, their taste delights my mouth, they enter my heart with love. I do have a cleric, a defender, and a peasant. The first pleases me like a bride whom an honest bridegroom yearns and longs for with divine love. His voice will be like the voice of clamorous speech that echoes in the woods. The second will be ready to give his life for me and will not fear the reproach of the world. I shall arm him with the weapons of my Holy Ghost. The third will have so firm a faith that he will say: 'I believe as firmly as if I saw what I believe. I hope for all the things God has promised.' He will have the intention of doing good and growing in virtue and avoiding evil.

In the first man's mouth I shall put three sayings for him to proclaim. His first proclamation will be: 'Let him who has faith put what he believes into practice!' The second: 'Let him who has a firm hope be steadfast in every good work.' The third: 'Let him who loves perfectly and with charity yearn fervently to see the object of his love!' The second man will work like a strong lion, taking careful precautions against treachery and persevering steadfastly. The third man will be as wise as a serpent that stands on its tail and lifts its head to the skies. These three will carry out my will. Others will follow them. Although I speak of three, by them I mean many." Then he spoke to the bride, saying: "Stand firm! Do not be concerned about the world or about its reproaches, for I, who heard every kind of reproach, am your God and your Lord."

The words of the glorious Virgin to her daughter about how Christ was taken down from the cross and about her own bitterness and sweetness at the passion of her Son, and about how the soul is symbolized by a virgin and the love of the world and the love of God by two youths, and about the qualities the soul should have as a virgin.

# Chapter 21

Mary spoke: "You should reflect on five things, my daughter. First, how every limb in my Son's body grew stiff and cold at his death and how the blood that flowed from his wounds as he was suffering dried up and clung to each limb. Second, how his heart was pierced so bitterly and mercilessly that the man speared it until the lance hit a rib, and both parts of the heart were on the lance. Third, reflect on how he was taken down from the cross! The two men who took him down from the cross made use of three stepladders: one reached to his feet, the second just below his armpits and arms, the third to the middle of his body.

The first man got up and held him by the middle. The second, getting up on another ladder, first pulled a nail out of one arm, then moved the ladder and pulled the nail from the other hand. The nails extended through the crossbeam. The man who had been holding up the weight of the body then went down as slowly and carefully as he could, while the other man got up on the stepladder that went to the feet and pulled out the nails from the feet. When he was lowered to the ground, one of them held the body by the head and the other by the feet. I, his mother, held him about the waist. And so the three of us carried him to a rock that I had covered with a clean sheet and in that we wrapped his body. I did not sew the sheet together, because I knew that he would not decay in the grave.

After that came Mary Magdalene and the other holy women. Angels, too, as many as the atoms of the sun, were there, showing their allegiance to their Creator. None can tell what sorrow I had at the time. I was like a woman giving birth who shakes in every limb of her body after delivery. Although she can scarcely breathe due to the pain, still she rejoices inwardly as much as she can because she knows that the child she has given birth to will never return to the same painful ordeal he has just left. In the same way, although no sorrow could compare with my sorrow over the death of my Son, still I rejoiced in my soul because I knew my Son would no longer die but would live forever.

Thus my sorrow was mixed with a measure of joy. I can truly say that there were two hearts in the one grave where my Son was buried. Is it not said: 'Where your treasure is, there is your heart as well'? Likewise, my heart and mind were constantly going to my Son's grave." Then the Mother of God went on to say: "I shall describe this man by way of a metaphor, how he was situated and in what kind of state and what his present situation is like. It is as though a virgin was betrothed to a man and two youths were standing before her. One of them, having been addressed by the virgin, said to her:

'I advise you not to trust the man to whom you are betrothed. He is unbending in his actions, tardy in payment, miserly in giving gifts. Rather, put your trust in me and in the words I speak to you, and I shall show you another man who is not hard but gentle in every way, who gives you what you want right away and gives you plenty of pleasant and delightful gifts.'

The virgin, hearing this and thinking about it to herself, answered: 'Your words are good to hear. You yourself are gentle and attractive to my eyes. I think I will follow your advice.' When she took off her ring in order to give it to the youth, she saw three sayings inscribed on it. The first was: 'When you come to the top of the tree, beware lest you lay hold of a dry branch of the tree to support yourself and fall!' The second saying was: 'Beware lest you take advice from an enemy!'

The third saying was: 'Place not your heart between the teeth of a lion!' When the virgin saw these sayings, she pulled her hand back and held onto the ring, thinking to herself: 'These three sayings I see may perhaps mean that this man who wants to have me as his bride is not to be trusted. It seems to me that his words are empty; he is full of hatred and will kill me.' While she was thinking this, she looked again and noticed another inscription that also had three sayings.

The first saying was: 'Give to the one who gives to you!' The second saying was: 'Give blood for blood!' The third saying was: 'Take not from the owner what belongs to him!' When the virgin saw and heard this, she thought again to herself: 'The first three sayings inform me how I can escape death, the other three how I can obtain life. Therefore, it is right for me to follow the words of life.' Then the virgin prudently summoned to herself the servant of the man to whom she had first been betrothed. When he came, the man who wanted to deceive her withdrew from them.

So it is with the soul of that person who was betrothed to God. The two youths standing before the soul represent the friendship of God and the friendship of the world. The friends of the world have come closer to him up until now. They spoke to him of worldly riches and glory and he almost gave the ring of his love to them and consented to them in every way. But by the aid of my Son's grace he saw an inscription, that is, he heard the words of his mercy and understood three things through them. First, that he should beware lest, the higher he rose and the more he relied on perishable things, the worse would be the fall that threatened him.

Second, he understood that there was nothing in the world but sorrow and care. Third, that his reward from the devil would be evil. Then he saw another inscription, I mean, he heard its consoling messages. The first message was that he should give his possessions to God from whom he had received them all. The second was that he should render the service of his own body to the man who had shed his blood for him. The third was that he should not alienate his soul from the God who had created and redeemed it. Now that he has heard and carefully considered these things, God's servants approach him and he is pleased with them, and the servants of the world draw away from him.

His soul is now like a virgin who has risen fresh from the arms of her bridegroom and who ought to have three things. First, she should have fine clothes so as not to be laughed at by the royal maidservants, should some defect be noticed in her clothes. Second, she should comply with the will of her bridegroom so as not to cause him any dishonor on her account, should anything dishonorable be discovered in her actions. Third, she should be completely clean lest the bridegroom discover in her any stain because of which he might scorn or repudiate her.

Let her also have people to guide her to the bridegroom's suite so as not to lose her way about the precincts or in the elaborate entrance. A guide should have two characteristics: first, the person following him should be able to see him; second, one should be able to hear his directions and where he steps. A person following another who leads the way should have three characteristics. First, he should not be slow and sluggish in following. Second, he should not hide himself from the person leading the way. Third, he should pay close attention and watch the footsteps of his guide and follow him eagerly. Thus, in order that his soul may reach the suite of the bridegroom, it is necessary that it be guided by the kind of guide who can successfully lead it to God his bridegroom."

The glorious Virgin's doctrinal teaching to her daughter about spiritual and temporal wisdom and about which of them one ought to imitate, and about how spiritual wisdom leads a person to everlasting consolation, after a little struggle, while temporal wisdom leads to eternal damnation.

# Chapter 22

Mary spoke: "It is written that 'if you would be wise you should learn wisdom from a wise person.' Accordingly, I give you the figurative example of a man who wanted to learn wisdom and saw two teachers standing before him. He said to them: 'I would really like to learn wisdom, if only I knew where it would lead me and of what use and purpose it is.' One of the teachers answered: 'If you would follow my wisdom, it will lead you up a high mountain along a path that is hard and rocky underfoot, steep and difficult to climb. If you struggle for this wisdom you will gain something that is dark on the outside but shining on the inside. If you hold onto it, you will secure your desire.

Like a circle that spins around, it will draw you to itself more and more, sweetly and ever more sweetly, until in time you are imbued with happiness from every side.' The second teacher said: 'If you follow my wisdom, it will lead you to a lush and beautiful valley with the fruits of every land. The path is soft underfoot and the descent is little trouble. If you persevere in this wisdom, you will gain something that is shiny on the outside, but when you want to use it, it will fly away from you. You will also have something that does not last but ends suddenly. A book, too, once you have read it through to the end, ceases to exist along with the act of reading, and you are left idle.'

When the man heard this, he thought to himself: 'I hear two amazing things. If I climb up the mountain, my feet get weak and my back grows heavy. Then, if I do obtain the thing that is dark on the outside, what good will it do me? If I struggle for something that has no end, when will there be any consolation for me? The other teacher promises something that is radiant on the outside but does not last, a kind of wisdom that will end with the reading of it. What use do I have of things with no stability?' While he was thinking this in his mind, suddenly another man appeared between the two teachers and said: 'Although the mountain is high and difficult to climb, nevertheless there is a bright cloud above the mountain that will give you comfort.

If the promised container that is dark on the outside can somehow be broken, you will get the gold that is concealed within and you will be in happy possession of it forever.' These two teachers are two kinds of wisdom, namely the wisdom of the spirit and the wisdom of the flesh. The spiritual kind involves giving up your self-will for God and aspiring to the things of heaven with your every desire and action.

It cannot be truly called wisdom if your actions do not accord with your words. This kind of wisdom leads to a blessed life. But it involves a rocky approach and a steep climb, inasmuch as resisting your passions seems a hard and rocky way. It involves a steep climb to spurn habitual pleasures and not to love worldly honors. Although it is difficult, yet for the person who reflects on how little time there is and how the world will end and who fixes his mind constantly on God, above the mountain there will appear a cloud, that is, the consolation of the Holy Ghost.

A person worthy of the Holy Ghost's consolation is one who seeks no other consoler but God. How would all the elect have undertaken such hard and arduous tasks, if God's Spirit had not cooperated with their goodwill as with a good instrument? Their good will drew this Spirit to them, and the divine love they had for God invited it, for they struggled with heart and will until they were made strong in works.

They won the consolation of the Spirit and also soon obtained the gold of divine delight and love that not only made them able to bear a great many adversities but also made them rejoice in bearing them as they thought of their reward. Such rejoicing seems dark to the lovers of this world, for they love darkness. But to the lovers of God it is brighter than the sun and shines more than gold, for they break through the darkness of their vices and climb the mountain of patience, contemplating the cloud of that consolation that never ends but begins in the present and spins like a circle until it reaches perfection. Worldly wisdom leads to a valley of misery that seems lush in its plenty, beautiful in reputation, soft in luxury. This kind of wisdom will end swiftly and offers no further benefit beyond what it used to see and hear.

Therefore, my daughter, seek wisdom from the wise one, I mean, from my Son! He is wisdom itself from whom all wisdom comes. He is the circle that never ends. I entreat you as a mother does her child: love the wisdom that is like gold on the inside but contemptible on the outside, that burns inside with love but requires effort on the outside and bears fruit through its works. If you worry about the burden of it all, God's Spirit will be your consoler.

Go and keep on trying like someone who keeps going on until the habit is acquired. Do not turn back until you reach the peak of the mountain! There is nothing so difficult that it does not become easy through steadfast and intelligent perseverance. There is no pursuit so noble at the outset that it does not fall into darkness by not being brought to completion. Advance, then, toward spiritual wisdom! It will lead you to physical toil, to despising the world, to a little pain, and to everlasting consolation. But worldly wisdom is deceitful and conceals a sting. It will lead you to the hoarding of temporary goods and to present prestige but, in the end, to the greatest unhappiness, unless you are wary and take careful precautions."

The glorious Virgin's words explaining her humility to her daughter, and about how humility is likened to a cloak, and about the characteristics of true humility and its wonderful fruits.

# Chapter 23

"Many people wonder why I speak with you. It is, of course, to show my humility. If a member of the body is sick, the heart is not content until it has regained its health, and once its health is restored the heart is all the more gladdened. In the same way, however much a person may sin, if he turns back to me with all his heart and a true purpose of amendment, I am immediately prepared to welcome him when he comes. Nor do I pay attention to how much he may have sinned but to the intention and purpose he has when he returns.

Everyone calls me 'Mother of mercy.' Truly, my daughter, the mercy of my Son has made me merciful and the disclosure of his mercy has made me compassionate. For that reason, that person is miserable who, when she or he is able, does not have recourse to mercy. Come, therefore, my daughter, and hide yourself beneath my cloak! My cloak is contemptible on the outside but very useful on the inside, for three reasons. First, it shelters you from the stormy winds; second, it protects you from the burning cold; third, it defends you against the rain-showers from the sky.

This cloak is my humility. The lovers of the world hold this in contempt and think that imitating it is a silly superstition. What is more contemptible than to be called an idiot and not to get angry or answer in kind? What is more despicable than the giving up of everything and being in every way poor? What seems sorrier to worldly souls than to conceal one's own pain and to think and believe oneself unworthier and lowlier than everyone else? Such was my humility, my daughter. This was my joy, this my one desire. I only thought of how to please my Son. This humility of mine was useful for those who followed me in three ways.

First, it was useful in pestilent and stormy weather, that is, against human taunts and scorn. A powerful and violent storm wind pounds a person from all directions and makes him freeze. In the same way, taunting easily crushes an impatient person who does not reflect on future realities; it drives the soul away from charity. Anyone carefully studying my humility should consider the kinds of things I, the Queen of the universe, had to hear, and so he should seek my praise and not his own.

Let him recall that words are nothing but air and he will soon grow calm. Why are worldly people so unable to put up with verbal taunts, if not because they seek their own praise rather than God's? There is no humility in them, because their eyes are made bleary by sin. Therefore, although the written law says one should not without due cause give one's ear to insulting speech or put up with it, still it is a virtue and a prize to listen patiently to and put up with insults for the sake of God.

Second, my humility is a protection from the burning cold, that is, from carnal friendship. For there is a kind of friendship in which a person is loved for the sake of present commodities, like those who speak in this way: 'Feed me for the present and I will feed you, for it is no concern of mine who feeds you after death! Give me respect and I will respect you, for it does not concern me in the least what kind of future respect there is to come.' This is a cold friendship without the warmth of God, as hard as frozen snow as regards loving and feeling compassion for one's fellow human being in need, and sterile is its reward.

Once a partnership is broken up and the desks are cleared away, the usefulness of that friendship immediately disappears and its profit is lost. Whoever imitates my humility, though, does good to everyone for the sake of God, to enemies and friends alike: to his friends, because they steadily persevere in honoring God; and to his enemies, because they are God's creatures and may become good in the future.

In the third place, the contemplation of my humility is a protection against rain-showers and the impurities coming from the clouds. Where do clouds come from, if not from the moisture and vapors coming from the earth? When they rise to the skies due to heat, they condense in the upper regions and, in this way, three things are produced: rain, hail, and snow. The cloud symbolizes the human body that comes from impurity. The body brings three things with it just as clouds do. The body brings hearing, seeing, and feeling.

Because the body can see, it desires the things it sees. It desires good things and beautiful forms; it desires extensive possessions.

What are all these things if not a sort of rain coming from the clouds, staining the soul with a passion for hoarding, unsettling it with worries, distracting it with useless thoughts and upsetting it over the loss of its hoarded goods? Because the body can hear, it would fain hear of its own glory and of the world's friendship. It listens to whatever is pleasant for the body and harmful to the soul. What do all these things resemble if not swiftly melting snow, making the soul grow cold toward God and blear-eyed as to humility?

Because the body has feeling, it would fain feel its own pleasure and physical rest. What does this resemble if not hail that is frozen from impure waters and that renders the soul unfruitful in the spiritual life, strong as regards worldly pursuits and soft as regards physical comforts? Therefore, if a person wants protection from this cloud, let him run for safety to my humility and imitate it. Through it, he is protected from the passion for seeing and does not desire illicit things; he is protected from the pleasure of hearing and does not listen to anything that goes against the truth; he is protected from the lust of the flesh and does not succumb to illicit impulses.

I assure you: The contemplation of my humility is like a good cloak that warms those wearing it; I mean those who not only wear it in theory but also in practice. A physical cloak does not give any warmth unless it is worn. Likewise, my humility does no good to those who just think about it, unless each one strives to imitate it, each in his own way. Therefore, my daughter, don the cloak of humility with all your strength, since worldly women wear cloaks that are a proud thing on the outside but are of little use on the inside. Avoid such garments altogether, since, if the love of the world does not first become abhorrent to you, if you are not continually thinking of God's mercy toward you and your ingratitude toward him, if you do not always have in mind what he has done and what you do, and the just sentence that awaits you in return, you will not be able to comprehend my humility.

Why did I humble myself so much or why did I merit such favor, if not because I considered and knew myself to be nothing and to have nothing in myself? This is also why I did not seek my own glory but only that of my Donor and Creator. Therefore, daughter, take refuge in the cloak of my humility and think of yourself as a sinner beyond all others! For, even if you see others who are wicked, you do not know what their future will be like tomorrow; you do not even know their intention or their awareness of what they are doing, whether they do it out of weakness or deliberately. This is why you should not put yourself ahead of anyone and why you must not judge anyone in your heart."

The Virgin's exhortation to her daughter, complaining about how few her friends are; and about how Christ speaks to the bride and describes his sacred words as flowers and explains who the people are in whom such words are to bear fruit.

# Chapter 24

Mary was speaking: "Imagine a large army somewhere and a person walking alongside it heavily weighed down, carrying a great load on his back and in his arms. With his eyes full of tears, he might look at the army to see if there should be someone to have compassion on him and relieve his burden. That is the way I felt. From the birth of my Son until his death, my life was full of tribulation. I carried a heavy load on my back and persevered steadfastly in God's work and patiently bore everything that happened to me. I endured carrying a most heavy load in my arms, in the sense that I suffered more sorrow of heart and tribulation than any creature.

My eyes were full of tears when I contemplated the places in my Son's body destined for the nails as well as his future passion, and when I saw all the prophesies I had heard foretold by the prophets being fulfilled in him. And now I look around at everyone who is in the world to see if there happens to be some who might have compassion on me and be mindful of my sorrow, but I find very few who think about my sorrow and tribulation. This is why, my daughter, although I am forgotten and neglected by many people, you must not forget me! Look at my struggles and imitate them as far as you can! Contemplate my sorrow and tears and be sorry that the friends of God are so few. Stand firm! Look, my Son is coming."

He came at once and said: "I who am speaking with you am your God and Lord. My words are like the flowers of a fine tree. Although all the flowers spring up from the tree's one root, not all of them come to fruition. My words are like flowers that spring up from the root of divine charity. Many people take them, but they do not bear fruit in all of them nor reach maturity in them all. Some people take them and keep them for a time but later reject them, for they are ungrateful to my Spirit. Some take and keep them, for they are full of love, and the fruit of devotion and holy conduct is produced in them.

You, therefore, my bride, who are mine by divine right, must have three houses. In the first, there should be the necessary nourishment to enter the body; in the second the clothes that clothe the body on the outside; in the third the tools necessary for use in the house. In the first there should be three things: first, bread; then drink; and third, meats. In the second house there should be three things: first, linen clothing; then woolen; then the kind made by silkworms. In the third house there should also be three things: first tools and vessels to be filled with liquids; second, living instruments, such as horses and asses and the like, by which bodies can be conveyed; and, third, instruments that are moved by living beings."

Christ's advice to the bride about the provisions in the three houses, and about how bread stands for a good will, drink for holy forethought, and meats for divine wisdom, and about how there is no divine wisdom in erudition but only in the heart and in a good life.

# Chapter 25

"I who am speaking with you am the Creator of all things, created by none. There was nothing before me and there can be nothing after me, since I always was and always am. I am the Lord whose power none can withstand and from whom all power and sovereignty come. I speak to you as a man speaks to his wife: My wife, we should have three houses. In one of them there should be bread and drink and meats. But you might ask: What does this bread mean? Do I mean the bread that is on the altar? This is indeed bread, prior to the words "This is my body," but, once the words have been spoken, it is not bread but the body that I took from the Virgin and that was truly crucified on the cross. But here I do not mean that bread. The bread that we should store in our house is a good and sincere will. Physical bread, if it is pure and clean, has two good effects. First, it fortifies and gives strength to all the veins and arteries and muscles. Second, it absorbs any inner impurity, bringing it along for removal as it goes out, and so the person is cleansed. In this way a pure will gives strength.

If a person wishes for nothing but the things of God, works for nothing but the glory of God, desires with every desire to leave the world and to be with God, this intention strengthens him in goodness, increases his love for God, makes the world loathsome to him, fortifies his patience and reinforces his hope of inheriting glory to the extent that he cheerfully embraces everything that happens to him. In the second place, a good will removes every impurity. What is the impurity harmful to the soul if not pride, greed, and lust? However, when the impurity of pride or of some other vice enters the mind, it will leave, provided the person reasons in the following way: 'Pride is meaningless, since it is not the recipient who should be praised for goods given him, but the giver. Greed is meaningless, since all the things of earth will be left behind. Lust is nothing but filth. Therefore I do not desire these things but want to follow the will of my God whose reward will never come to an end, whose good gifts never grow old: Then every temptation to pride or greed will leave him and he will persevere in his good intention of doing good.

The drink we should have in our houses is holy forethought about everything to be done. Physical drink has two good effects. First, it aids good digestion. When a person proposes to do something good and, before doing it, considers to himself and turns carefully over in his mind what glory will come out of it for God, what benefit to his neighbor, what advantage to his soul, and does not want to do it unless he judges there to be some divine usefulness in his work, then that proposed work will turn out well or be, so to speak, well digested. Then, if any indiscretion occurs in the work he is doing, it is quickly detected. If anything is wrong, it is quickly corrected and his work will be upright and rational and edifying for others.

A person who does not show holy forethought in his work and does not seek benefit to souls or the glory of God, even if his work turns out well for a time, nevertheless it will come to nothing in the end. In the second place, drink quenches thirst. What kind of thirst is worse than the sin of base greed and anger? If a person thinks beforehand what usefulness will come of it, how wretchedly it will end, what reward there will be if he makes resistance, then that base thirst is soon quenched through God's grace, zealous love for God and good desires fill him, and joy arises because he has not done what came into his mind. He will examine the occasion and how he can avoid in the future those things by which he was almost tripped up, had he not had forethought, and he will be more careful in the future about avoiding such things. My bride, this is the drink that should be stored in our pantry.

Third, there should also be meats there. These have two effects. First, they taste better in the mouth and are better for the body than just bread alone. Second, they make for tenderer skin and better blood than if there were only bread and drink. Spiritual meat has a like effect. What do these meats symbolize? Divine wisdom, of course. Wisdom tastes very good to a person who has a good will and wants nothing but what God wants, showing holy forethought, doing nothing until he knows it to be for God's glory.

Now, you might ask: 'What is divine wisdom?' For many people are simple and only know one prayer - the Our Father, and not even that correctly. Others are very erudite and have wide knowledge. Is this divine wisdom? By no means. Divine wisdom is not precisely to be found in erudition, but in the heart and a good life. That person is wise who reflects carefully on the path toward death, on how he will die, and on his judgment after death. That person has the meats of wisdom and the taste of a good will and holy forethought, who detaches himself from the vanity and superfluities of the world and contents himself with the bare necessities, and struggles in the love of God according to his abilities.

When a person reflects on his death and on his nakedness at death, when a person examines God's terrible court of judgment, where nothing is hidden and nothing is remitted without a punishment, when he also reflects on the instability and vanity of the world, will he not then rejoice and sweetly savor in his heart the surrender of his will to God together with his abstinence from sins? Is not his body strengthened and his blood improved, that is, is not every weakness of his soul, such as sloth and moral dissolution, driven away and the blood of divine love rejuvenated? This is because he reasons rightly that an eternal good is to be loved rather than a perishable one.

Therefore divine wisdom is not precisely to be found in erudition but in good works, since many are wise in a worldly way and after their own desires but are altogether foolish with regard to God's will and commandments and the disciplining of their body. Such people are not wise but foolish and blind, for they understand perishable things that are useful for the moment, but they despise and forget the things of eternity. Others are foolish with regard to worldly delights and reputation but wise in considering the things that are of God, and they are fervent in his service.

Such people are truly wise, for they savor the precepts and will of God. They have truly been enlightened and keep their eyes open in that they are always considering in what way they may reach true life and light. Others, however, walk in darkness, and it seems to them more delightful to be in darkness than to inquire about the way by which they might come to the light. Therefore, my bride, let us store up these three things in our houses, namely a good will, holy forethought, and divine wisdom. These are the things that give us reason to rejoice. Although I speak my advice to you, by you I mean all my chosen ones in the world, since the righteous soul is my bride, for I am her Creator and Redeemer."

The Virgin's advice to her daughter about life, and Christ's words to the bride about the clothes that should be kept in the second house, and about how these clothes denote the peace of God and the peace of one's neighbor and works of mercy and pure abstinence, and an excellent Explanation of all these things.

# Chapter 26

Mary spoke: "Place the brooch of my Son's passion firmly on yourself, just as St. Lawrence placed it firmly on himself. Each day he used to reflect in his mind as follows: 'My God is my Lord, I am his servant. The Lord Jesus Christ was stripped and mocked. How can it be right for me, his servant, to be clothed in finery? He was scourged and fastened to the wood. It is not right, then, that I, who am his servant, if I really am his servant, should have no pain or tribulation.' When he was stretched out over the coals and liquid fat ran down into the fire and his whole body caught fire, he looked up with his eyes toward heaven and said: 'Blessed are you, Jesus Christ, my God and Creator!

I know I have not lived my days well. I know I have done little for your glory. This is why, seeing that your mercy is great, I ask you to deal with me according to your mercy.' And at this word his soul was separated from his body. Do you see, my daughter? He loved my Son so much and endured such suffering for his glory that he still said he was unworthy of reaching heaven. How then can those people who live by their own desires be worthy? Therefore, keep ever in mind the passion of my Son and of his saints. They did not endure such sufferings for no reason, but in order to give others an example of how to live and to show what a strict payment will be demanded for sins by my Son who does not want there to be the least sin without correction."

Then the Son came and spoke to the bride, saying: "I told you earlier what should be stored in our houses. Among other things, there should be clothing of three kinds: first, clothing made of linen, which is produced in and grows from the earth; second, that made of leather, which comes from animals; third, that made of silk, which comes from silkworms. Linen clothing has two good effects. First, it is soft and gentle against the naked body. Second, it does not lose its color, but the more it is washed, the cleaner it becomes. The second kind of clothing, that is, leather, has two effects.

First, it covers a person's shame; second, it provides warmth against the cold. The third kind of clothing, that is, silken, also has two effects. First, it can be seen to be very beautiful and fine; second, it is very expensive to buy. The linen clothes that are good for the naked parts of the body symbolize peace and concord. A devout soul should wear this with respect to God, so that she can be at peace with God both by not wanting anything other than what God wants or in a different way than he wants, and by not exacerbating him through sins, since there is no peace between God and the soul unless she stops sinning and controls her concupiscence.

She should also be at peace with her neighbor, that is, by not causing him problems, by helping him if he has problems, and by being patient if he sins against her. What is a more unfortunate strain on the soul than always to be longing to sin and never to have enough of it, always to be desiring and never at rest? What stings the soul more sharply than to be angry with her neighbor and to envy his goods? This is why the soul should be at peace with God and with her neighbor, since nothing can be more restful than resting from sin and not being anxious about the world, nothing gentler than rejoicing in the good of one's neighbor and wishing for him what one wishes for oneself.

This linen clothing should be worn over the naked parts of the body, because, more properly and importantly than the other virtues, peace should be lodged closer to the heart, which is where God wants to take his rest. This is the virtue that God instills and keeps instilled in the heart. Like linen, this peace is born in and grows from the earth, since true peace and patience spring up from the consideration of one's own weakness. A man who is of the earth ought to consider his own weakness, namely that he is quick to anger if offended, quick to feel pain if hurt. And if he reflects in this way he will not do unto another what he himself cannot bear, reflecting to himself that: 'Just as I am weak, so too is my neighbor.

Just as I do not want to put up with such things, neither does he.' Next, peace does not lose its color, that is, its stability, but stays increasingly constant, since, considering his neighbor's weakness in himself, he becomes more willing to put up with injuries. If a man's peace gets soiled by impatience in any way, it grows ever cleaner and brighter before God the more frequently and quickly it is washed through penance. He also becomes so much the happier and more prudent in toleration, the more often he gets irritated and then gets washed again, since he rejoices in the hope of the reward that he hopes will come to him on account of his inner peace, and he is all the more careful about not letting himself fall due to impatience.

The second kind of clothing, namely leather, denotes works of mercy. These leather clothes are made from the skins of dead animals. What do these animals symbolize if not my saints, who were as simple as animals? The soul should be covered with their skins, that is, she should imitate and carry out their works of mercy. These have two effects. First, they cover the shame of the sinful soul and cleanse her so as not to appear stained in my sight. Second, they defend the soul against the cold. What is the cold of the soul if not the soul's hardness with respect to my love? Works of mercy are effective against such coldness, wrapping the soul so that she does not perish from the cold. Through these works God visits the soul, and the soul comes ever closer to God.

The third kind of clothing, that made of silk by silkworms, which seems very expensive to buy, denotes the pure habit of abstinence. This is beautiful in the sight of God and the angels and men. It is also expensive to buy, since it seems hard to people to restrain their tongue from idle and excessive talk. It seems hard to restrain the appetite of the flesh from superfluous excess and pleasure. It also seems hard to go against one's own will. But although it may be hard, it is in every way useful and beautiful. This is why, my bride, in whom I mean all the faithful, in our second house we should store up peace toward God and neighbor, works of mercy through compassion on and help for the wretched, and abstinence from concupiscence.

Although the latter is more expensive than the rest, it is also so much more beautiful than the other clothes that no other virtue seems beautiful without it. This abstinence should be produced by silkworms, that is, by the consideration of one's excesses against God, by humility, and by my own example of abstinence, for I became like a worm for the sake of humankind. A person should examine in his spirit how and how often he has sinned against me and in what way he has made amends. Then he will discover by himself that no amount of toil and abstinence on his part can make amends for the number of times he has sinned against me.

He should also ponder my sufferings and those of my saints as well as the reason why I endured such sufferings. Then he will truly understand that, if I demand such a strict repayment from my saints, who have obeyed me, how much more I will demand in vengeance from those who have not obeyed me. A good soul should therefore readily undertake to practice abstinence, recalling that her sins are evil and surround the soul like worms. Thus, from these low worms she will collect precious silk, that is, the pure habit of abstinence in all her limbs. God and all the host of heaven rejoice in this. Eternal joy will be awarded to the person storing this up who would otherwise have had eternal grief, had abstinence not come to his assistance."

Christ's words to the bride about the instruments in the third house, and about how such instruments symbolize good thoughts, disciplined senses, and true confession; there is also given an excellent Explanation of all these things in general and about the locks of these houses.

# Chapter 27

The Son of God spoke to the bride, saying: "I told you earlier that there should be instruments of three kinds in the third house. First, instruments or vessels into which liquids are poured. Second, instruments with which the land outside is prepared, such as hoes and axes and tools for repairing things that get broken. Third, living instruments, such as asses and horses and the like for conveying both the living and the dead. In the first house, where there are liquids, there should be two kinds of instruments or vessels: first those into which sweet and fluid substances are poured, such as water and oil and wine and the like; second, those into which pungent or thick substances are poured, such as mustard and flour and the like. Do you understand what these things signify? The liquids refer to the good and bad thoughts of the soul.

A good thought is like sweet oil and like delicious wine. A bad thought is like bitter mustard that makes the soul bitter and base. Bad thoughts are like the thick liquids that a person sometimes needs. Although they are not much good for nourishing the body, still they are beneficial for the purgation and curing of both body and brain. Although bad thoughts do not fatten and heal the soul like the oil of good thoughts, still they are good for the purgation of the soul, just as mustard is good for the purgation of the brain. If bad thoughts did not sometimes get in the way, human beings would be angels and not human, and they would think they got everything from themselves.

Therefore, in order that a man might understand his weakness, which comes from himself, and the strength that comes from me, it is sometimes necessary that my great mercy allows him to be tempted by bad thoughts. So long as he does not consent to them, they are a purgation for the soul and a protection for his virtues. Although they may be as pungent to take as mustard, still they are very healing for the soul and lead it toward eternal life and toward the kind of health that cannot be gained without some bitterness. Therefore, let the vessels of the soul, where the good thoughts are placed, be carefully prepared and always kept clean, since it is useful that even bad thoughts arise both as a trial and for the sake of gaining greater merit. However, the soul should strive diligently so as not to consent to them or delight in them. Otherwise the sweetness and the development of the soul will be lost and only bitterness will remain.

In the second house there should also be instruments of two kinds: first, outdoor instruments, such as the plow and the hoe, to prepare the ground outside for sowing and to root up brambles; second, instruments useful for both indoor and outdoor purposes, such as axes and the like. The instruments for cultivating the soil symbolize the human senses. These should be used for the benefit of one's neighbor just as the plow is used on the soil. Bad people are like the soil of the earth, for they are always thinking in an earthly fashion. They are barren of compunction for their sins, because they think nothing is a sin. They are cold in their love for God, because they seek nothing but their own will.

They are heavy and sluggish when it comes to doing good, because they are eager for worldly reputation. This is why a good person should cultivate them through his exterior senses, just as a good farmer cultivates the earth with a plow. First, he should cultivate them with his mouth, by saying things to them that are useful for the soul and by instructing them about the path to life; next, by doing the good deeds he can. His neighbor can be formed in this way by his words and motivated to do good. Next, he should cultivate his neighbor by means of the rest of his body in order that he may bear fruit.

He does this through his innocent eyes that do not look on unchaste things, so that his unchaste neighbor may also learn modesty in his whole body. He should cultivate him by means of his ears that do not listen to unsuitable things as well by means of his feet that are quick to do the work of God. I, God, shall give the rain of my grace to the soil thus cultivated by the work of the cultivator, and the laborer shall rejoice over the fruit of the once barren earth as it begins to put forth shoots.

The instruments needed for indoor preparations, such as the ax and similar tools, signify a discerning intention and the holy examination of one's work. Whatever good a person does should not be done for the sake of reputation and human praise but out of love for God and for the sake of an eternal reward. This is why a person should carefully examine his works and with what intention and for what reward he has done them. If he should discover any kind of pride in his works, let him immediately cut it out with the ax of discretion.

In this way, just as he cultivates his neighbor who is, as it were, outside the house, that is, outside the company of my friends due to his bad deeds, so too he may bear fruit for himself on the inside through divine love. Just as the work of a farmer will soon come to naught if he has no instruments with which to repair things that have been broken, so too, unless a person examines his work with discernment, and how it may be lightened if it is too burdensome or how it may be improved if it has failed, he will achieve no results. Accordingly, one should not only work effectively outdoors, one must also consider attentively on the inside how and with what intention one works.

There should be living instruments in the third house to convey the living and the dead, such as horses and asses and other animals. These instruments signify true confession. This conveys both living and dead. What does living denote if not the soul that has been created by my divinity and lives forever? This soul comes closer and closer to God each day through a true confession. Just as an animal becomes a stronger beast of burden and more beautiful to behold the more often and better it is fed, so too confession - the more often it is used and the more carefully it is made as to both lesser and greater sins - conveys the soul increasingly forward and is so pleasing to God that it leads the soul to God's very heart. What are the dead things conveyed by confession, if not the good works that die through mortal sin? Good works dying through mortal sins are dead in the sight of God, for nothing good can please God unless sin is first corrected either through a perfect intention or in deed.

It is not good to combine sweet-smelling and stinking substances in the same vessel. If anyone kills his good works through mortal sins and makes a true confession of his crimes with the intention to improve and to avoid sin in the future, his good works, which earlier were dead, come to life again through confession and the virtue of humility and they gain him merit for eternal salvation. If he dies without making confession, although his good works cannot die or be destroyed but cannot merit eternal life due to mortal sin, still they can merit a lighter punishment for him or contribute to the salvation of others, provided he has done the good works with a holy intention and for the glory of God. However, if he has done the works for the sake of worldly glory and his own benefit, then his works will die when their doer dies, inasmuch as he has received his reward from the world on whose behalf he labored.

Therefore, my bride, by whom I mean all my friends, we should store up in our houses those things that give rise to the spiritual delight God wants to have with a holy soul. In the first house, we should store, first, the bread of a sincere will that wants nothing but what God wants; second, the drink of holy forethought by not doing anything unless it is thought to be for God's glory; third, the meats of divine wisdom by always thinking on the life to come and on how the present should be ordered.

In the second house, let us store up the peace of not sinning against God and the peace of not quarreling with our neighbor; second, works of mercy through which we may be of practical benefit to our neighbor; third, perfect abstinence by which we restrain those things that tend to disturb our peace. In the third house, we should store up wise and good thoughts in order to decorate our home on the inside; second, temperate, well-disciplined senses to be a light for our neighbors on the outside; third, true confession that helps us to revive, should we grow weak.

Though we have the houses, the things stored in them cannot be kept safe without doors, and doors cannot swing without hinges or be locked without locks. This is why, in order that the stored goods be kept safe, the house needs the door of steadfast hope so as not to be broken down by adversity. This hope should have two hinges in order that a person may not despair of achieving glory or of escaping punishment, but always in every adversity have the hope of better things, being confident in the mercy of God. The lock should be divine charity that secures the door against the entrance of the enemy.

What good is it to have a door without a lock, or hope without love? If someone hopes for eternal rewards and in the mercy of God, but does not love and fear God, he has a door without a lock through which his mortal enemy can enter whenever he likes and kill him. But true hope is when a person who hopes also does the good deeds he can. Without these good deeds he cannot attain heaven, that is, if he knew and was able to do them but did not want to.

If anyone realizes that he has committed a transgression or has not done what he could, he should make the good resolution of doing what good he can. As to what he cannot do, let him hope firmly that he will be able to come to God thanks to his good intention and love for God. So, let the door of hope be secured with divine charity in such away that, just as a lock has many catches inside to prevent the enemy from opening it, this charity for God should also entail the concern not to offend God, the loving fear of being separated from him, the fiery zeal to see God loved, and the desire to see him imitated. It should also entail sorrow, for a person is not able to do as much as he would like or knows he is obliged to do, and humility, which makes a person think nothing of all that he accomplishes in comparison to his sins.

Let the lock be made strong by these catches, so that the devil cannot easily open the lock of charity and insert his own love. The key to open and close the lock should be the desire for God alone, along with divine charity and holy works, so that a person does not wish to have anything except God, even if he can get it, and all this because of his great charity. This desire encloses God in the soul and the soul in God, since their wills are one.

The wife and husband alone should have this key, that is, God and the soul, so that, as often as God wants to come in and enjoy good things, namely the virtues of the soul, he may have free access with the key of stable desire; as often again as the soul wants to go into the heart of God, she may do so freely, since she desires nothing but God. This key is kept by the vigilance of the soul and the custody of her humility, by which she ascribes every good she has to God. And this key is kept also by the power and charity of God, lest the soul be overturned by the devil.

Behold, my bride, what love God has for souls! Stand therefore firm and do my will!"

Christ's words to the bride about his unchanging nature and about how his words are accomplished, even if they are not immediately followed by deeds; and about how our will should be wholly entrusted to God's will.

# Chapter 28

The Son spoke to the bride, saying: "Why are you so upset because that man claimed my words were false? Am I worse off because of his disparagement or would I be better off because of his praise? I am, of course, unchangeable and can become neither greater nor less, and I have no need of praise. A person who praises me does gain a benefit from his praise of me, not for me but for himself. I am truth, and falsehood never proceeds or can proceed from my lips, since everything I have said through the prophets or other friends of mine, whether in spirit or in body, is accomplished as I intended it at the time.

My words were not false if I said one thing at one time, another at another time, first something more explicit, then something more obscure. The Explanation is that, in order to prove the reliability of my faith as well as the zeal of my friends, I revealed much that could be understood in different ways, both well and badly, by good and bad people according to the different effects of my Spirit, thus giving them the possibility of carrying out different good acts in their different circumstances.

Just as I assumed a human nature into one person in my divine nature, so too I have also spoken at times through my human nature as being subject to my divine nature, but at other times through my divine nature as the Creator of my human nature, as is clear from my gospel. And in this way, although ignorant people or detractors might see divergent meanings in them, still they are true words in agreement with truth. It was also not unreasonable for me to have handed down some things in an obscure manner, since it was right that my plan should in some way be hidden from the wicked, and at the same time that all good people should eagerly hope for my grace and obtain the reward for their hope. Otherwise, if it had been implied that my plan would come about at a specific point in time, then everyone would have given up both their hopes and their charity due to the great length of time.

I also promised a number of things that, however, did not occur because of the ingratitude of the people then living. Had they left off their evildoing, I would certainly have given them what I had promised. This is why you ought not be upset over claims that my words are lies. For what seems to be humanly impossible is possible for me. My friends are also surprised that the words are not followed up by deeds. But this, again, is not unreasonable.

Was not Moses sent to Pharaoh? Yet signs did not immediately follow. Why? Because, if the signs and portents had immediately followed, neither the hardheartedness of Pharaoh nor the power of God would have been manifested nor would the miracles have been clearly shown. Pharaoh would still have been condemned for his own wickedness, even if Moses had not come, although his hardheartedness would not have been so manifest. This is also what is happening now. So, be brave! The plow, though drawn by oxen, is still steered by the will of the plowman. Likewise, although you may hear and know my words, they do not turn out or get accomplished according to your will, but according to mine. For I know the lay of the land and how it should be cultivated. But you should entrust all your will to me and say: 'May your will be done!' "

John the Baptist admonishes the bride through a parable in which God is symbolized by a magpie, the soul by its chicks, the body by its nest, worldly pleasures by wild animals, pride by birds of prey, worldly mirth by a snare.

# Chapter 29

John the Baptist spoke to the bride, saying: "The Lord Jesus has called you out of darkness into light, from impurity into perfect purity, from a narrow into a broad place. Who is able to explain these gifts or how could you thank him as much as you should for them? Just do all that you can! There is a kind of bird called a magpie. She loves her chicks, because the eggs from which the chicks came were once in her womb. This bird makes a nest for herself out of old and used things for three purposes.

First, as a resting place; second, as a shelter from rain and heavy drought; third, in order to feed her young when they are hatched from the eggs. The bird hatches her young by lovingly settling herself on top of the eggs. When the chicks are born, the mother entices them to fly in three ways. First, by the distribution of food; second, by her solicitous voice; third, by the example of her own flying. Since they love their mother, the chicks, once they have got used to their mother's food, first travel little by little beyond the nest with their mother leading the way. Then they go further away as their strength allows, until they become accomplished in the use and skill of flight.

This bird stands for God, who exists eternally and never changes. From the womb of his divinity all rational souls proceed. A nest is prepared for each soul out of used things, inasmuch as the soul is joined to a body of earth through which God nourishes it with the food of good affections, defends it from the birds of evil thoughts, and gives it respite from the rain of bad actions. Each soul is joined to the body in order that it may rule the body and nowise be ruled by it and so that it may spur the body to struggle and provide for it intelligently. Thus, like a good mother, God teaches the soul to advance toward better things, and teaches it to leave its confinement for broader spaces. First, he feeds it by giving it intelligence and reason according to each one's capacity, and by pointing out to the mind what it should choose and what it should avoid.

As the magpie first leads its chicks beyond the nest, so too the human person first learns to think thoughts of heaven, and also to think how confined and base the nest of the body is, how bright the heavens and how delightful eternal things are. God also leads the soul out with his voice when he calls: 'He who follows me will have life; he who loves me will not die.' This voice leads toward heaven. Anyone who does not hear it is either deaf or ungrateful for his mother's love. Third, God leads the soul out through his own flying, that is, through the example of his human nature. This glorious human nature had, as it were, two wings. Its first wing was that there was only purity and no defilement in it; its second wing was that he did all things well. Upon these two wings God's human nature flew through the world. For this reason, the soul should follow them as far as it can, and if it cannot do so in deeds, let it at least try to do so in intention.

When the young chick is flying, it has to beware of three dangers. The first is wild animals. It must not land next to them on the ground, because the chick is not as strong as they are. Second, it must beware of birds of prey, since the chick does not yet fly as swiftly as those birds do, which is why it is safer to stay in hiding. Third, it should take care not to be lured by a baited snare. The wild animals that I mentioned are worldly pleasures and appetites. The young chick should beware of them, for they seem good to know, fine to own, beautiful to behold. But when you think you have got hold of them, they quickly go away. When you think they give you pleasure, they bite you without mercy.

In the second place, the chick should beware of birds of prey. These represent pride and ambition. These are the birds that always want to rise higher and higher and to be ahead of the other birds and hate all those behind them. The chick should beware of them and should want to remain in humble hiding, so that it does not grow proud of the grace it has received or despise those that are behind it and have less grace, and does not think itself better than others. Third, the chick should beware of being lured by a baited snare. This represents worldly mirth. It may seem good to have laughter on one's lips and pleasant sensations in one's body, but there is a barb in these things. Immoderate laughter leads to immoderate mirth, and the pleasure of the body leads to inconstancy of mind, which gives rise to sadness, either at death or earlier, along with distress. You should therefore hurry, my daughter, to leave your nest through the desire for heaven! Beware of the beasts of desire and the birds of pride! Beware of the bait of empty mirth!"

Then the Mother spoke to the bride and said: "Beware of the bird that is daubed with pitch, for anyone who touches it gets stained. This represents worldly ambition, unstable as the air, repulsive in its way of seeking favor and keeping bad company. Care nothing for honors, do not bother about favors, pay no attention to praise or reproach! From these things come inconstancy of soul and the lessening of love for God. Be steadfast! God, who has begun to bring you out of the nest, will keep nourishing you until death. After death, however, you will hunger no more. He will also protect you from sorrow and defend you in life, and after death you will have nothing to fear."

The Mother's entreaty to her Son for his bride and for another holy person, and about how the Mother's entreaty is received by Christ, and about certainty regarding the truth or falsity of a person's holiness in this life.

# Chapter 30

Mary spoke to her Son saying: "My Son, grant your new bride the gift that your most worthy body may take root in her heart, so that she herself may be changed into you and be filled with your delight!" Then she said: "This holy man, when he was living in time, was as steadfast in the holy faith as a mountain unbroken by adversity, undistracted by pleasure. He was as flexible toward your will as the moving air, wherever the force of your Spirit led him. He was as ardent in your love as fire, warming those grown cold and overtaking the wicked. Now his soul is with you in glory, but the vessel he used is buried and lies in a more humble place than is fitting. Therefore, my Son, raise his body up to a higher station, do it honor, for it honored you in its own small way, raise it up, for it raised you up on high as much as it could by means of its toil!"

The Son answered: "Blessed are you, who overlook nothing in the affairs of your friends. You see, Mother, it is no use for good food to be given to wolves. It is not right to bury in mud the sapphire that keeps all the members healthy and strengthens the weak. It is no use to light a candle for the blind. This man was indeed steadfast in faith and fervent in charity, just as he was ready to do my will with the greatest of continence. Therefore, he tastes to me like good food prepared through patience and tribulation, sweet and good in the goodness of his will and affections, even better in his manly struggles to improve, excellent and most sweet in his praiseworthy way of finishing his works. Therefore it is not right for such food to be lifted up before wolves, whose greed is never sated, whose lust for pleasure flees from the herbs of virtue and thirsts for rotten meat, whose shrewd speech is harmful to everyone.

He resembled the sapphire of a ring through the brightness of his life and reputation, proving himself to be a bridegroom of his church, a friend of his Lord, a preserver of the holy faith and a scorner of the world. Therefore, dear Mother, it is not right for such a lover of virtue and so pure a bridegroom to be touched by impure creatures, or for so humble a friend to be handled by lovers of the world. In the third place, by his fulfillment of my commandments and by the teaching of a good life, he was like a lamp on a lampstand. Through this teaching, he strengthened those who were standing, lest they fall. Through this teaching he raised up those who were falling down. Through it he also offered inspiration to those who would come after him to seek me.

They are unworthy to see this light, blinded as they are by their own love. They are unable to perceive this light, for their eyes are sick with pride. People with scabby hands cannot touch this light. This light is hateful to the greedy and to those who love their own will. This is why, before he can be raised up to a higher station, justice requires those who are unclean to be purified and those who are blind to be enlightened.

However, regarding that man whom the people of the earth are calling a saint, three things show that he was not holy. The first is that he did not imitate the life of the saints before he died; second, that he was not joyfully ready to suffer martyrdom for God's sake; third, that he did not have an ardent and discerning charity like the saints. Three things make someone appear holy to the crowd. The first is the lie of a deceiving and ingratiating man; the second is the easy credulity of the foolish; the third is the cupidity and lukewarmness of prelates and examiners. Whether he is in hell or in purgatory is not given you to know until the time comes for telling it."

# Book 3

Warnings and instructions to the bishop about how to eat and dress and pray, and about how he should behave before meals, at meals, and after meals, and likewise about his sleep and how he should carry out the office of bishop always and everywhere.

# Chapter 1

"Jesus Christ, God and man, who came to earth in order to take on a human nature and save souls through his blood, who disclosed the true way to heaven and opened its gates, he himself has sent me to all of you. Hear, daughter, you to whom it has been given to hear spiritual truths. If this bishop proposes to walk the narrow path taken by few and to be one of those few, let him first lay aside the burden that besets him and weighs him down - I mean his worldly desires - by using the world only for needs consistent with the modest sustenance of a bishop. This is what that good man Matthew did when he was called by God.

Leaving behind the heavy burden of the world, he found a light burden. In the second place, the bishop should be girded for the journey, to use the words of scripture. Tobias was ready for his journey when he found the angel standing there girded. What does it mean to say that the angel was girded? It means that every bishop should be girded with the belt of justice and divine charity, ready to walk the same path as he who said: 'I am the good shepherd and I lay down my life for my sheep.' He should be ready to speak the truth in his words, ready to perform justice in his actions both regarding himself and regarding others, not neglecting justice due to threats and taunts or false friendships or empty fears. To each bishop thus girded shall Tobias, that is, the righteous, come and they shall follow on his path.

In the third place, he should eat bread and water before he undertakes his journey, just as we read about Elijah, who, aroused from sleep, found bread and water at his head. What is this bread given to the prophet if not the material and spiritual goods bestowed upon him? For material bread was given to him in the desert as a lesson. Although God could have sustained the prophet without material food, he wanted material bread to be prepared for him so that people might understand it to be God's wish that they make use of God's good gifts in temperate fashion for the solace of the body. Moreover, an infusion of the Spirit inspired the prophet when he went on for forty days in the strength of that food. For, if no interior unction of grace had been inspired in his mind, he would certainly have given up during the toil of those forty days, for in himself he was weak but in God he had the strength to complete such a journey.

Therefore, inasmuch as man lives by God's every word, we urge the bishop to take the morsel of bread, that is, to love God above all things. He will find this morsel at his head, in the sense that his own reason tells him that God is to be loved above all things and before all things, both because of creation and redemption and also because of his enduring patience and goodness. We bid him also to drink a little water, that is, to think inwardly on the bitterness of Christ's passion. Who is worthy enough to be able to meditate on the agony of Christ's human nature, which he was suffering at the moment when he prayed for the chalice of the passion to be taken from him and when drops of his blood were flowing to the ground? The bishop should drink this water together with the bread of charity and he will be strengthened for journeying along the path of Jesus Christ.

Once the bishop has set out on the path to salvation, if he wants to make further progress, it is useful for him to give thanks to God with all his heart from the very first hour of the day, considering his own actions carefully and asking God for help to carry out his will.

Then, when he is getting dressed, he should pray in this manner: 'Ashes must with ashes be, dust with dust. Yet, since I am bishop by the providence of God, I am putting these clothes made from the dust of the earth on you, my body, not for the sake of beauty or ostentation but as a covering, so that your nakedness might not be seen. Nor do I care whether your clothing is better or worse, but only that the bishop's habit should be acknowledged out of reverence for God, and that through his habit the bishop's authority may be recognized for the correction and instruction of others. And so, kind God, I beg you to give me steadfastness of mind so that I do not take pride in my precious ashes and dust nor foolishly glory in the colors of mere dust. Grant me fortitude so that, just as a bishop's garb is more distinguished and respected than that of others due to his divine authority, the garb of my soul may be acceptable before God, lest I be thrust down all the deeper for having held authority in an undistinguished and unworthy manner or lest I be ignominiously stripped for having foolishly worn my venerable garb to my own damnation.'

After that he should read or sing the hours. The higher the rank a person rises to, the more glory he or she should render to God. However, a pure heart pleases God just as much in silence as in singing, provided a person is occupied with other righteous and useful tasks. After Mass has been said, the bishop should fulfill his episcopal duties, taking diligent care not to give more attention to material things than to spiritual. When he comes to the dinner table, this should be his thought: 'O Lord Jesus Christ, you command that the corruptible body be sustained with material food, help me to give my body what it needs in such a way that the flesh does not grow shamelessly insolent against the soul due to superfluous eating nor sluggish in your service out of imprudent abstinence.

Inspire in me a suitable moderation so that when this man of earth nourishes himself with things of the earth, the Lord of the earth may not be provoked to anger by his creature of earth.' While at table, the bishop is allowed to have the kind of moderate refreshment and conversation in which foolish vanity is avoided and no word is uttered or heard that may offer the hearers an occasion of sin. Rather, it should all be proper and salutary.

If bread and wine are missing from the material table, everything loses its taste; in the same way, if good doctrine and exhortation are missing from the episcopal and spiritual table, everything set on it seems tasteless to the soul. And so, in order to avoid any occasion of frivolity, something should be read or recited at table that can be of profit to those seated there. When the meal is ended and the thanksgiving blessing has been prayed to God, the bishop should plan what he has to do or read books that can lead him on toward spiritual perfection. After dinner, though, he may entertain himself with the companions of his household. However, just as a mother giving milk to her baby anoints her nipples with ashes or some other bitter substance until she weans the baby from milk and accustoms it to solid foods, so too the bishop should bring his companions closer to God through the kind of conversation by which they may come to fear and love God, becoming in this way not only their father through the divine authority in him but also their mother through the spiritual formation he gives them.

If he is consciously aware that anyone in his household is in the state of mortal sin and has not repented despite admonishments, then he should separate himself from him. If he retains him out of convenience and temporal consolation, he will have no immunity from the other's sin. When he goes to bed, he should carefully examine the deeds and impressions of the day that has gone, thinking the following thoughts: 'O God, Creator of my body and soul, look on me in your mercy.

Grant me your grace, so that I do not grow lukewarm in your service by oversleeping nor grow weak in your service due to disturbed sleep, but grant me for your glory that measure of sleep that you have prescribed for us in order to give the body rest. Give me fortitude so that my enemy, the devil, may not disturb me nor drag me away from your goodness.' When he gets up out of bed, he should wash away in confession any lapses that the flesh may have suffered, so that the sleep of the following night might not begin with the sins of the previous."

The Virgin's words to her daughter about the opportune solution to the difficulties meeting the bishop on the narrow path, and about how patience is symbolized by clothing and the Ten Commandments by ten fingers, and the longing for eternity and the distaste for worldliness by two feet, and about three enemies to the bishop along his way.

# Chapter 2

Again the Mother of God speaks: "Tell the bishop that, if he sets out on this path, he will meet with three difficulties. The first difficulty is that it is a narrow path; the second, that there are sharp thorns on it; the third, that it is a rocky and uneven path. I will give you three pieces of advice in this regard. The first is that the bishop should wear rugged and tightly knit clothes in preparation for the narrow path. The second is that he should hold his ten fingers in front of his eyes and look through them as through bars so as not to be scratched by the thorns.

The third is that he should step cautiously and test each and every step he takes to see if his foot gets a firm hold when he sets it down, and he should not hastily set down both feet at the same time without first assuring himself of the condition of the path. This narrow path symbolizes nothing other than the malice of wicked people toward the righteous, the kind of people who deride righteous deeds and pervert the paths and upright warnings of the righteous, who give little weight to anything having to do with humility and piety. In order to confront such people the bishop should clothe himself in the garment of steadfast patience, since patience makes burdens pleasant and joyfully accepts the insults it receives.

The thorns symbolize nothing other than the hardships of the world. In order to confront them, the ten fingers of God's commandments and counsels should be held up so that, when the thorn of hardship and poverty scratches him, he may recall the sufferings and poverty of Christ. When the thorn of anger and envy scratches him, he should recall the love of God that we are commanded to keep. True love does not insist on getting what is its own, but opens itself up wholly to the glory of God and the benefit of one's neighbor.

That the bishop ought to step cautiously means that he should everywhere have an attitude of intelligent caution. For a good person should have two feet, so to speak. One foot is a longing for eternity. The other is a distaste for the world. His longing for eternity should be circumspect, in the sense that he must not long for eternal things for himself alone as though he were worthy of them; rather, he should place all his longing and desire as well as his reward in the hands of God. His distaste for the world should be cautious and full of fear, in the sense that this distaste must not be the result of his hardships in the world or impatience with life nor should it be for the sake of living a quieter life or being released from carrying out work beneficial to others. Rather, it should only be the result of his abhorrence of sin and his longing for eternity.

Once these three difficulties have been overcome, I would warn the bishop about three enemies on his path. You see, the first enemy tries to whistle in the bishop's ears so as to block his hearing. The second stands in front of him in order to scratch out his eyes. The third enemy is at his feet, shouting loudly and holding a noose in order to ensnare his feet when he lifts them off the ground. The first are those people or those impulses that try to draw the bishop away from the right path, saying: 'Why do you take so much work on yourself and why are you making your way on so narrow a path? Go off instead to the verdant path where so many people are walking. What does it matter to you how this person or those people behave? Why do you bother to offend or censure those people who could honor and appreciate you? If they do not offend you and those close to you, what do you care how they live or whether they are offending God? If you yourself are a good man, why do you bother to be judging others? Better to exchange gifts and services! Make use of human friendships in order to win praise and a good reputation during your lifetime.'

The second enemy wants to blind you like the Philistines did Samson. This enemy is worldly beauty and possessions, sumptuous clothing, the various trappings of pomp, human privileges and favors. When such things are presented to you and please the eyes, reason is blinded, love for God's commandments grows lukewarm, sin is carried out freely and, once committed, is taken lightly. Therefore, when the bishop has a moderate supply of necessary goods, he should be content. For all too many people nowadays find it more pleasant to stand around with Samson at the millstone of desire rather than to love the church with a praiseworthy disposition for pastoral ministry.

The third enemy shouts loudly and carries a noose and says: 'Why are you walking with such caution and with your head bowed down? Why do you humble yourself so much, you who should be and could be honored by many people? Be a priest so as to sit among those of the first rank! Be a bishop so as to be honored by the many! Advance to higher ranks in order to obtain better service and enjoy greater relaxation! Store up a treasure with which you can help yourself as well as others and be comforted by others in return and happy wherever you are!'

When the heart becomes inclined to such feelings and suggestions, the mind soon steps toward earthly appetites, lifting as it were the foot of base desire, with which it gets so entangled in the trap of worldly care that it can scarcely rise up to the consideration of its own wretchedness or to that of the rewards and punishments of eternity. Nor is this surprising, since scripture says that whoever aspires to the office of bishop desires a noble task for the honor of God. Now, however, there are many who want the honors but shirk the task in which is found the eternal salvation of the soul. This is why this bishop should stay in the position that he holds and not seek a higher one, until it pleases God to give him another."

A complete Explanation to the bishop from the Virgin about how he should exercise his episcopal office in order to give glory to God, and about the double reward for having held the rank of bishop in a true way and about the double disgrace for having held it in a false way, and about how Jesus Christ and all the saints welcome a true and up right bishop.

# Chapter 3

The Mother of God was speaking: "I wish to explain to the bishop what he should do for God and what will give glory to God. Every bishop must hold his miter carefully in his arms. He must not sell it for money nor give it up to others for the sake of worldly friendship nor lose it through negligence and lukewarmness. The bishop's miter signifies nothing other than the bishop's rank and power to ordain priests, to prepare the chrism, to correct those who go astray, and to encourage the negligent by his example. To hold his miter carefully in his arms means that he should reflect carefully on how and why he received his episcopal power, how he wields it, and what its effects and purpose are.

If the bishop would examine how he received his power, he should first examine whether he desired the episcopate for his own sake or for God's. If it was for his own sake, then his desire was no doubt carnal; if it was for God's sake, that is, in order to give glory to God, then his desire was meritorious and spiritual.

If the bishop would consider for what purpose he has received the episcopate, then surely it was in order that he might become a father to the poor and a consoler and intercessor for souls, because the bishop's goods are intended for the good of souls. If his means are consumed inefficaciously and wasted in a prodigal manner, then those souls will cry out for revenge on the unjust steward. I will tell you the reward that will come from having held the rank of bishop. It will be a double reward, as Paul says, both corporal and spiritual.

It will be corporal, because he is God's vicar on earth and is therefore accorded divine honor by men as away of honoring God. In heaven it will be corporal and spiritual because of the glorification of body and soul, because the servant will be there with his Lord, due both to the way he lived as a bishop on earth and to his humble example by which he incited others to the glory of heaven along with himself. Everyone who has the rank and garb of a bishop but flees the episcopal way of life will merit a double disgrace.

That the bishop's power is not to be sold means that the bishop should not knowingly commit simony or exercise his office for the sake of money or human favor or promote men whom he knows to be of bad character because people petition him to do so. That the miter should not be given up to others on account of human friendship means that the bishop should not disguise the sins of the negligent or let those whom he can and should correct go unpunished, or pass over the sins of his friends in silence due to worldly friendship or take the sins of his subordinates on his own back, for the bishop is God's sentinel.

That the bishop should not lose his miter through negligence means that the bishop should not delegate to others what he should and can do more profitably himself, that he should not, for the sake of his own physical ease, transfer to others what he himself is more perfectly able to carry out, since the bishop's duty is not to rest but to work. Nor should the bishop be ignorant of the life and conduct of those to whom he delegates his tasks. Instead he should know and review how they observe justice and whether they conduct themselves prudently and without cupidity in their assignments. I want you to know, too, that the bishop, in his role as shepherd, ought to carry a bouquet of flowers under his arms in order to entice sheep both far and near to run gladly after its scent.

This bouquet of flowers signifies the bishop's pious preaching. The two arms from which the bouquet of divine preaching hangs are two kinds of works necessary to a bishop, namely, public good works and hidden good works. Thus, the nearby sheep in his diocese, seeing the bishop's charity in his works and hearing it in his words, will give glory to God through the bishop. Likewise, the faraway sheep, hearing of the bishop's reputation, will want to follow him. This is the sweetest bouquet: not to be ashamed of God's truth and humility, to preach good doctrine and to practice as one preaches, to be humble when praised and devout in humiliation. When the bishop has traveled to the end of this path and reaches the gate, he must have a gift in his hands to present to the high king. Accordingly, may he have in his hands a vessel precious to him, an empty one, to offer to the high king.

The empty vessel to be offered is his own heart. He must struggle night and day in order for it to be empty of all lusts and the desire for fleeting praise. When such a bishop is led into the kingdom of glory, Jesus Christ, true God and man, will come out to meet him together with the whole host of saints. Then he will hear the angels saying: 'Our God, our joy and every good! This bishop was pure in body, manly in his conduct. It is befitting that we should present him to you, for he longed for our company everyday. Satisfy his longing and magnify our joy at his coming!' Then, too, other saints will say: 'O God, our joy is both from you and in you and we need nothing else.

Yet, our joy is heightened by the joy of the soul of this bishop who longed for you while he was still able to long. The sweet flowers of his lips increased our numbers. The flowers of his works consoled those dwelling far and near. Therefore, let him rejoice with us, and rejoice yourself over him for whom you longed so much when you died for him.' Finally the King of glory shall say to him: 'Friend, you have come to present to me the vessel of your heart emptied of your selfish will. Therefore, I will fill you with my delight and glory. My happiness will be yours and your glory in me will never cease.' "

The Mother's words to her daughter about the covetousness of bad bishops; she explains in a long parable that many persons through their good intentions attain the spiritual rank that intemperate bishops reject despite having been called to it in a physical sense.

# Chapter 4

The Mother of God speaks to the Son's bride saying: "You are crying because God loves people so much but people love God so little. So it is. Where, indeed, is that ruler or bishop who does not covet his office in order to obtain worldly honors and wealth but, rather, desires it in order to help the poor with his own hands? Since rulers and bishops do not want to come to the wedding feast prepared for everyone in heaven, the poor and weak will come instead, as I will show you by way of an example.

In a certain city lived a wise, handsome, and wealthy bishop who was praised for his wisdom and handsome looks, but did not, as he ought to, return thanks to God who had given him that very wisdom. He was praised and honored for his wealth, too, and he handed out numerous gifts with a view to worldly favor. He longed for even greater possessions so as to be able to give more gifts and win greater honor. This bishop had a learned priest in his diocese who thought to himself as follows: 'This bishop,' he said, 'loves God less than he should. His whole life tends toward worldliness.

Therefore, if it is pleasing to God, I would like to have his episcopate in order to give glory to God. I do not desire it for worldly reasons, seeing that worldly honor is but empty air, nor for the sake of wealth, which is as heavy as the heaviest of burdens, nor for the sake of physical rest and comfort, since I only need a reasonable amount of rest so as to keep my body fit for God's service. No, I desire it for the sake of God alone. And, although I am unworthy of any honor, still, in order to win more souls for God and to benefit more people by my word and example and to support more people through church revenues, I would gladly take on the burdensome task of being bishop.

God knows that I would rather die a painful death or put up with bitter hardships than to have the rank of bishop. I am as susceptible to suffering as the next man, but, still, he who aspires to the office of bishop desires a noble task. For this reason, I readily desire the honorable title of bishop along with a bishop's burden, although I do so in the same way as I desire death. I desire the honor as a means to saving more souls. I desire the burden for my own salvation and in order to show my love for God and souls. I desire the office for the sole purpose of being able to distribute the goods of the church to the poor more generously, to instruct souls more outspokenly, to instruct those in error more boldly, to mortify my flesh more completely, to exercise self-control more assiduously as an example to others.'

This canon prudently reproved his bishop in private. However, the bishop took it badly and embarrassed the priest in public, imprudently boasting of his own competence and moderation in everything. The canon, however, saddened over the bishop's improprieties, bore the insults with patience. But the bishop ridiculed the charity and patience of the canon and spoke against him so much that the canon was given the blame and thought to be a lying fool, while the bishop was seen as being just and circumspect.

At length, as time went by, both the bishop and the canon passed away and were called to God's judgment. In his sight and in the presence of the angels, a golden throne appeared with the miter and insignia of a bishop next to it. A large number of demons were following the canon, desirous of finding some fatal fault in him. As to the bishop, they felt as sure about having him as a whale does of the calves that she keeps alive in her belly amid the waves. There were many indictments leveled against the bishop; why and with what intention he undertook the office of bishop, why he grew proud about the goods intended for souls, the way he directed the souls entrusted to him, in what way he had responded to the grace God had given him.

When the bishop could make no just reply to the charges, the judge replied: 'Put excrement on the bishop's head instead of a miter and pitch on his hands instead of gloves, mud on his feet instead of sandals. Instead of a bishop's shirt and linen garment put the rags of a whore on him. Let him have disgrace instead of honor. Instead of a train of servants, let him have a raging mob of demons.' Then the judge added: 'Put a crown as radiant as the sun on the canon's head, gilded gloves on his hands, place shoes on his feet. Let him don the clothes of a bishop with every honor.'

Dressed in his episcopal garb, surrounded by the heavenly host, he was presented to the judge as an honored bishop. The bishop, however, went off like a thief with a rope about his neck. At the sight of him the judge averted his merciful eyes as did all his saints with him.

That is the way in which many persons through their good intentions and in a spiritual sense attain the rank of honor scorned by those who were called to it in a physical sense. All these things took place instantaneously before God, although, for your sake, they were acted out in words, for a thousand years are as a single hour before God. It happens every day that, inasmuch as bishops and rulers do not want to have the office to which they were called, God chooses for himself poor priests and parish clerks who, living according to their own better conscience, would be glad to be of benefit to souls for the glory of God if they could, and they do what they can. For this reason, they will take the places prepared for the bishops.

God is like a man who hangs a golden crown outside the door of his house and cries out to passersby: 'Anyone of any social standing can earn this crown! He who is most nobly clothed in virtue will obtain it.' Know that if bishops and rulers are wise in worldly wisdom, God is wiser than they in a spiritual sense, for he raises up the humble and does not give his approval to the proud. Know, too, that this canon who was praised did not have to groom his horse when he went off to preach or carry out his duties, nor did he have to light the fire when he was about to eat.

No, he had the servants and the means he needed to live in a reasonable fashion. He had money, too, although not for his own greedy use, for not even if he had had all the wealth in the world would he have given a single shilling to become bishop. But not for all the world would he have refused to become bishop, if that was God's will. He gave his will to God, ready to be honored for the honor of God and ready to be cast down out of love and fear of God."

Ambrose's words to the bride about the prayer of good persons for the people; rulers of the world and the church are compared to helmsmen, while pride and the rest of the vices are compared to storms, and the passage into truth is compared to a haven; also, about the bride's spiritual calling.

# Chapter 5

"It is written that the friends of God once cried out asking God to rend the heavens and come down to free his people of Israel. In these days, too, God's friends cry out saying: 'Kindest God, we see innumerable people perishing in perilous storms, for their helmsmen are greedy and are always desirous of putting to land in those countries where they think they will get a greater profit. They lead the people toward places where there is a tremendous hurling of the waves, while the people themselves do not know any safe haven. So this countless people is therefore in awful peril and very few of them ever reach their proper haven. We beg you, King of all glory, graciously light up the haven so that your people may escape their danger, not having to obey the wicked helmsmen but being led to the haven by your blessed light.'

By these helmsmen I mean all those who wield either material or spiritual power in the world. Many of them love their own will so much that they do not bother themselves about the needs of the souls under them or about the fierce storms of the world, since they are of their own free will caught up in the storms of pride, greed, and impurity. The wretched populace imitates their deeds, thinking that they are on a straight course. In this way the rulers bring themselves and their subjects to perdition by following their every selfish desire. By the haven I mean the passageway to truth.

For many people this passageway has grown so dark that when someone describes for them how to get to the haven of their celestial fatherland by way of the sacred gospel of Christ, then they call him a liar and instead follow the ways of those who wallow in each and every sin, rather than trusting in the words of those who preach the gospel truth.

By the light requested by the friends of God I mean a divine revelation made in the world in order that God's love might be renewed in human hearts and his justice not be forgotten or neglected. Therefore, because of his mercy and the prayers of his friends, it has pleased God to call you in the Holy Ghost in order that you may spiritually see, hear, and understand so that you may reveal to others that which you hear in the Spirit according to the will of God."

Ambrose's words to the bride offering an allegory about a man, his wife and his housemaid, and about how this adulterer symbolizes a wicked bishop while his wife symbolizes the church and his housemaid the love of this world, and about the harsh sentence on those more attached to the world than to the church.

# Chapter 6

"I am Bishop Ambrose. I am appearing to you and speaking with you in allegory because your heart is unable to receive a spiritual message without some physical comparison. Once there was a man whose lawfully wedded wife was charming and prudent. However, he liked the housemaid better than his wife. This had three consequences. The first is that the words and gestures of the housemaid delighted him more than those of his wife. The second is that he dressed the housemaid up in fine clothes without caring that his wife was dressed in common rags. The third is that he was accustomed to spending nine hours with the housemaid and only the tenth hour with his wife. He spent the first hour at the housemaid's side, enjoying himself in gazing on her beauty. He spent the second hour sleeping in her arms. He spent the third hour cheerfully doing manual labor for the sake of the housemaid's comfort.

He spent the fourth hour taking physical rest with her after his physical toil. He spent the fifth hour restless in his mind and worrying about how to provide for her. He spent the sixth hour at rest with her, seeing now that she fully approved of what he had done for her. At the seventh hour the fire of carnal lust entered into him. He spent the eighth hour satisfying his willful lust with her. In the ninth hour he neglected certain tasks that he nevertheless would have liked to carry out. He spent the tenth hour doing some tasks that he did not feel like doing. And only during this hour did he stay with his wife. One of his wife's relatives came to the adulterer and reproached him strongly, saying: 'Turn the affection of your mind toward your lawfully wedded wife. Love her and clothe her as is fitting, and spend nine hours with her and only the tenth hour with the housemaid. If not, beware, because you will die a horrible and sudden death.'

By this adulterer I refer to someone who holds the office of bishop for the sake of providing for the church but, in spite of that, leads an adulterous life. He is joined to the holy church in spiritual union so that she should be his dearest bride, but he withdraws his affections from her and loves the servile world much more than his noble lady and bride. Thus, he does three things. First, he rejoices more in the fraudulent adulation of the world than in an obedient disposition toward the holy church. Second, he loves worldly decorations, but cares little about the lack of material or spiritual decoration of the church. Third, he spends nine hours on the world and only one of ten on the holy church. Accordingly, he spends the first hour in good cheer, gazing on the beauty of the world with delight.

He spends the second hour sleeping sweetly in the arms of the world, that is, amid its high fortifications and the vigilance of its armies, happily confident in possessing physical security because of these things. He spends the third hour cheerfully doing manual labor for the sake of worldly advantage in order that he might obtain the physical enjoyment of the world. He spends the fourth hour gladly taking physical rest after his physical toil, now that he has sufficient means. He spends the fifth hour restless in his mind in different ways, worrying about how he can appear to be wise in worldly matters.

During the sixth hour he experiences an agreeable restfulness of mind, seeing that worldly people everywhere approve of what he has done. In the seventh hour he hears and sees worldly pleasures and readily opens his lust for them. This causes a fire to burn impatiently and intolerably in his heart. In the eighth hour he carries out in act what before had merely been his burning desire. During the ninth hour he negligently omits certain tasks he had wanted to do for worldly motives, so as not to offend those for whom he has a mere natural affection. In the tenth hour he cheerlessly performs a few good deeds, afraid that he might be held in scorn and gain a bad reputation or receive a harsh sentence if for some reason he wholly neglected to do them.

He is accustomed to spending only this tenth hour with the holy church, doing what good he does not out of love but out of fear. He is, of course, afraid of the punishment of the fires of hell. If he could live forever in physical comfort and with plenty of worldly possessions, he would not care about losing the happiness of heaven.

Therefore, I swear by that God who has no beginning and who lives without end, and affirm with certainty that, unless he returns to the holy church soon and spends nine hours with her and only the tenth with the housemaid, that is, with the world - not by loving it but by possessing the wealth and honor of his episcopal office with reluctance, and arranging everything in humility and reasonably for the glory of God - then the spiritual wound in his soul will be as grave as - to make a physical comparison - the wound of a man struck so horribly on his head that his whole body is destroyed down to the soles of his feet, with his veins and muscles bursting, and his bones getting shattered and the marrow flowing out terribly in all directions.

As harshly tormented as seems the heart in a body struck so violently in its head and the parts of the body closest to the head that the very soles of its feet are in pain, although they are at the farthest remove, equally harshly tortured will that miserable soul closest to the blast of divine justice appear when in its conscience it sees itself being unbearably wounded on every side."

The Virgin's words to the bride comparing a world-loving bishop to a bellows full of air or to a snail lying in filth, and about the sentence dealt out to such a bishop who is the very opposite of Bishop Ambrose.

# Chapter 7

"Scripture says: 'He who loves his own soul in this world will lose it.' Now this bishop loved his own soul with his every desire, and there were no spiritual inclinations in his heart. He might well be compared to an air-filled bellows next to a forge. Just as there is air left in the bellows once the coals are spent and the red-hot metal is flowing, so too, although this man has given his nature everything it craves, uselessly wasting his time, the same inclinations are still left in him like the air in the bellows. His will is inclined to worldly pride and lust. Because of these vices, he offers an excuse and a sinful example to people with hardened hearts who, wasted in sins, are flushed down to hell.

This was not the attitude of the good bishop Ambrose. His heart was filled with God's will. He ate and slept with temperance. He expelled the desire for sin and spent his time usefully and morally, He might well be called a bellows of virtue. He healed the wounds of sin with words of truth. He inflamed those who had grown cold in God's love by the example of his own good works. He cooled those who were burning with sinful desire by the purity of his life. In this way, he helped many people to avoid entering the death of hell, for divine love remained in him as long as he lived.

This bishop, on the other hand, is like a snail that reclines in its native filth and drags its head on the ground. In similar fashion, this man reclines and has his delight in sinful abomination, letting his mind be drawn to worldliness rather than to the thought of eternity, I would have him reflect on three things: First, the way in which he has exercised his priestly ministry. Second, the meaning of that gospel phrase: 'They have sheep's clothing but are ravenous wolves on the inside.' Third, the reason why his heart burns for temporal things but is cold toward the Creator of all things."

The Virgin's words to the bride about her own perfection and excellence, and about the inordinate desires of modern teachers and about their false reply to the question asked them by the glorious Virgin.

# Chapter 8

The Mother speaks: "I am the woman who has always been in God's love. I was from my infancy entirely in the company of the Holy Ghost. If you want an example, think of how a nut grows. Its outer shell grows and widens, while its inner kernel also widens and grows, so that the nut is always full and there is no room in it for anything extraneous. In the same manner, too, I was full of the Holy Ghost from my infancy. As my body grew and I became older, the Holy Ghost filled me up with such abundance that he left no room in me for any sin to enter. Thus, I am she who never committed either venial or mortal sin. I so burned with love for God that I liked nothing but to carry out God's will, for the fire of divine love blazed in my heart.

God, blessed above all forever, who created me through his power and filled me with the power of his Holy Ghost, had an ardent love for me. In the fervor of his love he sent me his messenger and gave me to understand his decision that I should become the Mother of God. When I understood what the will of God was, then, through the fire of love that I bore in my heart towards God, a word of true obedience at once left my lips, and I gave this answer to the messenger, saying: 'May it be done to me according to your word.' At that very instant the Word was made flesh in me. The Son of God became my son.

The two of us had one son who is both God and man, as I am both Mother and Virgin. As my Son Jesus Christ, true God and wisest of men, lay in my womb, I received such great wisdom through him that I not only could understand the learning of scholars, I could even discern whether their hearts were true, whether their words proceeded from love for God or from mere scholarly cleverness. Therefore, you who hear my words should tell that scholar that I have three questions for him: First, whether he desires to win the favor and friendship of the bishop in a corporal sense more than he desires to present the bishop's soul to God in a spiritual sense.

Second, whether his mind rejoices more in owning a great many florins or in owning none. Third, which of the following two choices he prefers: to be called a scholar and take his seat among the honored ranks for the sake of worldly glory or to be called a simple brother and take his seat among the lowly.

Let him ponder these three questions carefully. If his love for the bishop is corporal rather than spiritual, then it follows that he tells him things the bishop likes to hear rather than prohibiting him from doing all the sinful things he likes to do.

If he is happier about owning a lot of florins rather than none, then he loves riches more than poverty. He then gives the impression of advising his friends to acquire as much as they can rather than to give up gladly what they can do without. If, for the sake of worldly honor, he prefers his scholarly reputation and sitting in a seat of honor, then he loves pride more than humility and, therefore, appears to God more like an ass than a scholar. In that case he is chewing on empty straw, which is the same as scholarly knowledge without charity, and he does not have the fine wheat of charity, since divine charity can never grow strong in a proud heart."

After the scholar had excused himself with the excuse that he had a greater desire to present the soul of the bishop to God in a spiritual sense and that he would rather have no florins and, in the third place, that he did not care about the title of scholar, the Mother said again: "I am she who heard the truth from the lips of Gabriel and believed without doubting. This is why Truth took for himself flesh and blood from my body and remained in me.

I gave birth to that same Truth who was in himself both God and man. Inasmuch as Truth, who is the Son of God, willed to come to me and to dwell in me and to be born from me, I know fully well whether people have truth on their lips or not. I asked the scholar three questions. I would have approved of his answer, had there been truth in his words. However, there was no truth in them. Therefore, I will give him three warnings. The first is that there are some things that he loves and desires in this world but which he will not obtain at all. The second is that he will soon lose the thing that he has worldly joy in possessing. The third is that the little ones will enter heaven. The great ones will be left standing outside, because the gate is narrow."

The Virgin's words to the bride about how those who can see and hear and so forth escape dangers by virtue of the sunlight and so forth, but dangers befall those who are blind and deaf and so forth.

# Chapter 9

The Mother speaks: "Although a blind man does not see it, the sun still shines clearly in splendor and beauty even while he is falling down the precipice. Travelers who have clear eyesight are thankful for the clear light that helps them avoid the dangers of their journey. Although the deaf man does not hear it, still the violent avalanche comes crashing down upon him terribly from on high, but he who can hear it coming escapes to safer places. Although a dead man cannot taste it while he lies rotting among worms, a good drink still tastes sweet. A living man can sip it and be glad at heart, feeling himself emboldened for any brave deed."

The Virgin speaks to her daughter, offering assurance about the words spoken to her; and about the danger and approaching collapse of the church, and about how, unfortunately, the overseers of the church largely devote themselves nowadays to a life of debauchery and greed and waste the goods of the church in their pride, and about how the wrath of God is aroused against such as these.

# Chapter 10

The Mother speaks: "Do not be afraid of the things you are about to see, thinking they come from the evil spirit. Just as light and heat accompany the approach of the sun but do not follow after a dark shadow, in the same way two things accompany the coming of the Holy Ghost into the heart: ardent love for God and the complete illumination of holy faith. You are experiencing both these things now. These two do not follow upon the devil whom we can liken to a dark shadow. Therefore, send my messenger to the man I mentioned to you. Although I know his heart and how he will respond, and the imminent end of his life, you should still send him the following message.

I would have him know that the foundation of the holy church is so heavily deteriorated on its right side that its vaulted roof has many cracks at the top, and that this causes the stones to fall so dangerously that many of those who pass beneath it lose their lives. Several of the columns that should stand erect are almost level with the ground and even the floor is so full of holes that blind people entering there have dangerous falls. Sometimes it even happens that, along with the blind, people with good eyesight have bad falls because of the dangerous holes in the floor. As a result of all this, the Church of God is dangerously tottering, and if she is tottering so badly, what awaits next if not her collapse?

I assure you that if she is not helped by repairs, her collapse will be so great that it will be heard throughout all of Christendom.

I am the Virgin whose womb the Son of God condescended to enter, without the least contagious trace of carnal lust. The Son of God was born from my closed womb, giving me solace but no pain at all. I stood next to the cross when he victoriously overcame hell through his patient suffering and opened up heaven with the blood of his heart. I was also on the mountain when God's Son, who is also my Son, ascended into heaven. I have the clearest knowledge of the whole of the catholic faith that he preached and taught to everyone who wanted to enter heaven.

I am that same woman, and now I stand over the world in continuous prayer, like a rainbow above the clouds that appears to bend toward the earth and to touch it with both ends. I see myself as a rainbow bending down toward both the good and the wicked inhabitants of the earth by means of my prayers. I bend down toward good people in order that they may be steadfast in the commandments of the holy church, and I bend down toward bad people in order that they may not add to their wickedness and grow worse. I would have the man I mentioned to you know that foul and horrible clouds are rising up in one direction against the shining rainbow. By these clouds I mean those who lead a life of carnal debauchery, those who are as insatiable as the ocean chasm in their greed for money, and those who arrogantly and irrationally spend their means as wastefully as a torrential stream pours out its water.

Many of the overseers of the church are guilty of these three things, and their horrendous sins rise up to heaven in the sight of God, as opposed to my prayers as foul clouds are opposed to the shining rainbow. The men who should be placating the wrath of God along with me are instead provoking God's wrath against themselves. Such men should not be promoted in the church of God. I, the Queen of Heaven, will come to the aid of anyone who, knowing his own insufficiency, is willing to take on the task of making the church's foundation stable and restoring the blessed vineyard that God founded with his blood, and, together with the angels, I will root up loose roots and throw any trees without fruit into the fire and plant fruitful shoots in their stead. By this vineyard I mean the church of God in which the two virtues of humility and divine charity must be restored."

## Addendum

The Son of God speaks of the papal nuncios: "You have entered the company of rulers and are going to rise still higher. Worthy is he who works to exalt humility, for pride has already risen far too high. He who has charity for souls will also receive the highest honors, for ambition and simony are now prevalent among many people. Happy is he who tries to root out the vices of the world as far as he can, for vice is now grown abnormally strong.

It is also most efficacious to have patience and to pray for it, for, in the days of many who are yet living, the sun will be rent in two, the stars thrown into confusion, wisdom will be made foolish, the humble on earth will groan and the bold will prevail. The understanding and interpretation of these things belongs to the wise men who know how to make the rough smooth and to provide for the future." The foregoing revelation was for the cardinal of Albano who was then a prior.

The bride's trusting words to Christ, and about how John the Baptist offers assurance to the bride that Christ speaks to her, and about the happiness of the good rich man, and about how an imprudent bishop is compared to a monkey because of his foolishness and wicked life.

# Chapter 11

The bride spoke to Christ humbly in her prayer saying: "O my Lord Jesus Christ, so firmly do I believe in you that even if the serpent lay in front of my mouth, he should not enter unless you permitted it for my own good."

John the Baptist answered: "The one who appears to you is the very Son of God by nature, whom I myself heard the Father bearing witness to when He said: 'This is my Son.' From him proceeds the Holy Ghost who appeared above him in the form of a dove as I was baptizing him. He is the son of the Virgin according to the flesh. I touched his body with my very own hands.

Believe firmly in him and enter into his life. He is the one who has shown the true path by which poor and rich can enter heaven. But you might ask, what should the inner disposition of a rich person be if he is to enter heaven, given that God himself has said that it is easier for a camel to go through the eye of a needle than for a rich man to enter heaven? To this I answer you: A rich man who is disposed in such away that he is afraid to have any ill-gotten goods, who is concerned not to spend his means wastefully or contrary to God's will, who holds his possessions and honors with reluctance and would willingly be separated from them, who is disturbed by the loss of souls and the dishonor done to God, and, although he is compelled by the plans of God to own the world to some extent, is vigilant concerning the love of God in his every intention, this is the kind of rich man who bears fruit and is happy and dear to God.

This bishop, however, is not rich in that way. He is like a monkey with four distinguishing features. The first is a costume that has been made for him that hangs down and hides his torso but leaves his private parts completely exposed. The second is that he touches stinking things with his fingers and puts them to his mouth. The third is that he has a humanlike face, although the rest of his coloring and appearance is that of a brute animal. The fourth is that, although he has both hands and feet, he tramples on the dirt with his hands and fingers. This foolish bishop is like a monkey, curious about the vanity of the world, too deformed for any action deserving praise.

He wears a costume, that is, his episcopal ordination, which is honorable and precious in the sight of God, but his naked private parts are exposed, since the frivolity of his character and his carnal lust are displayed to others and bring ruin to souls. This goes against what that noble knight says about how a man's more shameful parts are given the greater honor, meaning by this that the animal urges of priests should be hidden by good works, so that the weak may not be scandalized by their example.

A monkey also touches and sniffs at stinking things. What do you do with a finger if not point to something you have seen, just as when I beheld God in his human nature and pointed to him with my finger, saying, 'Behold the Lamb of God'? What are the fingers of a bishop if not his praiseworthy virtues through which he should point to God's justice and charity?
But, instead, this man's actions point to the fact that he is nobleborn and rich, worldly wise and lavish with his money. What is this if not to touch stinking rot with his fingers? Is glorying in the flesh or in a great household anything else than glorying in puffed-up sacks? A monkey has a human face but looks like a brute animal in other respects.

This man, too, possesses a soul stamped with the seal of God but deformed through his own greed. In the fourth place, just as a monkey touches and tramples on the dirt with his feet and hands, so too this man covets the things of the earth in his appetites and actions, turning his face away from heaven and lowering it to the earth like an oblivious animal. Does a man like that lessen the wrath of God? No, indeed, he rather provokes God's justice against himself."

## Addendum

The following revelation was made about a cardinal legate during the jubilee year. The Son of God speaks: "O proud debater, where is your pomp, where is your equestrian finery now? You did not want to understand while you were being held in honor. This is why you have now fallen into dishonor. Answer my question then, although I know all things, while this new bride is listening." And immediately it was as if an amazingly misshapen person appeared, trembling and naked. The judge said to him: "O soul, you taught that the world and its riches should be spurned. Why then did you follow after them?"

The soul answered: "Because their filthy stench smelled better to me than your sweet fragrance." And as soon as he said this, a daemon poured a vessel of sulphur and poison into the soul. Again the judge spoke: "O soul, you were set up to be a shining lamp for the people, why did you not shine forth by word and example?" The soul answered: "Because your love had been wiped out from my heart. I roamed about like one who had lost his memory and like a vagabond, looking at things in the present and not thinking of the future." When the soul had said this, it was deprived of the light of its eyes. The daemon who was seen to be present said: "O judge, this soul is mine. What shall I do?" The judge said: "Purge and scrutinize it as in a winepress until the council is held at which the allegations of both friends and enemies will be discussed."

The bride speaks to Christ, pouring forth prayers for the bishop mentioned above, and about the answers that Christ, the Virgin, and Saint Agnes gave to the bride.

# Chapter 12

"O my Lord, I know that no one can enter heaven unless drawn by the Father. Therefore, most kind Father, draw this ailing bishop to you. And you, Son of God, help him if he makes the effort. And you, Holy Ghost, fill this cold and empty bishop with your love."

God the Father answers: "If he who draws something is strong but the thing drawn too heavy, his effort is soon wasted and comes to naught. Besides, if the one drawn is bound up, then he can neither help himself nor the person drawing him. If the one drawn is unclean, then he is loathsome to the one who draws him and comes in contact with him. The attitude of this bishop is like that of a man standing at a fork in the road trying to decide which way to take."

The bride answered: "O my Lord, is it not written that no one stands still in this life but advances either toward that which is better or toward that which is worse?"

The Father answered: "Both things could be said here, since this man stands, as it were, between two roads, one of joy and one of sorrow. The horror of eternal punishment upsets him, and he would prefer to obtain the joy of heaven. However, he thinks the road that leads to joy is too rough to tread. But he certainly does start walking when he goes after objects he fervently desires."

Blessed Agnes speaks: "The attitude of this bishop is like that of a man standing between two roads. He knew one of them was narrow at first but delightful in the end; he knew the other was pleasant for a while but ended in a bottomless pit of anguish. As the traveler thought about these two roads, he was more attracted to the road that was pleasant at the start. However, since he was afraid of the bottomless pit, the following thought occurred to him. He said: 'There must be a shortcut on the pleasurable road. If I can find it, I can go safely on for a long time and, when I get to the pit at the end, provided I find the shortcut, nothing will harm me.' So he walked safely on along the road, but when he came to the pit, he took a terrible fall right into it, since he had not found the shortcut he was expecting.

Nowadays there are a lot of people with the same idea as this man. They think to themselves as follows. They say: 'It is burdensome to take the narrow path. It is hard to give up our self-will and our privileges.' In this way they place a false and dangerous confidence in themselves. They say: 'The road is long. God's mercy is great. The world is pleasant and was made for pleasure. There is nothing to prevent me from making use of the world for a time as I wish, since I mean to follow God at the end of my life. After all, there is a kind of shortcut from the path of worldliness and that is contrition and confession. If I can manage that, I will be saved.'

The thought that a person can keep desiring sin until the end of life and then go to confession is a very weak hope, because they fall into the pit sooner than they expect. At times, too, they undergo such pain and so sudden a death that they are completely incapable of repenting in a fruitful manner. It serves them right. For, when they had the opportunity, they did not want to have any foresight for coming evils, but they arbitrarily set the time for God's mercy by their definition. They made no resolution not to sin so long as they could continue enjoying sin. In the same way, too, this bishop was standing between these two roads. Now, however, he is drawing nearer to the more pleasurable path of the flesh. Let us say that he has three pages set before him to read.

He reads the first page over and over with pleasure, but he reads the second page only once in a while and with no pleasure at all, while he reads the third only rarely and does so with sadness. The first page represents the wealth and privileges he delights in. The second is the fear of Gehenna and the future judgment that is upsetting to him. The third is the love and filial fear of God that he rarely peruses. If he would take to heart all that God has done for him or how much he has lavished on him, the love of God would never be extinguished in his heart."

The bride answered: "O Lady, pray for him." And then Blessed Agnes said: "What is the role of justice if not to judge and what is the role of mercy if not to encourage?" The Mother of God speaks: "The bishop will be told this: Although God can do all things, a man's personal cooperation is still necessary if he is to avoid sin and gain the love of God. There are three means to avoid sin and three means to obtain love. The three by which sin is avoided are: Perfect penance; second, the intention of not wanting to commit the sin again; third, to improve one's life according to the advice of those whom one knows to have given up the world. The three means that work together to obtain love are humility, mercy, and the effort to love. Whoever prays even one Our Father for the sake of gaining God's love will soon experience the effect of God's love drawing close to him.

About the other bishop, about whom I was speaking with you before, I must say in conclusion that the pits appear too wide for him to leap over, the walls too high to climb, the bars too strong to break. I stand here waiting for him, but he turns his head away toward the activities of three groups of people that he enjoys watching. The first group is a dancing chorus. He tells them: 'I like listening to you, wait up for me!' The second group is engaged in speculation. He tells them: 'I want to see what you see - I enjoy that sort of thing a lot.' The third group is enjoying itself and relaxing in quiet, and he wants to enjoy privilege and quiet with them.

To be a dancing chorus in the world means nothing other than to pass from one fleeting delight to another, from one desire for honor to another. To stand and speculate means nothing other than to take the soul away from divine contemplation and to think about the collecting and distributing of temporal goods. To relax in quiet means nothing other than to relax in body. While watching these three crowds, the bishop has climbed up a high mountain but he does not care about the words I have sent to him, nor does he care about the terms of my message that are that, if he keeps his promise, I will also keep mine."

The bride answers: "O gentle Mother, do not abandon him!" The Mother says to her: "I will not abandon him until dust returns to dust. More than that, if he breaks through the bars, I will come to meet him like a handmaid and will help him like a mother." And the Mother added: "Are you, daughter, thinking of what would have been the reward of that canon of Orléans, if his bishop had been converted? I will answer you: You see how the earth bears grass and flowers of different species and kinds. In the same way, too, if every person had uprightly remained in their own station from the beginning of the world, then everyone would have received a great reward, inasmuch as everyone who is in God would have gone from one delight to the next, not because of any sense of tediousness in their pleasure, but because their delight grows continuously more delightful and their indescribable joy is continuously made new."

## Explanation

This was the bishop of Växjö. When he was in Rome, he was greatly worried about his return. It was heard in the spirit: "Tell the bishop that his delay is more useful than his haste. Those in his company who have gone ahead of him will follow after him. This is why when he returns to his country, he will find my words to be true." This is the way it all turned out. On his return, he found the king in capture and the whole kingdom in an uproar. Those in his company who had gone ahead of him were impeded for a long time on the way and arrived after him. "Know also that the lady who is in the company of the bishop will return safely but will not die in her home country." And so it turned out, for she went a second time to Rome, and she died and was buried there.

## About the same bishop

When Lady Bridget came down from Monte Gargano to the city of Mafredonia in the kingdom of Sicily, the same bishop was in her company. On the mountain it happened that he had such a bad fall from his horse that he broke two ribs. When the lady was about to go out to St. Nicholas of Bari in the morning, he called her to him saying: "Lady, it is so hard for me to stay here without you. It is also a burden that you should be delayed on my account, especially given the raids going on. I ask you," he said, "for the love of Jesus Christ, to pray to God for me and touch your hand to my aching side!

I hope that my pain will be lessened through the touch of your hands." With tears in her eyes, she answered in compassion: "Sir, I regard myself as nothing, for I am a great sinner in God's sight. But let us all pray to God and he will answer your faith." They prayed, and when she stood up, she touched the bishop's side, saying: "May the Lord Jesus Christ heal you." Immediately the pain went away. And the bishop got up and followed her all the way back to Rome.

The Mother's words to the daughter in which the words and deeds of Christ are explained and wonderfully described as a treasure, his divine nature as a castle, sin as bars, virtues as walls, and the beauty of the world and the delight of friendship as two moats, and about how a bishop ought to behave with respect to the care of souls.

# Chapter 13

The Mother speaks to the bride of her Son, saying: "This bishop prays to me in his love, and, for that reason, he should do what pleases me most. There is a treasure I know of that whoever possesses it will never be poor, whoever sees it will never know distress and death, and whoever desires it will joyfully receive whatever he wishes. The treasure is locked up in a strong castle behind four bars. Outside the castle stand high walls large and thick. Beyond the walls are two wide and deep moats. And so I ask the bishop to jump over the two moats in a single leap, and climb the walls in a single bound, and break through the bars with a single blow and then to bring me the thing that pleases me most.

I will now tell you the meaning of all this. When you use the word 'treasure,' you refer to something that is rarely used or moved about. In this case, the treasure is my dearest Son's precious words and the deeds he did during and before his passion, along with the miracles he worked when the Word was made flesh in my body and that he continues to do when, at God's word, the bread on the altar each day is changed into that same flesh. All these things are a precious treasure that has become so neglected and forgotten that there are very few people who recall it or draw any profit from it. However, the glorious body of God my Son is to be found in a fortified castle, that is, in the strength of his divine nature. Just as a castle is a defense against enemies, so the strength of my Son's divine nature is a defense for the body of his human nature, so that no enemy can harm him. The four bars are four sins that exclude many people from the participation in and the goodness of the strength of the body of Christ.

The first sin is pride along with the desire for worldly honors. The second is the desire for worldly possessions. The third is the repulsive lust to fill the body up intemperately, and its utterly repulsive satisfaction. The fourth is anger and envy and the neglect of one's own salvation. Many people have an excessive love for these four sins and possess them habitually, which takes them very far away from God. They see and receive the body of God, but their soul is as far from God as thieves are when the way to what they want to steal is blocked by strong bars.

This is why I said that he should break through the bars with a single blow. The blow symbolizes the zeal for souls with which a bishop ought to break sinners through deeds of justice done for the love of God in order that, once the bars of vice have been broken, the sinner can reach the precious treasure. Although he cannot strike down every sinner, he should do what he can and ought to do, especially for those who are under his care, sparing neither great nor small, neighbor nor relation, friend nor enemy. This is what Saint Thomas of England did. He suffered much for the sake of justice and met with a harsh death in the end, all because he did not refrain from striking bodies with the justice of the church in order that souls might endure less suffering.

This bishop should imitate Thomas's way of life, so that everyone who hears him may understand that he hates his own sins as well as other people's sins. The blow of divine zeal will then be heard throughout the heavens before God and his angels. Many people will then be converted and mend their ways, saying: 'He does not hate us but our sins.' They will say: 'Let us repent and we will become friends both of God and of the bishop.'

The three walls surrounding the castle are three virtues. The first virtue is giving up carnal pleasures and doing the will of God. The second is to prefer to suffer reproaches and curses for the sake of truth and justice rather than to obtain worldly honors and possessions by dissimulating the truth. The third is to be ready to forgo both life and possessions for the sake of any Christian's salvation. However, look at what people do nowadays. They think these walls are too high to climb over at all.

Accordingly, neither their hearts nor their souls approach the glorious body with any constancy, for they are far from God. This is why I told my friend to climb the walls in a single bound. A bound is what you call it when the feet are held far apart in order for the body to move quickly. A spiritual bound is similar, for, when the body is on earth and the love of the heart is in heaven, then you climb the three walls quickly. When a man meditates on the things of heaven, he is ready to give up his own will, to suffer rejection and persecution for the sake of justice, and to die willingly for the glory of God.

The two moats outside the wall represent the beauty of the world and the company and enjoyment of worldly friends. There are many people who are content to take it easy in these moats and never care whether they will see God in heaven. The moats are wide and deep, wide because the wills of such people are far from God, and deep because they confine many souls in the depths of hell. This is why the moats should be jumped over in a single leap. A spiritual leap is nothing other than to detach one's whole heart from things that are empty and to take the leap from earthly goods to the kingdom of heaven.

I have shown how to break through the bars and leap over the walls. Now I will show how this bishop should bring me the most precious thing there ever was. God's divine nature was and is from eternity without beginning, since neither beginning nor end can be found in it. But his human nature was in my body and took flesh and blood from me. Therefore, it is the most precious thing there ever was or is. Accordingly, when the righteous soul receives God's body with love and when his body fills the soul, the most precious thing there ever was is there. Although the divine nature exists in three Persons without beginning and without end in itself, when God sent his Son to me with his divine nature and the Holy Ghost, he received his blessed body from me. I will now show the bishop how this precious thing is to be brought before the Lord. Wherever God's friend comes across a sinner whose words show little love for God but much love for the world, that soul is empty with respect to God.

Accordingly, God's friend should show his love for God by his sorrow that a soul redeemed by the Creator's blood should be an enemy to God. He should show compassion for the wretched soul by using two voices, as it were, toward it: one in which he entreats God to have pity on the soul, and another in which he shows the soul its own danger. If he can reconcile and unite the two of them, God and the soul, then the hands of his love will offer to God the most precious gift, for the thing most dear to me is when the body of God, which was once inside me, and the human soul, which God has created, come together in friendship.

This is hardly surprising. You know well that I was present when my Son, the great knight, went forth from Jerusalem to fight a battle so brutal and difficult that all the sinews of his arms were strained. His back was bloodied and livid, his feet pierced by nails, his eyes and ears full of blood. His head sank when he gave up his spirit. His heart was sundered by the point of a spear. He won souls by suffering greatly. He who now dwells in glory stretches out his arms to men, but few there are who bring him his bride. Consequently, a friend of God should spare neither life nor possessions in helping others while he helps himself by bringing them to my Son.

Tell this bishop that, given that he prays for my friendship, I will bind myself to him with a bond of faith. The body of God, which was once within me, will welcome his soul with great love. As the Father was in me together with the Son who had my body and soul in himself, and as the Holy Ghost who is in the Father and the Son was everywhere with me and had my Son within him, so too my servant will be bound to the same Spirit. If he loves the sufferings of God and has his precious body in his heart, then he will have God's human nature that has the divine nature within and without it. God will be in him and he in God, just as God is in me and I in him. As my servant and I share one God, we will also share one bond of love and one Holy Ghost who is one God with the Father and the Son.

One thing more: If this bishop keeps his promise with me, I will help him during his lifetime. At the end of his life I will help and assist him and bring his soul before God, saying: 'My God, this man served you and obeyed me, and therefore I present his soul to you!' O daughter, what is a person thinking of when he despises his own soul? Would God the Father in his unfathomable divinity have let his own innocent Son suffer so much in his human nature, if he had not an honest desire and longing for souls and for the eternal glory that he has prepared for them?"

This revelation was about the bishop of Linköping who was afterwards made archbishop. There is more on the same bishop in Book 6,Chapter 22, beginning: "This prelate."

## Addendum about the same man

"The bishop for whom you weep came to an easy purgatory. Know for certain that, although in the world he had many who blocked his way, they have now received their sentence, and he shall be glorified due to his faith and purity."

The Mother's words to her daughter, using a marvelous comparison to describe a certain bishop, likening the bishop to a butterfly, his humility and pride to its two wings, the three facades covering up the vices of the bishop to the insect's three colors, his deeds to the thickness of its coloring, his double will to the butterfly's two feelers, his greed to its mouth, his puny love to its puny body.

# Chapter 14

The Mother speaks to the bride of her Son, saying: "You are a vessel that the owner fills and the teacher empties. However, it is one and the same person who fills and empties you. A person who can pour wine and milk and water together into a vessel would be called an expert teacher if he could separate each of these liquids blended together and restore each to its own proper nature. This is what I, the Mother and Teacher of all mankind, have done and am doing to you. A year and a half ago, all sorts of matters were spoken to you, and now they all seem to be blended together in your soul, and it would seem disgusting if they were all poured out together, since their purpose would not be understood. This is why I gradually distinguish them as I see fit.

Do you recall that I sent you to a certain bishop whom I called my servant? Let us compare him to a butterfly with two wide wings spattered in the colors white, red, and blue. When you touch it, the pigment sticks to your fingers like ashes. This insect has a puny body but a big mouth, two feelers on its forehead, and a hidden place in its belly through which it emits the filth of its belly. The wings of this insect, that is, the bishop's wings, are his humility and pride. Outwardly he appears humble in his words and gestures, humble in his dress and actions, but inwardly there is a pride that makes him great in his own sight, rendering him swollen up with his own reputation, ambitious for people's appreciation, judgmental of others, and arrogant in preferring himself to others. On these two wings he flies before people with the apparent humility that aims at pleasing individuals and being the talk of everyone, as well as with the pride that makes him consider himself to be holier than others.

The three colors of the wings represent his three facades that cover up his vices. The color red means that he continually lectures on the sufferings of Christ and the miracles of the saints in order to be called holy, but they are far from his heart indeed, since he has not much liking for them. The color blue means that, on the outside, he does not seem to care about temporal goods, seeming to be dead to the world and to be all for the things of heaven under his facade of heavenly blue. But this second color makes him no more stable or fruitful before God than the first. The color white implies that he is a religious in his dress and commendable in his ways. However, his third color holds just as much charm and perfection as the first two. As a butterfly's pigment is thick and stays on your fingers, leaving behind nothing but a kind of ashy substance, so too his deeds seem to be admirable, inasmuch as he desires solitude , but they are empty and ineffectual as to their usefulness to him, since he does not sincerely yearn for or love that which is lovable.

The two feelers represent his duplicitous will. You see, he wants to lead a life of comfort in this world and to have eternal life after death. He does not want to be cheated out of being held in great esteem on earth while receiving an even more perfect crown in heaven. This bishop is just like a butterfly, thinking he can carry heaven on one feeler and earth on the other, although he cannot put up with the least little difficulty for God's glory. So he relies on God's church and thinks he can benefit it by his word and example, as if the church could not thrive without him. He presumes that his own good deeds will make worldly people bear spiritual fruit. Hence he reasons like a soldier who has already fought the fight. 'Since,' he says, 'I am already called devout and humble, why should I strive after a life of greater austerity? Although I may sin in a few pleasures without which my life would be unhappy, still my greater merits and good deeds will be my excuse. If heaven can be won for a cup of cold water, what need is there to struggle beyond measure?'

A butterfly has a big mouth as well, but its greed is even bigger, so much so that if it could eat up every single fly but one, it would want to eat that one up, too. Likewise, if this man could add a shilling to the many he already has in such away that it would go unnoticed in secret, he would take it, although the hunger of his greed would not be stilled even then.

A butterfly also has a hidden outlet for its impurities. This man, too, gives improper vent to his anger and impatience, displaying his secret impurities to others. And as a butterfly has a little body, this man has little charity, while his lack of charity is made up for only by the width and breadth of his wings." The bride answered: "If he has just one spark of charity, there is always some hope of life and charity and salvation for him." The Mother said: "Did not Judas also have some charity left when he said after he had betrayed his Lord: 'I have sinned in betraying innocent blood'? He wanted to make it look as though he had charity, but he had none."

The Mother's words to her daughter in which another such bishop is allegorically described as a gadfly, his wordy eloquence as flying, his two concerns as two wings, his flattery of the world as a sting; and about the Virgin's amazement at the life of these two bishops; also, about preachers.

# Chapter 15

The Mother speaks again to the bride, saying: "I have shown you another bishop whom I called the pastor of the flock. Let us compare him to a gadfly with an earthy color that flies about noisily. Wherever he alights, his bite is terrible and painful. This pastor has an earthy color, for, although he was called to poverty, he would rather be rich than poor, he would rather be in charge than submit, he would rather have his own will than be disciplined through obedience to others. He flies about noisily in the sense that he is full of wordy eloquence in his pious preaching, and lectures about worldly vanities instead of spiritual doctrine, praising and following worldly vanities rather than the holy simplicity of his order.

He has two wings as well, that is, two ideas: The first is that he wants to offer people charming and soothing speech so that he may win their esteem. The second is that he wants everyone to yield to him and obey him. The sting of a gadfly is unbearable. Likewise, this man stings souls to damnation. Although he should be a doctor of souls, he does not tell the people who come to him about their danger and infirmity nor does he use a sharp scalpel, but speaks soothingly to them in order to be called meek and so as not to cause anyone to avoid him. These two bishops are quite simply astonishing. One of them makes an appearance of being poor, solitary, and humble in order to be called spiritual. The other one wants to possess the world in order to be called merciful and generous. The one wants to seem to own nothing and yet longs to possess everything secretly. The other openly wants to have many possessions in order to have a lot to give away and thus win the esteem of others. Accordingly, as the proverb goes, since they serve me in a way I cannot see (because I do not accept it), I shall reward them in a way they will not see.

Do you wonder why such men are praised for their preaching? I will tell you: Sometimes a bad man speaks to good people and the good Spirit of God is poured into them, not because of the goodness of the teacher but through the teacher's words in which the good Spirit of God is found for the good of the listeners. Sometimes a good man speaks to bad people who are made good by hearing it both because of the good Spirit of God and the goodness of the teacher. Sometimes a cold man speaks to cold people in such away that these cold hearers recount what they have heard to fervent people who had not been there, rendering their listeners more fervent. So, do not worry about what kind of people you are sent to. Wonderful is God who tramples gold underfoot and places mud amidst the rays of the sun!"

The Son's Explanation to the bride that the damnation of souls does not please God; also, about the astonishing questions of the younger bishop to the older bishop, and about the answers of the older bishop to the younger one.

# Chapter 16

The Son speaks to the bride, saying: "Why do you think these two men are being shown to you? Is it because God enjoys censuring and condemning them? Of course not. No, it is done in order better to reveal God's patience and glory and also so that those who hear it may fear God's judgment. But now, come and listen to an astonishing conversation. Look there, the younger bishop has asked the older one a question, saying: 'Brother, hear and answer me. Once you had been bound to the yoke of obedience, why did you forsake it? Once you had chosen poverty and the religious state, why did you abandon them? Once you had entered the religious state and made yourself dead to the world, why did you seek the episcopate?' The older man answered: 'The obedience that taught me to be an inferior was a burden to me. That is why I preferred my freedom. The yoke that God says is pleasant was bitter to me.

That is why I sought and chose bodily comfort. My humility was pretended. That is why I craved honors. And, since it is better to push than to pull, I desired the episcopate accordingly.' The younger man asked again: 'Why did you not do honor to your episcopal see by giving it worldly honor? Why did you not acquire riches by means of worldly wisdom? Why did you not spend your possessions according to the demands of worldly honor? Why did you humble yourself outwardly rather than acting in accord with worldly ambition?'

The older man answered: 'The reason I did not strew worldly honors upon my see was that I was hoping myself to be honored so much the more by appearing to be humble and spiritual rather than worldly minded. Therefore, in order to be praised by worldly people, I made a show of holding everything in contempt; I appeared humble and devout in order to be held in esteem by spiritual men. The reason I did not acquire riches through worldly wisdom was in order that spiritual men might not notice it and hold me in contempt because of my secularity. The reason I was not liberal in giving gifts was that I preferred to have few rather than many companions for the sake of my own peace and quiet. I preferred having my money-chest full to handing away gifts.'

Again the younger man asked: 'Tell me, why did you give a pleasant and sweet drink out of a dirty vessel to an ass? Why did you give the bishop husks from the pigsty? Why did you fling down your crown under your feet? Why did you spit out wheat but chew weeds? Why did you free others from their chains but bind yourself with fetters? Why did you apply medicine to the wounds of others but poison to your own?' The older man answered: 'I gave my ass a sweet drink from a disgusting, dirty vessel in the sense that, although a scholar, I preferred to handle the divine sacraments of the altar for the sake of my worldly reputation rather than to apply myself to everyday cares. Inasmuch as my secrets were unknown to men but known to God, I grew a great deal in presumption and in that way added to the heavy justice of my terrible condemnation.

To the second question, I answer that I gave the bishop husks from the pig-sty in the sense that I followed the promptings of nature through self-indulgence and did not stand firm in self-restraint. As to the third question, I cast my episcopal crown underfoot in the sense that I preferred to do acts of mercy for the sake of human favor rather than acts of justice for the glory and love of God.

As to the fourth question, I spat out wheat but chewed straw in the sense that I did not preach God's words out of love for God nor did I like doing the things I told others to do. As to the fifth question, I freed others but bound myself in the sense that I absolved the people who turned to me with contrition, but I myself liked doing the things that they lamented through their penance and rejected through their tears. As to the sixth question, I anointed others with healing ointment but myself with poison in the sense that while I preached about purity of life and made others better, I made myself worse. I laid down precepts for others but was myself unwilling to lift a finger to do those very things. Where I saw others making progress, that is where I failed and wasted away, since I preferred to add a load to my already committed sins than to lessen my load of sins by making reparation.'

After this a voice was heard, saying: 'Give thanks to God that you are not among these poisonous vessels that, when they break, return to the poison itself.' Immediately, the death of one of the two was then announced."

The Virgin's words to her daughter praising the life and order of St. Dominic, and about how he turned to the Virgin at the hour of his death, and about how in modern times few of his friars live by the sign of Christ's passion given them by Dominic, but many of them live by the mark of incision given them by the devil.

# Chapter 17

Again the Mother speaks to the bride, saying: "Yesterday I told you about two men who belonged to the Rule of St. Dominic. Dominic held my Son as his dear Lord and loved me his Mother more than his own heart. My Son gave this holy man the inspired thought that there are three things in the world that displease my Son: pride, greed, and carnal desire. By his sighs and entreaties, St. Dominic procured help and medicine so as to combat these three evils. God had compassion on his tears and inspired him to set up a codified rule of life in which the holy man opposed three virtues to the three evils of the world.

Against the vice of greed he laid it down that one should own nothing without the permission of one's superior. Against pride he prescribed wearing a humble and simple habit. Against the bottomless voracity of the flesh, he prescribed abstinence and times for practicing self-discipline. He placed a superior over his friars in order to preserve peace and protect unity.

In his desire to give his friars a spiritual sign, he symbolically impressed a red cross on their left arm near the heart, I mean through his teaching and fruitful example, when he taught and admonished them continually to recall the suffering of God, to preach God's word more fervently, not for the world's sake but out of love for God and souls. He also taught them to submit rather than to govern, to hate their self-will, to bear insults patiently, to want nothing beyond food and clothing, to love truth in their hearts and to proclaim it with their lips, not to seek their own praise but to have the words of God on their lips and to teach them always, without omitting them out of shame or uttering them in order to win human favor.

When the time came for his deliverance, which my Son had revealed to him in spirit, he came in tears to me, his Mother, saying:

'O Mary, Queen of Heaven, whom God predestined for himself to unite his divine and human natures, you alone are that virgin and you alone are that most worthy mother. You are the most powerful of women from whom Power itself went forth. Hear me as I pray to you! I know you to be most powerful and therefore I dare to come before you. Take my friars, whom I have reared and nurtured beneath the austerity of my scapular, and protect them beneath your wide mantle! Rule them and nurture them anew, so that the ancient enemy may not prevail against them and may not ruin the new vineyard planted by the right hand of your Son! My Lady, by my scapular with its one piece in front and one at the back, I am referring to nothing other than the twofold concern that I have shown for my friars.

I was anxious night and day for them and about how they might serve God by practicing temperance in a reasonable and praiseworthy fashion. I prayed for them that they might not desire any worldly thing that could offend God or that might blacken their reputation for humility and piety among their fellows. Now that the time for my reward has come, I entrust my members to you. Teach them as children while you carry them as their mother.' With these and other words, Dominic was called to the glory of God.

I answered him as follows, using figurative language: 'O Dominic, my beloved friend, since you love me more than yourself, I shall protect your sons beneath my mantle and rule them, and all those who persevere in your role shall be saved. My mantle is wide with mercy and I deny mercy to no one who happily asks for it. All those who seek it find protection in the bosom of my mercy.'

But, my daughter, what do you think the rule of Dominic consists in? Surely, it consists in humility, continence, and the contempt of the world. All those who make a commitment to these three virtues and lovingly persevere in them will never be condemned. They are the ones who keep the rule of Blessed Dominic. Now hear something truly amazing: Dominic placed his sons beneath my wide mantle, but, look and see, now there are fewer of them beneath my wide mantle than there were in the austerity of his scapular. Yet not even during Dominic's lifetime did everyone have a true sheepskin or a Dominican character. I can illustrate their character better by way of a parable.

If Dominic came down from the heights of heaven where he lives and said to the Thief who was coming back from the valley and had been looking over the sheep with a view to slaughtering and destroying them, he would say 'Why are you calling after and leading away the sheep that I know to be mine by evident signs?' The Thief might answer: 'Why, Dominic, do you appropriate to yourself what is not your own? It is outrageous pilferage to usurp another's property for oneself.' If Dominic tried to reply that he had raised and tamed them and led and taught them, the Thief would say: 'You may have brought them up and taught them, but I have led them back to their own self-will by gentle coaxing.

You may have mixed leniency with austerity for them, but I enticed them more coaxingly and showed them things better to their liking, and, see, more of them are running to my pasture at my call. This is how I know the sheep eagerly following me are mine, given that they are free to choose to follow the one who attracts them more.' If Dominic should answer in turn that his sheep are marked with a red sign in the heart, the Thief would say; 'My sheep are marked with my sign, a mark of incision on their right ear. Since my sign is more obvious and visible than your sign, I recognize them as my sheep.'

The Thief stands for the devil who has incorporated many of Dominic's sheep into himself. They have an incision on the right ear in the sense that they do not listen to the words of life of the one saying: 'The path to heaven is narrow.' They only put into practice those words they like hearing. Dominic's sheep are few, and they have a red sign in their heart in the sense that they lovingly keep in mind God's suffering and lead a happy life in all chastity and poverty, fervently preaching the word of God.

For this is the Rule of Dominic as people commonly express it; 'To be able to carry all that you own on your back, to want to own nothing but what the Rule allows, to give up not only superfluous things but even at times to refrain from licit and necessary things on account of the impulses of the flesh.' ”

The Mother's words to her daughter about how friars would now listen and in fact do listen sooner to the devil's voice than to that of their father Dominic, about how few of them follow in his footsteps now, about how those seeking the episcopate for worldly honor and for their own comfort and freedom do not belong to the rule of St. Dominic, about the terrible condemnation of such men, and about the condemnation experienced for one such episcopate.

# Chapter 18

The Mother speaks to the bride, saying: "I told you that all those who belong to the Rule of Dominic are beneath my mantle. Now you are going to hear just how many they are. If Dominic were to come down from the place of delights where he has true happiness and were to cry out as follows: 'My dear brothers, you my followers, there are four good things in reserve for you: honor in return for humility, everlasting riches in return for poverty, satisfaction without boredom in return for continence, eternal life in return for the contempt of the world,' they would scarcely listen to him. On the contrary, if the devil suddenly came up from his hollow and proclaimed four different things, and said: 'Dominic promised you four things. Look here, I have what you want in my hand.

I offer honors, I hold wealth in my hand, instant gratification is there, the world will be delicious to enjoy. Take what I offer you, then! Use these things that are certain! Lead a life of joy so that after death you may rejoice together!' If these two voices were now to sound in the world, more people would run to the voice of the robber and devil than to the voice of Dominic, my great good friend. What shall I say of the friars of Dominic?

Those who are in his rule are indeed few, fewer still those who follow in his footsteps by imitating him. For not everyone listens to the one voice, because not everyone is of one and the same sort - not in the sense that not everyone comes from God or that not everyone can be saved, if they want, but in the sense that not everyone listens to the voice of the Son of God saying: 'Come to me and I will refresh you, by giving you myself!'

But what shall I say of those friars who seek the episcopate for worldly reasons? Do they really belong to the rule of Dominic? Certainly not. Or are those who accept the episcopate for a good reason excluded from the Rule of Dominic? Of course not. Blessed Augustine lived by a Rule before he became a bishop, but when he was bishop he did not give up his rule of life, although he attained the highest honors. For he accepted the honor with reluctance, and they did not bring more comfort to him but more work, because, when he saw he could do good to souls, he gladly gave up his own desires and physical comfort for God's sake in order to win more souls for God. Accordingly, those men who aspire to and accept the episcopate in order to be of greater benefit to souls do belong to the Rule of Dominic. Their reward will be twofold, both because of the noble order that they had to leave and of the burden of the episcopal office to which they were called.

I swear by that God by whom the prophets swore, who did not swear their oath in impatience but because they took God as a witness to their words.

Likewise, by the same God I declare and swear that to those friars who have scorned the rule of Dominic there will come a mighty hunter with ferocious hounds. It is as if a servant were to say to his master: 'There have come into your garden many sheep whose meat is poisoned, whose fleeces are matted with filth, whose milk is useless, and who are very insolent in their lusts. Command them to be slaughtered, so that there will be no shortage of pasture for the profitable sheep and so that the good sheep will not be confused by the insolence of the bad.'

The master would answer him: 'Shut the entrances so that only such sheep as approved by me can get in, such sheep as it is right to foster and nourish, such as are upright and peaceful.' I tell you that some of the entrances will be shut at first, but not all of them. Later the hunter will come with his hounds and he will spare neither their fleeces from arrows nor their bodies from wounds until their life has been put to an end. Then guards will come and carefully inspect and examine the kind of sheep that get admitted to the pasture of the Lord."

The bride said in reply: "My Lady, do not be angry if I ask a question.

Given that the pope relaxed the austerity of the rule for them, should they be censured for eating meat or anything else set before them?" The Mother answered: "The pope, taking into consideration the weakness and inadequacy of human nature, as put forward by some, reasonably allowed them to eat meat so that they might be more able to work and more fervent in preaching, not that they might appear lazy and lax. For this reason, we excuse the pope for permitting it." Then the bride said: "Dominic arranged for a habit made not of the best nor the worst cloth, but something in between. Should they be censured for wearing finer clothing?" The Mother answered: "Dominic, who dictated his rule inspired by the Spirit of my Son, prescribed that they should not have clothing made from better or more expensive materials so as not to be criticized and branded for wearing a fine and expensive habit and become proud because of it.

He also arranged that they should not have clothing made of the poorest or roughest material so as not to be bothered too much by the roughness of their clothing when they rested after work. Instead, he arranged for them to have clothing of moderate and adequate quality that they would not grow proud over or feel vain about, but that would keep out the cold and safeguard their continual progress in a life of virtue. Therefore, we commend Dominic for his arrangements but rebuke those friars of his who make changes in their habit for the sake of vanity rather than usefulness."

Again the bride said: "Should those friars who build tall and sumptuous churches for your Son be rebuked? Or are they to be censured and criticized if they ask for a lot of donations in order to construct such buildings?" The Mother answered: "When a church is wide enough to hold all the people coming into it, when its walls are tall enough that the people going into it are not crowded together, when its walls are thick and strong enough to withstand any wind, when its roof is tight and firm enough that it does not leak then they have built it sufficiently. A humble heart in a humble church is more pleasing to God than high walls in which there are bodies inside but hearts outside. Accordingly, they have no need to fill their chests with gold and silver for works of construction, for it did not do Solomon any good to have built such sumptuous buildings when he neglected to love God for whom they were being built."

As soon as these things had been both said and heard, the older bishop, who above was said to have died, shouted out saying: "O! O! O! My miter is gone! That which was hidden beneath it can now be seen. Where is the honorable bishop now? Where is the venerable priest? Where is the poor friar? Gone is the bishop who was anointed with oil for his apostolic office and a life of purity. Left behind is the slave of dung stained with grease. Gone is the priest who was consecrated by holy words so as to be able to transform inanimate lifeless bread into the living God. Left behind is the deceitful traitor that greedily sold him who redeemed all men in his love.

Gone is the poor friar who renounced the world through his vow. Now I stand condemned by my pride and ostentation. Yet am I compelled to say the truth: He who condemned me is a just judge. He would rather have set me free through as bitter a death as that which he suffered when he hung on the wood of the cross than that I should receive such a condemnation as I now experience - but his justice, which he cannot contravene, spoke against it."

The bride's reply to Christ about how she is afflicted by various useless thoughts, and about how she cannot get rid of them, and Christ's reply to the bride about why God permits this, and about the usefulness of such thoughts and fears with respect to her reward, provided she detests the thoughts and has a prudent fear of God, and about how she should not make light of venial sin lest it lead to mortal sin.

# Chapter 19

The Son speaks to the bride: "What are you worried and anxious about?" She answered: "I am afflicted by various useless thoughts that I cannot get rid of, and hearing about your terrible judgment upsets me." The Son answered: "This is truly just. Earlier you found pleasure in worldly desires against my will, but now different thoughts are allowed to come to you against your will.

But have a prudent fear of God, and put great trust in me, your God, knowing for certain that when your mind does not take pleasure in sinful thoughts but struggles against them by detesting them, then they become a purgation and a crown for the soul. But if you take pleasure in committing even a slight sin, which you know to be a sin, and you do so trusting to your own abstinence and presuming on grace, without doing penance and reparation for it, know that it can become a mortal sin. Accordingly, if some sinful pleasure of any kind comes into your mind, you should right away think about where it is heading and repent. After human nature was weakened, sin has frequently arisen out of human infirmity. There is no one who does not sin at least venially, but God has in his mercy given mankind the remedy of feeling sorrow for each sin as well as anxiety about not having made sufficient reparation for the sins for which one has made reparation.

God hates nothing so much as when you know you have sinned but do not care, trusting to your other meritorious actions, as if, because of them, God would put up with your sin, as if he could not be glorified without you, or as if he would let you do something evil with his permission, seeing all the good deeds you have done, since, even if you did a hundred good deeds for each wicked one, you still would not be able to pay God back for his goodness and love. So, then, maintain a rational fear of God and, even if you cannot prevent these thoughts, then at least bear them patiently and use your will to struggle against them. You will not be condemned because of their entering your head, unless you take pleasure in them, since it is not within your power to prevent them.

Again, maintain your fear of God in order not to fall through pride, even though you do not consent to the thoughts. Anyone who stands firm stands by the power of God alone. Thus fear of God is like the gateway into heaven. Many there are who have fallen headlong to their deaths, because they cast off the fear of God and were then ashamed to make a confession before men, although they had not been ashamed to sin before God. Therefore, I shall refuse to absolve the sin of a person who has not cared enough to ask my pardon for a small sin. In this manner, sins are increased through habitual practice, and a venial sin that could have been pardoned through contrition becomes a serious one through a person's negligence and scorn, as you can deduce from the case of this soul who has already been condemned.

After having committed a venial and pardonable sin, he augmented it through habitual practice, trusting to his other good works, without thinking that I might take lesser sins into account. Caught in a net of habitual and inordinate pleasure, his soul neither corrected nor curbed his sinful intention, until the time for his sentencing stood at the gates and his final moment was approaching. This is why, as the end approached, his conscience was suddenly agitated and painfully afflicted because he was soon to die and he was afraid to lose the little, temporary good he had loved. Up until a sinner's final moment God abides him, waiting to see if he is going to direct his free will away from his attachment to sin.

However, if a soul's will is not corrected, that soul is then confined by an end without end. What happens is that the devil, knowing that each person will be judged according to his conscience and intention, labors mightily at the end of life to distract the soul and turn it away from rectitude of intention, and God allows it to happen, since the soul refused to remain vigilant when it ought to have.

Furthermore, do not grow overconfident and presumptuous, if I call anyone my friend or servant as I once called this man. I also called Judas a friend and Nebuchadnezzar a servant. I myself said: 'You are my friends if you carry out my commandments.' In the same way, I now say: 'The people who imitate me are my friends; those who persecute me by scorning my commandments are my enemies.' After it had been said that I had found a man after my own heart, did not David commit the sin of murder? Solomon, who received such wonderful gifts and promises, sinned against goodness and, due to his ingratitude, the promise was fulfilled not in him but in me, the Son of God.

Accordingly, just as when you dictate you add a closing formula at the end, I will also add this closing formula to my locution: If anyone does my will and gives up his own, he will receive the inheritance of eternal life. He who hears my will but does not persevere in doing it, will end up like the worthless and ungrateful servant. However, you should not lose hope, if I call anyone an enemy, since as soon as an enemy changes his will for the better he will be a friend of God. Was not Judas together with the twelve when I said: 'You, my friends, who have followed me will also sit on twelve thrones.' At the time Judas was indeed following me, but he will not sit with the twelve. In what way, then, have the words of God been fulfilled? I answer: God, who sees people's hearts and wills, judges and rewards according as he sees.

A human being judges according to what she or he sees on the surface. Therefore, in order that no good person should grow proud or any bad person should lose hope, God has called both good and bad to the apostolate, just as every day he calls both good and bad to higher rank so that everyone whose way of life accords with his office will be glorified in eternity. He who assumes the honor but not the burden is glorified in time and perishes in eternity. Because Judas did not follow me with a perfect heart, the words 'you who have followed me' did not apply to him, inasmuch as he did not persevere to the point of reward. However, the words did apply to those persons who were to persevere both then and in the time to come, for the Lord, for whom all things are present, sometimes says things in present time that apply to the future, and sometimes speaks about things that are going to be accomplished as if they have already been accomplished. Sometimes, too, he mixes past and future and uses the past for the future, so that no one may presume to analyze the immutable purpose of the Trinity.

Hear one thing more: 'Many are called, but few are chosen.' This man was called to the episcopate but he was not chosen, for he proved ungrateful to the grace of God. Hence, he is a bishop in name but is unworthy of his service and is numbered among those who go down but do not come up again."

Addendum

The Son of God speaks: "Daughter, you are wondering why the one bishop died peacefully, but the other one died a horrible death when the wall fell and utterly crushed him, and he survived for a short while but with a great deal of pain. I answer you: Scripture says - no rather, I myself have said it - that the righteous person, no matter what kind of death he dies, is in the hands of God, but worldly people consider a person righteous only if his departure is peaceful and without pain or shame. God, however, recognizes as righteous the one who has been proved by longstanding temperance or who suffered for the sake of righteousness. The friends of God suffer in this world in order to receive a lesser punishment in the future or to win a greater crown in heaven.

Peter and Paul died for the sake of righteousness, although Peter died a more painful death than Paul, for he loved the flesh more than Paul; he also had to be more conformed to me through his painful death since he held the primacy of my church. Paul, however, inasmuch as he had a greater love of continence and because he had worked harder, died by the sword like a noble knight, for I arrange all things according to merit and measure. So, in God's judgment it is not how people end their lives or their horrible death that leads to their reward or condemnation, but their intention and will. The case is similar concerning these two bishops. One of them suffered more painfully and died a more terrible death. This reduced his punishment, although it did not gain him the reward of glory, because he did not suffer with a right intention. The other bishop died in glory, but this was due to my hidden justice and did not gain an eternal reward for him, because he did not rectify his intention while he was alive."

The Mother's words to the daughter about how the talent represents the gifts of the Holy Ghost, and about how St. Benedict added to the gifts of the Holy Ghost given to him, and about how the Holy Ghost or the demonic spirit enters the human soul.

# Chapter 20

The Mother speaks: "Daughter, it is written that the man who received five talents earned another five. What does a talent signify if not a gift of the Holy Ghost? Some receive knowledge, others wealth, others wealthy contacts. However, everyone should yield double profits to the Lord, for example, as regards knowledge, by living usefully for themselves and instructing others, as regards wealth and other gifts, by using them rationally and charitably helping others. In this way the good abbot Benedict added to the gift of grace he had received by scorning the goods that are fleeting, by forcing his body to serve his soul, by putting nothing ahead of charity. Anxious not to let his ears be corrupted by empty talk or his eyes by seeing pleasurable sights, he fled to the desert in imitation of that man who, when he had not yet been born, recognized the coming of his dear Savior and leaped for joy in the womb of his mother.

Benedict would have gained heaven without the desert, inasmuch as the world was dead to him and his heart was completely full of God. However, it pleased God to call Benedict to the mountain so that many would come to know him and many would be inspired by his example to seek a life of perfection. This blessed man's body was like a sack of earth that enclosed the fire of the Holy Ghost and shut out the fire of the devil from his heart. Physical fire is enkindled by both air and a man's breath. Similarly, the Holy Ghost enters the human soul, either through personal inspiration or by lifting the mind up to God through some human action or divine locution. The spirit of the devil likewise visits its own people. However, the two spirits differ immeasurably, for the Holy Ghost makes the soul hot in her search for God but does not make her burn in her body. He shines his light in purity and modesty but does not darken the mind with evil. The evil Spirit, on the other hand, causes the mind to burn with carnal desires and makes it terribly embittered. He darkens the soul by making her unreflective and pushes her remorselessly toward the things of the earth.

In order that the good fire that was in Benedict might ignite many people, God called him to the mountain and, after many other flames had been called together along with him, Benedict made a great bonfire of them by the Spirit of God. He composed a rule of life for them through the Spirit of God. Through this rule many people have attained the same perfection as he. Now, however, there are many firebrands cast off from the bonfire of St. Benedict and they lie spread out everywhere, having coldness instead of heat, darkness instead of light. If they were gathered together in the fire, they would surely give off fire and heat."

The Mother's words to her daughter, showing the greatness and perfection of the life of St. Benedict by means of a comparison; also, the soul that bears worldly fruit is represented as a fruitless tree, the pride of mind as flint, and the cold soul as crystal; and about three noteworthy sparks arising from these three things, i.e., from the crystal, the flint, and the tree.

# Chapter 21

The Mother speaks: "I told you before that the body of blessed Benedict was like a sack that was disciplined and ruled but did not rule. His soul was like an angel, giving off a lot of heat and flame. I will show you this by means of a comparison. It is as though there were three fires. The first of them was lit with myrrh and produced a sweet odor. The second was lit with dry kindle. It produced hot embers and a splendid blaze. The third was lit with olive oil. It produced flames, light, and heat. These three fires refer to three persons, and the three persons refer to three states in the world.

The first was the state of those who reflected on God's love and surrendered their wills into the hands of others. They accepted poverty and humility in place of worldly vanity and pride, and loved continence and purity in place of intemperance. Theirs was the fire of myrrh, for, just as myrrh is pungent but keeps demons away and quenches thirst, so too their abstinence was pungent to the body yet quenched their inordinate desires and drained away all the power of the demons.

The second state was that of those who had the following thought: 'Why do we love worldly honors? They are nothing but the air that brushes past our ears. Why do we love gold? It is nothing but yellow dirt. What is the end of the body if not rot and ashes? How does it help us to desire earthly goods?

All things are vanity. Therefore, we shall live and work for one purpose alone, that God may be glorified in us and that others may burn with love for God through our word and example.' The fire of such people was that of the dry kindle, inasmuch as they were dead to the love of the world and all of them produced hot embers of justice and the blaze of holy evangelization.

The third state was that of those with a fervent love for the passion of Christ who longed with all their hearts to die for Christ. Theirs was the fire of olive oil. The olive contains oil that gives off a scorching heat when it is burned. In the same way, these people were drenched in the oil of divine grace. Through it they produced the light of divine knowledge, the heat of fervent charity, the strength of upright conduct.

These three fires spread far and wide. The first of them was lit in hermits and religious, as described by Jerome who, inspired by the Holy Ghost, found their lives wonderful and exemplary. The second fire was lit in the confessors and doctors of the church, while the third was in the martyrs who despised their own flesh for God's sake, and others who would have despised it had they obtained help from God. Blessed Benedict was sent to people belonging to these three states or fires. He fused the three fires together in such away that the unwise were enlightened, the cold-hearted were inflamed, the fervent became more fervent still. Thus, with these fires began the Benedictine order that guided each person according to his disposition and intellectual capacity along the way of salvation and eternal happiness.

From the sack of Blessed Benedict blew the sweetness of the Holy Ghost through which many monasteries were started. However, now the Holy Ghost has left the sack of many of his brothers, for the heat of the ashes has been extinguished and the firebrands lie scattered about, giving off neither heat nor light but the smoke of impurity and greed. However, God has given me three sparks so as to bring consolation to many people. The three stand for many sparks. The first spark was obtained with a crystal from the heat and light of the sun and has already settled on the dry kindle in order that a great fire may be made from it. The second spark was obtained with hard flint.

The third spark came from a fruitless tree whose roots were growing and that was spreading its foliage. The crystal, that cold and fragile stone, represents the soul who, while she may be cold in her love for God, still seeks perfection in her heart and will and prays for God's help. Her intention thus leads her to God and earns for her an increase of trials that makes her grow cold toward base temptations, until God enlightens the heart and settles in the soul now emptied of desire, so that she no longer wants to live for anything but the glory of God. Flint represents pride. What is harder than the intellectual pride of a person who wants to be praised by everyone, yet longs to be called humble and to seem devout?

What is more loathsome than a soul that places herself ahead of everyone else in her thoughts and cannot put up with being rebuked or taught by anyone? Nevertheless, many proud persons pray humbly to God that pride and ambition be removed from their hearts. God, therefore, with the cooperation of their good will, presents adversities to their hearts and at times consolations that draw them away from worldly things and spur them on toward heavenly. The fruitless tree represents the soul that is fed on pride and bears worldly fruit and desires to have the world and all its privileges.

However, because this soul has a fear of eternal death, she uproots many of the saplings of sins she would otherwise commit if she had no such fear. Because of her fear, God draws near to the soul and inspires his grace in her so that the useless tree might become fruitful. By means of such sparks of fire, the order of Blessed Benedict, which now seems abject and abandoned to many people, should be renewed."

The Mother's words to her daughter about a monk with a harlot's heart in his breast, and about how he apostatized from God through his own will and greed and his desertion of the angelic life.

# Chapter 22

The Mother speaks to the bride again: "What do you see that is blameworthy in this man here?" She answered: "That he rarely says Mass." The Mother said to her: "It is not for that reason that he is to be sentenced. There are many men who, mindful of their deeds, refrain from saying Mass but are no less acceptable to me. What else do you see in him?" And she said: "That he does not wear the habit established by blessed Benedict." The Mother replied: "It often happens that a custom gets started, and those who know it to be a bad custom but still follow it deserve blame. However, those who do not know the correct traditions and would even prefer a simpler habit, had it not been for the long-standing custom, are not to be so easily and thoughtlessly condemned. Listen, however, and I will tell you three reasons why he should be blamed.

First, because his heart, in which God should rest, is in the breast of harlots. Second, because he has given up the little he possessed but longs for the greater possessions of others; having promised to deny himself, he completely follows his own will and whim. Third, because God made his soul as beautiful as an angel and for that reason he should be leading an angelic life, but now his soul instead bears the image of that angel who apostatized from God through pride. People account him a great man, but God knows what sort he is before God. God is like a person who closes his fist about something and keeps it hidden from others until he opens his fist. God chooses weak creatures and keeps their crowns hidden in the present life until he rewards each person according to his deeds."

## Explanation

This man was a very worldly minded abbot who cared nothing for souls and who died suddenly without the sacraments. The Holy Ghost said about him: "O soul, you loved the earth and now the earth has received you. You were dead in your life and now you will not have my life nor be a sharer with me, since you loved the company of him who apostatized from me through pride and despised true humility."

The answer of God the Father to the bride's prayers for sinners, and about three witnesses on earth and three in heaven, and about how the whole Trinity bears witness to the bride, and about how she is his bride through faith, like all those who follow the orthodox faith of the holy church.

# Chapter 23

"O my most sweet God, I pray for sinners, to whose company I belong, that you deign to have mercy on them." God the Father answered: "I hear and know your intention, your loving entreaty will therefore be fulfilled. As John says in today's epistle, or, rather, as I say through John: 'There are three witnesses on earth, the Spirit, the water, and the blood, and three in heaven, the Father, the Son, and the Holy Ghost, and these three are your witnesses. The Spirit, who protected you in the womb of your mother, bears witness concerning your soul that you belong to God through the baptismal faith that your parents professed in your stead.

The baptismal water bears witness that you are the daughter of Christ's human nature through regeneration and the healing of original sin. The blood of Jesus Christ that redeemed you bears witness that you are the daughter of God and removed from the power of the devil by the sacraments of the church. The Father, the Son, and the Holy Ghost, three Persons but one in substance and power, we bear witness that you are ours through faith, just as are all those who follow the orthodox faith of the holy church. And so that you give witness that you want to do our will, go and receive the body and blood of Christ's human nature from the hand of the priest in order that the Son may bear witness that you belong to him whose body you receive to strengthen your soul. The Father, who is in the Son, bears witness that you belong to the Father and to the Son. The Holy Ghost, who is in the Father and the Son, the Spirit being in both, bears witness that, through true faith and love, you belong to the Three Persons and One God."

To the prayers of the bride for infidels, Jesus Christ replies that God is glorified through the evil of evil men, although not by their own power and volition; he illustrates this for her by means of an allegory in which a maiden represents the church or the soul and her nine brothers represent the nine orders of angels, the king represents Christ, while his three sons represent the three states of mankind.

# Chapter 24

"O my Lord Jesus Christ, I pray that your faith may be spread among the infidels, and that good people may be set even more aflame with your love and that wicked people may convert." The Son answered: "You are grieved because little honor is given to God and with all your heart you wish that God's honor were perfected. I will offer you an allegory that will help you to understand that honor is given to God even through the evil of evil men, although not by their own power and volition. Once there was a wise and beautiful, rich and virtuous maiden. She had nine brothers, each of whom loved her as his very heart, and you might say that each one's heart was in her. In the kingdom where the maiden lived, there was a law that said that whoever showed honor would be honored, whoever robbed would be robbed, whoever committed rape would be beheaded.

The king of the realm had three sons. The first son loved the maiden and offered her golden shoes and a golden belt, a ring for her hand and a crown for her head. The second son coveted the property of the maiden and robbed her. The third son coveted her maidenhood and sought to rape her. The king's three sons were captured by the maiden's nine brothers and presented to the king. Her brothers told him: 'Your sons desired our sister.

The first honored and loved her with his whole heart. The second one despoiled her. The third was ready to risk his life just to rape her. They were seized at the very moment when they were fully intent on carrying out what we have said.' Once the king heard this, he answered them, saying: 'They are all my sons, and I love all of them equally. However, I neither can nor wish to go against justice. Instead I intend to judge my sons as I would my servants. You, my son, who wanted to honor the maiden, come and receive honor and the crown along with your father! You, my son, who coveted the maiden's property and snatched it away, you shall go to prison until the stolen goods have been restored. Indeed, I have heard evidence concerning you that you were sorry for your crime and would have returned the stolen goods, but were prevented from doing so by your sudden and unexpected arrest. For this reason you will remain incarcerated until the last farthing is restored. But you, my son, who made every attempt to rape this maiden, are not sorry for your crime.

Therefore, your punishment will be multiplied by the number of ways in which you attempted to deflower the maiden.' All the brothers of the maiden answered: 'May you, the judge, be praised for your justice! For you would never have issued such a judgment had there not been virtue in you and fairness in your justice and mercy in your fairness.'

The maiden symbolizes the holy church. She is by nature outstanding by reason of her faith, beautiful by reason of the seven sacraments, laudable by reason of her conduct and virtue, lovable by reason of her fruits, for she reveals the true way to eternity. The holy church has three sons, so to speak, and these three stand for many. The first are those who love God with their whole heart. The second are those who love temporal goods for their own honor. The third are those who put their own will ahead of God. The maidenhood of the church represents human souls created solely by divine power.

Accordingly, the first son offers golden shoes by having contrition for his misdeeds, omissions, and sins. He offers clothes by following the precepts of the law and keeping the evangelical counsels as far as possible. He puts together a belt by firmly resolving to persevere in continence and chastity. He places a ring on her hand by firmly believing in what the catholic church teaches about the future judgment and life everlasting. The gem of the ring is hope, steadfastly hoping that no sin is so abominable that it cannot be wiped away through penance and the resolution to improve. He puts a crown on her head by having true charity. Just as a crown has various jewels, so too charity has various virtues. And the head of the soul or, rather, of the church is my Body. Whoever loves and reverences it is rightly called a son of God.

A person who loves the holy church and his own soul in such away has nine brothers, that is, the nine orders of angels, for he will be their companion and fellow in eternal life. The angels embrace the holy church with all their love, as if she were in the heart of each one of them. It is not stones and walls that make up the holy church but the souls of the righteous, and, for this reason, the angels rejoice over their honor and progress as though over their own.

The second brother or, rather, son, represents those who reject the authority of the holy church and live for worldly honor and the love of the flesh, who deform the beauty of virtue and live after their own desires, but repent toward the end and are sorry for their evil deeds. They must go to purgatory until they can be reconciled to God through the works and prayers of the church. The third son represents those who are a scandal to their own soul, not caring whether they perish forever, as long as they can carry out their desires. The nine orders of angels seek justice because of these people, inasmuch as they refuse to be converted through penance.

Thus, when God delivers his sentence, the angels praise him for his unbending fairness. When God's honor is thus perfected, they rejoice over his might, because even the evil of evil men serves to give him honor. This is why, when you see immoral persons, you should have compassion on them and rejoice over the eternal honor of God. God does not will anything evil, for he is the Creator of all things and the only being truly good in himself, but, as a most just judge, he still permits many things to be done in regard to which he is honored in heaven and on earth on account of his fairness and his hidden goodness."

The Mother's lament to her daughter that the most innocent lamb, Jesus Christ, is neglected by his creatures in modern times.

# Chapter 25

The Mother speaks: "My lament is that on this day the most innocent lamb was carried who best knew how to walk. On this day, that little boy was silent who best knew how to speak. On this day, the most innocent little boy who never sinned was circumcised. This is why, although I cannot be angry, still I seem to be angry because the supreme Lord who became a little boy is forgotten and neglected by his creatures."

Christ's Explanation to the bride of the ineffable mystery of the Trinity, and about how diabolical sinners obtain God's mercy through contrition and a will to improve, and his response as to how he has mercy on everyone, both Jews and others, and about the double judgment, that is, the sentence for those who are to be condemned and for those who are to be saved.

# Chapter 26

The Son speaks: "I am the Creator of heaven and earth, one with the Father and the Holy Ghost, true God. The Father is God, the Son is God, the Holy Ghost is God, not three gods but one God. Now you might ask, if there are three Persons, why are there not three gods? My answer is that God is nothing other than power itself, wisdom itself, goodness itself, from which come all power beneath or above the heavens, all conceivable wisdom and the kindness. Thus, God is triune and one, triune in Persons, one in nature. The power and the wisdom is the Father, from whom all things come and who is prior to all, deriving his power from nowhere else but himself for all eternity.

The power and wisdom are also the Son, equal to the Father, deriving his power not from himself but as begotten ineffably from the Father, the beginning from the beginning, never separated from the Father. The power and wisdom are also the Holy Ghost, who proceeds from the Father and the Son, eternal with the Father and the Son, equal in majesty and might. Thus, one God and three Persons. The three have the same nature, the same operation and will, the same glory and might.

God is thus one in essence, but the Persons are distinct in the proper quality of each. The Father is wholly in the Son and Spirit, and the Son is wholly in the Father and Spirit, and the Spirit is wholly in both, in one divine nature, not as prior and posterior but in an ineffable way. In God there is neither prior nor posterior, nothing greater or less than another, but the Trinity is wholly and ineffably equal. Well has it been written that God is great and greatly to be praised.

However, now I can complain that I am little praised and unknown to many people, because everyone is following his own will but few follow mine. Be you steadfast and humble, and do not exalt yourself in your mind if I show you other people's trials, and do not betray their names unless you are instructed to do so. Their trials are not shown to you to shame them but in order that they may be converted and come to know God's justice and mercy. Nor should you shun them as condemned, for even if I should say today that a certain person is wicked, should he call on me tomorrow with contrition and a will to improve, I am prepared to forgive him. And that person whom I yesterday called wicked, today, due to his contrition, I declare him to be so dear a friend of mine that if his contrition remains steadfast, I forgive him not only his sin but even remit the punishment of sin.

You might understand this with a metaphor. It is as though there were two drops of quicksilver and both were heading toward each other in haste. If nothing but a single atom remained to keep them from joining, still God would be powerful enough to prevent them from coming together. Likewise, if any sinner were so rooted in diabolical deeds that he was standing at the very brink of destruction, he could still obtain forgiveness and mercy, if he called upon God with contrition and a will to improve. Now, given that I am so merciful, you might ask why I am not merciful toward pagans and Jews, some of whom, if they were instructed in the true faith, would be ready to lay down their lives for God. My response is that I have mercy on everyone, on pagans as well as Jews, nor is any creature beyond my mercy.

With leniency and mercy I will judge both those people who, learning that their faith is not the true one, fervently long for the true faith, as well as those people who believe the faith they profess to be the best one, because no other faith has ever been preached to them, and who wholeheartedly do what they can. You see, there is a double judgment, namely the one for those to be condemned and the one for those to be saved. The sentence of condemnation for Christians will have no mercy in it. To them will belong eternal punishment and shadows and a will hardened against God. The sentence for those Christians to be saved will be the vision of God and glorification in God and goodwill toward God. Excluded from these rewards are pagans and Jews as well as bad and false Christians. Although they did not have the right faith, they did have conscience as their judge and believed that the one whom they worshipped and offended was God.

But the ones whose intention and actions were and are for justice and against sin will, along with the less bad Christians, share a punishment of mercy in the midst of sufferings due to their love of justice and their hatred of sin. However, they will not have consolation in the service of glory and of the vision of God. They will not behold him due to their lack of baptism, because some temporal circumstance or some hidden decision of God made them draw back from profitably seeking and obtaining salvation. If there was nothing that held them back from seeking the true God and being baptized, neither fear nor the effort required nor loss of goods or privileges, but only some impediment that overcame their human weakness, then I, who saw Cornelius and the centurion while they were still not baptized, know how to give them a higher and more perfect reward in accordance with their faith.

One thing is the ignorance of sinners, another that of those who are pious but impeded. Likewise, too, one thing is the baptism of water, another that of blood, another that of wholehearted desire. God, who knows the hearts of all people, knows how to take all of these circumstances into account. I am begotten without beginning, begotten eternally from the beginning. I was born in time at the end of times. From the commencement I have known how to give individual persons the rewards they deserve and I give to each according as he deserves. Not the least little good done for the glory of God will go without its reward. This is why you should give many thanks to God that you were born of Christian parents in the age of salvation, for many people have longed to obtain and see that which is offered to Christians and yet have not obtained it."

The bride's prayer to the Lord for Rome, and about the vast multitude of holy martyrs resting in Rome, and about the three degrees of Christian perfection, and about a vision of hers and how Christ appears to her and expounds and explains the vision to her.

# Chapter 27

"O Mary, I have been unkind, but still I call you to my aid. I pray to you that you may graciously pray for the excellent and holy city of Rome. I can physically see that some of the churches are abandoned where the bones of the saints lie in rest. Some of them are inhabited, but the heart and conduct of their rectors are far from God. Procure mercy for them, for I have heard it is written that there are seven thousand martyrs for any day in the year at Rome. Although their souls do not receive less honor in heaven because their bones are held in contempt here on earth, nevertheless I ask you that greater honor may be given to your saints and to the relics of your saints here on earth and that the devotion of the people may be stirred up in this way."

The Mother answered: "If you measured out a plot of land a hundred feet in length and as much in width and sowed it so full of pure grains of wheat that the grains were so close together that there was just the space of a thumb left between them, and even if each grain gave fruit a hundredfold, there would still be more Roman martyrs and confessors from the time when Peter came to Rome in humility until Celestine left from the throne of pride and returned to his solitary life.

But I am referring to those martyrs and confessors who against infidelity preached true fidelity and against pride preached humility and who died or were ready in intention to die for the truth of the faith. Peter and many others were so wise and zealous in spreading the word of God that they would readily have died for each and every person if they had been able. However, they were also concerned lest they be taken suddenly from the presence of those people whom they nourished with their words of consolation and preaching, for they desired to save souls more than to save their own lives and reputation. They were also prudent and hence went to work in secret during times of persecution in order to win and gather together a greater number of souls. Between these two, I mean, between Peter and Celestine, not everyone has been good, but not everyone has been bad either.

Now let us set up three degrees or ranks, as you yourself were doing: positive, comparative, and superlative, or good, better, and best. To the first rank belong those whose thoughts were the following: 'We believe whatever the holy church teaches. We do not want to defraud anyone but to give back whatever has been fraudulently taken, and we want to serve God with all our heart.' There were people like that in the time of Romulus, the founder of Rome, and, after their own beliefs, they thought as follows: 'We understand and recognize through creatures that God is the Creator of all things and therefore we want to love him above all else.' There were also many who thought like this: 'We have heard from the Hebrews that the true God has revealed himself through manifest miracles. So, if we only knew where to place our trust, we would place it there.' We can say that all of these belonged to the first rank.

At the appointed time, Peter arrived in Rome. He raised some people to the positive rank, others to the comparative rank, and still others to the superlative. To the positive rank belonged those who accepted the true faith and lived in matrimony or in another honorable state. To the comparative rank belonged those who gave up their possessions out of love for God, and set others the example of a good life in words and example and deed and did not put anything ahead of Christ. To the superlative rank belonged those who offered their physical lives out of love for God. But let us make a search of these ranks to find out where there is now a more fervent love of God. Let us search among the knights and the learned. Let us search among the religious and those who have scorned the world. These people would be thought to belong to the comparative and superlative ranks. Yet, indeed, very few are found.

There is no life more austere than the life of a knight, if he truly follows his calling. While a monk is obliged to wear a cowl, a knight is obliged to wear something heavier, namely, a coat of mail. While it is hard for a monk to fight against the will of the flesh, it is harder for a knight to go forth among armed enemies. While a monk must sleep on a hard bed, it is harder still for the knight to sleep with his weapons. While a monk finds abstinence a burden and trouble, it is harder for the knight to be constantly burdened by fear for his life.

Christian knighthood was not established out of greed for worldly possessions but in order to defend the truth and spread the true faith. For this reason, the knightly rank and the monastic rank should be thought to correspond to the superlative or comparative rank. However, those in every rank have deserted their honorable calling, since the love for God has been perverted into worldly greed. If but a single florin were offered them, most of them in all three ranks would keep silent about the truth rather than lose the florin and speak the truth."

The bride speaks again: "I also saw what looked like many gardens on earth. I saw roses and lilies in the gardens. In one spacious plot of land I saw a field a hundred feet in length and as much in width. In each foot of land there were seven grains of wheat sown and each grain gave fruit a hundredfold.

Then I heard a voice saying: 'O Rome, Rome, your walls have crumbled. Your city gates are therefore unguarded. Your vessels are being sold. Your altars have therefore been abandoned. The living sacrifice along with the incense of matins is burned in the portico. The sweet and holy fragrance does not come from the holy of holies.'"

At once the Son of God appeared and said to the bride: "I will tell you the meaning of the things you have seen. The land you saw represents the entire territory where the Christian faith is now. The gardens represent those places where God's saints received their crowns. However, in paganism, that is, in Jerusalem and in other places, there were many of God's elect, but their places have not been shown to you now. The field that is a hundred paces in length and as much in width stands for Rome. If all the gardens of the whole world were to be brought alongside Rome, Rome would certainly be as great as to the number of martyrs (I am speaking materially), because it is the place chosen for the love of God.

The wheat you saw in each foot of land represents those who have entered heaven through mortification of the flesh, contrition, and innocence of life. The few roses represent the martyrs who are red from the blood they shed in different regions. The lilies are the confessors who preached and confirmed the holy faith by word and deed. Today I can say of Rome what the prophet said of Jerusalem:

'Once righteousness lodged in her and her princes were princes of peace. Now she has turned to dross and her princes have become murderers.'

O Rome, if you knew your days, you would surely weep and not rejoice. Rome was in olden days like a tapestry dyed in beautiful colors and woven with noble threads. Its soil was dyed in red, that is, in the blood of martyrs, and woven, that is, mixed with the bones of the saints. Now her gates are abandoned, in that their defenders and guardians have turned to avarice. Her walls are thrown down and left unguarded, in that no one cares that souls are being lost. Rather, the clergy and the people, who are the walls of God, have scattered away to work for carnal advantage. The sacred vessels are sold with scorn, in that God's sacraments are administered for money and worldly favors.

The altars are abandoned, in that the priest who celebrates with the vessels has hands empty as to love for God but keeps his eyes on the collection; although he has God in his hands, his heart is empty of God, for it is full of the vain things of the world. The holy of holies, where the highest sacrifice used to be consumed, represents the desire to see and enjoy God. From this desire, there should rise up love for God and neighbor and the fragrance of temperance and virtue. However, the sacrifice is now consumed in the portico, that is, in the world, in that the love for God has completely turned into worldly vanity and lack of temperance.

Such is Rome, as you have seen it physically. Many altars are abandoned, the collection is spent in taverns, and the people who give to it have more time for the world than for God. But you should know that countless souls ascended into heaven from the time of humble Peter until Boniface ascended the throne of pride. Yet Rome is still not without friends of God. If they were given some help, they would cry out to the Lord and he would have mercy on them."

The Virgin instructs the bride about knowing how to love and about four cities where four loves are found and about which of these is properly called perfect love.

# Chapter 28

The Mother speaks to the bride, saying: "Daughter, do you love me?" She answers: "My Lady, teach me to love, for my soul is defiled with false love, seduced by a deadly poison, and cannot understand true love." The Mother says: "I will teach you. There are four cities where there are four kinds of love, that is, if we are to call each of them love, given that no love can properly be found except where God and the soul are united in the true union of the virtues. The first city is the city of trial. This is the world.

A man is placed there to be tested as to whether he loves God or not.

This is in order that he may come to know his own weakness and acquire the virtues by which he may return to glory, so that, having been cleansed on earth, he may receive a glorious crown in heaven. One finds disordered love in this city, because the body is loved more than the soul, because there is a more fervent desire for temporal than spiritual good, because vice is honored and virtue despised, because travels abroad are more appreciated than one's home country, because a little mortal being gets more respect and honor than God whose reign is everlasting.

The second city is the city of cleansing where the dirt of the soul is washed away. God has willed to set up places where a person who has become proud in the negligent use of his freedom yet without losing his fear of God may be cleansed before receiving his crown. One finds imperfect love in this city, inasmuch as God is loved because of a person's hope of being released from captivity but not out of an ardent affection. This is due to weariness and bitterness in atoning one's guilt. The third city is the city of sorrow. This is hell. Here one finds a love for every kind of evil and impurity, a love for every kind of envy and obstinacy. God governs this city as well. This he does by means of balanced justice, the due moderation of punishments, the restraint of evil, and the fairness of the sentences that takes each sinner's merits into account.

Some of the condemned are greater sinners, others lesser. The conditions for their punishment and retribution are set up accordingly. Although all the condemned are enclosed in darkness, not all of them experience it in one and the same way. Darkness differs from darkness, horror from horror, hell-fire from hell-fire. God's rule is one of justice and mercy everywhere, even in hell. Thus, those who have sinned deliberately have their particular punishment, those who have sinned out of weakness have a different one, those who are being held only because of the damage done by original sin have a different one again. While the torment of these latter consists in the lack of the beatific vision and of the light of the elect, still they come close to mercy and joy in the sense that they do not experience horrible punishments, since they bear no effects of any evil deeds of their own doing. Otherwise, if God did not ordain the number and limit of the punishments, the devil would never show any limits in tormenting them.

The fourth city is the city of glory. Here one finds perfect love and the ordered charity that desires nothing but God or but for the sake of God. Hence, if you would reach the perfection of this city, your love needs four qualities: it must be ordered, pure, true, and perfect. Your love is ordered when you love the body only for the sake of sustaining yourself, when you love the world without superfluities, your neighbor for God's sake, your friend for the sake of purity of life, and your enemy for the sake of the reward. Love is pure when sin is not loved alongside virtue, when bad habits are scorned, when sin is not taken lightly.

Love is true when you love God with all your heart and affections, when you take the glory and fear of God into prior consideration in all your actions, when you commit not the least little sin while trusting to your good deeds, when you practice temperance prudently without growing weak from too much fervor, when you do not have an inclination to sin out of cowardice or ignorance of temptations. Love is perfect when nothing is as enjoyable to a person as God. This kind of love begins in the present but is consummated in heaven. Love, then, this perfect and true kind of love! Everyone who does not have it shall be cleansed, no matter whether he is faithful or fervent or a child or baptized. Otherwise he will go to the city of horror.

Just as God is one, so too there is one faith, one baptism, one perfection of glory and reward in the church of Peter. Accordingly, anyone who longs to reach the one God must have one and the same love and will as the one God. Miserable are those who say: 'It is enough for me to be the least in heaven. I do not want to be perfect.' What a senseless thought! How can someone who is imperfect be there where everyone is perfect either through innocence of life or the innocence of childhood or by cleansing or by faith and goodwill?"

The bride's praise for the Virgin containing an allegory about Solomon's temple and the unexplainable truth of the unity of the divine and human natures, and about how the temples of priests are painted with vanity.

# Chapter 29

"Blessed are you, Mary, Mother of God. You are Solomon's temple whose walls were of gold, whose roof shone brightly, whose floor was paved with precious gems, whose whole array was shining, whose whole interior was fragrant and delightful to behold. In every way you are like the temple of Solomon where the true Salomon walked and sat and where he placed the ark of glory and the bright lamp. You, Blessed Virgin, are the temple of that Salomon who made peace between God and man, who reconciled sinners, who gave life to the dead and freed the poor from their oppressor. Your body and soul became the temple of the Godhead. They were a roof for God's love, beneath which the Son of God lived with you in joy after having proceeded from the Father.

The floor of the temple was your life arrayed in the careful practice of the virtues. No privilege was lacking to you, but everything you had was stable, humble, devout, and perfect. The walls of the temple were foursquare, for you were not troubled by any shame, you were not proud about any of your privileges, no impatience disturbed you, you aimed at nothing but the glory and love of God. The paintings of your temple were the constant inspirations of the Holy Ghost that raised your soul so high that there is no virtue in any other creature that is not more fully and perfectly in you. God walked in this temple when he poured his sweet presence into your limbs. He rested in you when the divine and human natures became joined.

Blessed are you, Virgin most blessed! In you God almighty became a little boy, the Lord most ancient became a tiny child, God the eternal and invisible Creator became a visible creature. I beg you, therefore, since you are the kindest and most powerful Lady, look upon me and have mercy on me! You are indeed the Mother of Solomon, although not of him who was the son of David but of him who is the Father of David and the Lord of that Solomon who built the wonderful temple that truly prefigured you. A son will listen to his Mother, especially to so great a Mother as you. Your son Solomon was, as it were, once asleep in you.

Entreat him, then, that he may be wakeful and watch over me so that no sinful pleasure may sting me, so that my contrition for sins may be lasting, so that I may be dead to the love of the world, patient in perseverance, fruitful in penance. There is no virtue in me but there is this prayer: 'Have mercy, Mary!' My temple is completely the opposite of yours. It is dark with vice, muddied with lust, ruined by the worms of desire, unsteady due to pride, ready to fall due to worldly vanity."

The Mother answered: "Blessed be God who has inspired your heart to offer this greeting to me so that you may understand how much goodness and sweetness there is in God. But why do you compare me to Solomon and to the temple of Solomon, when I am the Mother of him whose lineage has neither beginning nor end, of him who is said to have neither father nor mother, that is, of Melchisedech? He is said to have been a priest and it is to priests that the temple of God is entrusted, which is why I am Virgin and Mother of the high priest. And yet, I tell you that I am both the mother of King Solomon and the Mother of the peace-making priest, for the Son of God, who is also my Son, is both priest and King of kings.

It was indeed in my temple that he dressed himself spiritually in the priestly garb in which he offered a sacrifice for the world. In the royal city he was crowned with a royal but cruel crown. Outside the city, like a mighty warrior, he held the field and kept the war away. My grievance is that this same Son of mine is now forgotten and neglected by priests and kings. The kings pride themselves on their palaces, their armies, their worldly successes and honors. The priests grow proud of the goods and possessions that belong to souls. You said the temple was painted in gold. But the temples of priests are painted in worldly vanity and curiosity, since simony rules at the highest levels. The ark of the covenant has been taken away, the lamp of the virtues extinguished, the table of devotion abandoned."

The bride answered: "O Mother of mercy, have mercy on them and pray for them!" The Mother said to her: "From the beginning God so loved his own that not only are they heard when they pray for themselves, but others also experience the effects of their prayers thanks to them. Two things are necessary if prayers for others are to be heard, namely the intention of giving up sin and the intention of making progress in virtue. My prayers will benefit anyone who has both of these."

Saint Agnes's words to the bride about the love the bride should have for the Virgin, using the metaphor of flowers, and the glorious Virgin's description of God's boundless and everlasting kindness as compared to our lack of kindness and ingratitude, and about how the friends of God should not lose their peace in the midst of hardship.

# Chapter 30

Blessed Agnes speaks to the bride, saying: "My daughter, love the Mother of mercy. She is like the flower or reed shaped like a sword. This flower has two sharp extremities and a graceful tip. In height and width it excels all other flowers. Similarly, Mary is the flower of flowers, a flower that grew in a valley and extended over all the mountains. A flower, I say, that was raised in Nazareth and spread itself on Mount Lebanon. This flower had, first of all, height, in the sense that the blessed Queen of heaven excels every creature in dignity and power. Mary also had two sharp edges or leaves, that is, the sorrow in her heart over her Son's passion along with her steadfast resistance to the attacks of the devil by never consenting to sin.

The old man prophesied truly when he said: 'A sword shall pierce your soul. In a spiritual sense she received as many sword-strokes as the number of wounds and sores she saw her Son receive and that she also had already foreseen. Mary had also a great width, I mean, her mercy. She is and was so kind and merciful that she preferred to suffer any hardship rather than let souls be lost. United now with her Son, she has not forgotten her native goodness but, rather, extends her mercy to all, even to the worst of men. Just as the sun brightens and sets ablaze the heavens and earth, so too there is no one who does not experience Mary's sweet kindness, if he asks for it. Mary also had a graceful tip, I mean, her humility.

Her humility made her pleasing to the angel when she called herself the Lord's handmaid, although she was being chosen to be his Lady. She conceived the Son of God in humility, not wanting to please the proud. She ascended the highest throne through humility, loving nothing but God himself. Come forward, then, Conduit, and greet the Mother of mercy, for she has now arrived!"

Then Mary appeared and replied: "Agnes, you used a noun, add an adjective, too!" Agnes said to her: "I might say 'most beautiful' or 'most virtuous,' for that belongs rightfully to no one but you, the Mother of everyone's salvation." The Mother of God answered Blessed Agnes: "You speak truthfully, for I am the most powerful of all. Therefore, I myself will add an adjective and a noun, namely 'Conduit' of the Holy Ghost. Come, Conduit, and listen to me! You are sad because this saying is bandied about among men: 'Let us live as we like, since God is easily pleased. Let us make use of the world and its honor while we can, since the world was made for the sake of mankind.' Indeed, my daughter, a saying like that does not come from love of God nor does it tend or lead toward the love of God. However, God does not forget his love because of it but in every hour displays his kindness in return for human ingratitude. He is like a craftsman crafting some great work. At times he heats up the iron, at times he lets it cool. God is the supreme craftsman who made the world out of nothing and has shown his love to Adam and his posterity.

But the human race cooled down to such an extent that they committed enormous crimes and almost regarded God as nothing. For that reason, God had mercy and gave a benevolent warning first, but then revealed his justice by means of the flood. After the flood, God made his pact with Abraham, showing him signs of affection, and led his children by means of great signs and wonders. He gave the law to his people from his own lips, confirming his words and precepts by the most evident of signs. As time went by, again the people grew cold and fell into such insanity that they started to worship idols. Wanting to heat up the cold-hearted once more, God in his kindness sent his own Son into the world.

He taught the true way to heaven and gave an example of true humility to imitate. Although many have now quite forgotten him in their neglect, he still displays and reveals his merciful words. However, things will not be accomplished all at once, no more now than before. Prior to the coming of the flood, the people were warned first and were given time for repentance. Similarly, before Israel entered the promised land, the people were first tested and the promise was delayed for a time. God could have led the people for forty days without delaying for forty years, but his justice demanded that the ingratitude of the people should become apparent and that

God's mercy should be made manifest so as to render his future people so much the more humble.

It would be great audacity to ask why God made his people suffer so much or why there can be eternal punishment, given that a life in sin cannot last forever. It would be as great audacity as to try to reason out and comprehend the eternity of God. God is eternal and incomprehensible. His justice and recompensation is eternal, his mercy is beyond understanding. If God had not already shown justice to the first angels, how would we know of his justice and his fair judgment of everything?

If, again, he had not had mercy on humanity by creating it and then freeing it through innumerable miracles, how would we know that his goodness was so great or his love so immense and so perfect? Because God is eternal, his justice is eternal and there is neither increase nor decrease in it. It is as when someone plans ahead to do his work in such a way and on such a day.

When God exercises his justice or mercy, he manifests it by accomplishing it, since present, past, and future are known to him from eternity.

God's friends should persevere patiently in the love of God and not lose their peace, even though they may see worldly men and women prospering. God is like a good washing-woman who puts the dirty clothes in the waves to make them cleaner and brighter by the motion of the water, paying close attention to the water currents so that the clothes do not sink beneath the waves. Likewise, God places his friends in the waves of poverty and hardship in the present time in order to cleanse them for eternal life, while keeping close watch so that they are not plunged into excessive sorrow or unbearable hardship."

Christ's words to the bride offering the admirable allegory of a doctor and king, and about how the doctor symbolizes Christ, and about how those whom people think will be condemned are frequently saved while those whom people or worldly opinion think will be saved are condemned.

# Chapter 31

The Son speaks to the bride, saying: "A doctor came to a distant and unknown realm in which the king did not rule but was ruled, because he had the heart of a hare. Seated on his throne, he seemed like an ass with a crown. His people devoted themselves to gluttony, forgetting honesty and justice, and hating everyone who spoke to them about the good that awaited in the future. When the doctor presented himself to the king, saying he was from a lovely country and affirming that he had come because of his knowledge of human infirmities, the king, in wonder at the man and his words, answered:

'I have two prisoners to be beheaded tomorrow. One of them can scarcely breathe, but the other is more robust and stouter now than when he entered prison. Go to them, look at their faces and see which of them is in better health.' After the doctor had gone and examined them, he said to the king: 'The man whom you say is robust is almost a corpse and will not survive. As for the other, however, there is good hope.' The king asked him: 'How do you know that?'

The doctor said: 'Because the first man is full of harmful humors and vapor and cannot be cured. The other man, who is exhausted, can easily be saved with some fresh air.' Then the king said: 'I shall call together my noblemen and counselors so that they may see your wisdom and skill and you will win honor in their sight.' The doctor said to him: 'No, do that by no means.

You know your people are jealous of honor. If they cannot persecute a man with their actions, they destroy him with talk. Wait and I will make my wisdom known to you alone in private. This is how I have been taught. I have learned to display more wisdom in private than in public. I do not seek to win glory in your land of darkness, but I glory in the light of my fatherland. Besides, the healing time will not come until the south wind begins to blow and the sun appears at the meridian.' The king to him: 'How can that happen in my country? The sun rarely rises here, since we are beyond the climates, and the north wind always prevails among us. What good to me is your wisdom or such a long delay for healing? I see that you are full of talk.' The doctor answered: 'The wise man must not be hasty. However, in order that I may not seem to you to be unreliable and unfriendly, let me take charge of these two men. I will take them to the borders of your kingdom where the air is more suitable, and then you will see how much actions are worth and how much talk is worth.'

The king said to him: 'We are occupied with greater and more useful matters. Why do you distract us? Or what benefit does your teaching confer on us? We have our delight in present goods, in the things we see and own. We do not aspire to future and uncertain rewards. But, take the men, as you request. If you manage to show us something great and wonderful through them, we ourselves will proclaim you glorious and have you proclaimed glorious.' So he took the men and led them off to a temperate clime. One of them passed away and died, but the other, refreshed by the gentle air, recuperated.

I am that doctor who sent my words to the world in my longing to cure souls. Although I see the infirmities of many people, I only showed you two through whom you might admire my justice and mercy. I showed you one person whom the devil secretly possessed and who was to receive an eternal punishment. However, to people his works seemed to be righteous and were praised as such. I showed you a second person whom the devil openly controlled, but whom I said was to be healed in his time, although not in away open for men to see, as you were thinking. It was divine justice that the evil spirit began to control him by degrees, but the same justice also demanded that it should leave him by degrees, as in fact it did leave him up until the soul had been released from the body. Then the devil accompanied the soul to her judgment.

The judge said to him: 'You have chastised and sifted her like wheat. Now it belongs to me to crown her with a double crown because of her confession. Go away from the soul whom you chastised for so long.' And he said: 'Come, happy soul, perceive my glory and joy with the senses of your spirit!' To the other soul he said: 'Since you did not have the true faith and yet were honored and praised as being one of the faithful, and since you did not have the perfect deeds of the righteous, you will not have the wages of the faithful. During your lifetime you wondered why I would die for you and why I humbled myself for you.

Now I answer you that the faith of the holy church is true and leads souls upward, while my passion and blood allows them to enter heaven. Therefore, your faithlessness and your false love will press you down into nothingness, and you will be nothing with respect to eternal spiritual goods. As to why the devil did not go out of that other man in the sight of everyone, I answer: 'This world is like a lowly hovel compared to the tabernacle that God inhabits, and the people provoke God to anger. This is why he went out by degrees just as he had entered him.' "

The Virgin's words to the bride that show in an allegory how God the Father chose her from among the saints to be his mother and the port of salvation.

# Chapter 32

The Mother speaks to the bride saying: "A certain person searching for precious stones came upon a magnet. He took it in his hand and kept it in his treasury. With its help he led his ship to a safe port. Likewise, my Son searched among the many precious stones that are the saints, but he chose me especially as his mother in order that by my help humanity might be led to the port of heaven. As a magnet attracts iron to itself, so too I attract hard hearts to God. This is why you should not be troubled if your heart sometimes feels hard, because this is for your greater reward."

# Chapter 33

The Son of God speaks to the bride: "You are wondering about two men, one of whom was like a square-set stone, the other like a pilgrim to Jerusalem. However, neither of them achieved what you expected. The first man to whom you were sent was like a square-set stone, firm in his convictions but, like Thomas, piously doubting. Accordingly, since it was not yet the time when wicked deeds were fulfilled, he tasted the wine but did not drink it. Regarding the second man, I said that he would be a fellow traveler to Jerusalem. This happened so that you might learn the true state of the man who was reputed to be righteous and holy. He is a religious in his habit and a monk in his profession but an apostate in his ways, a priest by his rank but a slave to sin, a pilgrim by reputation but a vagabond in intention, rumored to be bound for Jerusalem but really headed for Babylon. Moreover, he left in disobedience and against the apostolic rules.

Also, he is so infected with heresy that he believes and says that he will become pope in the future and bring about a complete restoration. His books give evidence of this as well. This is why he will die a sudden death and, if he does not beware, he will join the company of the father of lies. Thus, you should not be troubled if certain things are said in an obscure way or if predictions do not turn out as you expect, since God's words can be understood in various ways. Whenever this happens I will point out the truth. But I am God, the true pilgrim bound for Jerusalem. I myself will be your fellow traveler."

## Explanation

The Spirit of God speaks: "You have heard that the man I told you was like a square-set stone and a pious doubter has died. May you know that he will not be in the number of those who tempted God in the desert nor with those who sought a sign like that of the prophet Jonah, nor with those who stirred up persecution against me. No, he will be with those who had zeal and charity although not yet perfectly."

The Mother's words to her daughter symbolizing the soul by a ring and the body by a cloth, and about how the soul should be purified through discretion and the body should be cleansed but not killed by abstinence.

# Chapter 34

The Mother speaks: "A ring is given to someone but it is too tight for his finger. So he asks advice of an enemy as to what should be done. The enemy answers him: 'Cut the finger off so the ring will fit on it.' A friend says to him: 'Certainly not! Instead, make the ring wider with a hammer.' Someone wants to filter and strain a drink for a powerful lord by using an unclean cloth and asks advice of an enemy. He answers: 'Cut everything that is unclean from the cloth and use the clean parts you find to filter your lord's drink.'

A friend tells him: 'By no means do that! Instead, the cloth should be washed and cleansed first and then the drink should be filtered!' The same thing applies even in spiritual matters. The ring represents the soul, the cloth represents the body. The soul, which should be placed on God's finger, should be made wider with the hammer of discretion and purification. The body should not be killed but cleansed through abstinence so that the words of God can be spread abroad by means of it."

# Table of Contents